WITHDRAWN
HARVARD LIBRARY
WITHDRAWN

AUTHORITY, DOGMA,
AND HISTORY

PUNCH'S FANCY PORTRAITS.—No. 113.

HIS EMINENCE CARDINAL MANNING.
(*Regarding a Fancy Portrait of what he might have been.*)

AND IN SPITE OF ALL TEMPTATIONS,
IF YOU READ HIS "PROTESTATIONS,"
HE REMAINS "AN ENGLISHMAN."
(*Vide an "Englishman's Protest" in the "Nineteenth Century."*)

AUTHORITY, DOGMA, AND HISTORY

THE ROLE OF THE OXFORD MOVEMENT CONVERTS IN THE PAPAL INFALLIBILITY DEBATES

Edited by
Kenneth L. Parker
Michael J. G. Pahls

ACADEMICA PRESS
BETHESDA - DUBLIN - PALO ALTO

Library of Congress Cataloguing-in-Publication Data

Authority, dogma, and history : the role of the Oxford Movement converts in the papal infallibility debates / edited by Kenneth L. Parker, Michael J.G. Pahls.
    p. cm.   Includes bibliographical references (p.) and index.
    ISBN-13: 978-1-933146-44-7
    ISBN-10: 1-933146-44-3

    1. Popes—Infallibility—History of doctrines—History of doctrines. 2. Catholic converts—England—History—19th century. 3. Vatican Council (1st : 1869-1870) 4. Oxford movement. I. Parker, Kenneth L. II. Pahls, Michael J. G.

BX1806.A88 2008   282.092'242—dc22   2008052287

Copyright 2009 by Kenneth L. Parker and Michael J.G. Pahls

All rights reserved. Printed in the United States of America.
No part of this book may be used or reproduced in any manner whatsoever without written permission except in the case of brief quotations embodied in critical articles and reviews.

Academica Press, LLC
Box 60728 Cambridge Station Palo Alto, CA. 94306
Website: www.academicapress.com to order: 650-329-0685

This collection is dedicated to
Professor Lawrence Barmann,
admired colleague and distinguished scholar

We celebrate his legacy of meticulous scholarship
and teaching excellence that has profoundly influenced
the work of historical theologians
at Saint Louis University

If the Past has been an obstacle and a burden,
Knowledge of the Past is the safest and the surest emancipation

Lord John Acton

Faith has nothing to fear from historical research

John Paul II

Contents

Acknowledgements	ix
Contributors	xi
List of Abbreviations	xiii

1. The Converts and the Council — 1
   Kenneth L. Parker and the Contributors

2. An Introduction to the Oxford Movement — 9
   Benjamin O'Connor

3. The Interplay of Hermeneutics and Heresy in the Process of Newman's Conversion from 1830 to 1845 — 45
   Jay Hammond, III

4. The Role of Newman's Theory of the Development of Christian Doctrine in the Events Leading to the Definition of Papal Infallibility at the First Vatican Council — 77
   C. Michael Shea

5. Henry Manning and Neo-Untramontanism: The Anglican Context for an Oxford Movement Convert's Faith in Papal Infallibility — 95
   Kenneth L. Parker

6. Canterbury's Rejoinder: Pusey, Gladstone, and the Neo-Ultramontanism of Manning — 115
   Michael J. G. Pahls

7. William George Ward, the *Dublin Review*, and Papal Infallibility — 129
   Hudson Russell Davis

8. Engaging in the Debates from the Periphery: The Contributions of Neglected Oxford Movement Converts in the Infallibility Debates — 157
   Donna Reinhard

Development in the Service of Rectification: 195
Newman's Understanding of the *Schola Theologorum*
   Michael J. G. Pahls

   Select Bibliography 213
   Index 239

Acknowledgements

Collaborative projects, especially with seven authors involved, run the risk of tension and fracture as the work progresses. This endeavor has been happily exempt from such drama. We have learned from one another and grown in respect for each other as the work moved forward. Many debts have accumulated along the way, and we wish to express our thanks.

First, we are deeply grateful to Dr. Ronald Crown, John Waide, and the rest of the Pius XII Library staff, who have always assisted us with grace and enthusiasm as we have pursued our work. Professor Parker has been the beneficiary of great kindness from archivists at the Bodleian Library in Oxford, the Pitts Library at Emory University, Cambridge University Library, and the British Library. Peter Erb has generously shared portions of his pre-publication critical edition of the Gladstone-Manning letters. For these and other acts of kindness we are deeply grateful.

Several of us have benefited from presenting early versions of these essays at the meetings of the American Catholic Historical Association in the spring of 2007, at the European Studies Conference in the fall of 2007, and at the National Conference of the Venerable John Henry Newman Association in the summer of 2008. We wish to thank friends and colleagues who have read and critiqued our work, especially Professor Paul Misner of Marquette Univeristy. Their insights and helpful suggestions have improved our essays. As current and former members of the Department of Theological Studies of Saint Louis University, we are grateful for the support and encouragement of our colleagues, as well as their helpful critiques in seminars and colloquia. This project would not have been possible without the dynamic and vibrant intellectual life that we enjoy in our community of scholarship.

Professor Parker is grateful for Mellon grants received to finance archival research. We also wish to thank the Graduate Student Association of Saint Louis University for its generous provision of funding for travel to conferences.

Acknowledgments

We are deeply grateful to Erick Moser, who shared proofreading and editorial burdens late in the project. R.H. Redfern-West, Director of Academica Press, deserves special thanks for his gracious invitation to publish this work and his longsuffering during its production.

We each have loved ones who could be singled out for their support and forbearance. Their love and generosity have made our work easier. We are deeply grateful to each of you.

Kenneth L. Parker
Michael J.G. Pahls

The Feast of All Saints, 1 November 2008
On the occasion of the translation of the
Venerable John Henry Newman's
remains to the Birmingham Orator

Contributors

Hudson Davis,
Adjunct Faculty, Saint Louis University

Jay Hammond, III
Assistant Professor of Historical Theology, Saint Louis University

Kenneth L. Parker
Associate Professor of Historical Theology, Saint Louis University

Benjamin O'Connor
Instructor in Theology, Loyola Academy, Wilmette, Illinois

Michael J. G. Pahls
Adjunct Faculty, Saint Louis University

Donna Reinhard
Adjunct Faculty, Saint Louis University

Charles M. Shea
Adjunct Faculty, Aquinas College, Grand Rapids, Michigan

INTRODUCTION:
THE CONVERTS AND THE COUNCIL

In the months before the First Vatican Council (1869-1870), Ignaz von Döllinger published *Der Papst und das Concil*. Writing under the pseudonym Janus—after the Roman god who guarded the past and presaged the future—Döllinger articulated a strident case against the rumored plan to define papal infallibility in a manner consonant with neo-ultramontane ideals. In the opening pages he dismissed this effort as the obsession of converts:

> The remark has frequently been made that it is chiefly converts, with little theological cultivation, but plenty of youthful zeal, who surrender themselves in willing and joyful mental slavery to the infallible ruler of souls; rejoicing and deeming themselves fortunate to have a master, visible, palpable, and easily inquired of.[1]

Indeed Döllinger's assessment proved a staple in the polemics of those who opposed a dogmatic definition of papal infallibility. This accusation even appeared in arguments among bishops at Vatican I. During the final days of the council, Archbishop Peter Kenrick of Saint Louis published his final effort to avert the definition. In that speech—published outside the Papal States because new rules barred its delivery before the council fathers—Kenrick lashed out at Henry Manning, who had become the *de facto* head of the English Church just fourteen years after his conversion to Catholicism. Lavishing praise on the oratorical skill recently displayed by the Archbishop of Westminster in defense of an expansive understanding of papal infallibility, the Irish-American prelate noted,

> And yet, while I listened, I could not help thinking of what used to be said of the English settlers in Ireland, that they were more Irish than the Irishmen. The Most Reverend Archbishop is certainly more Catholic than any Catholic I ever knew before. He has no doubt himself of the infallibility, personal, separate, and absolute, of the Pope, and he is not willing to allow other people to have

---

[1] Janus [Ignaz von Döllinger], *The Pope and the Council* (London: Rivingtons, 1869), xxvi.

any. ... As for myself, whom the experience of well nigh sixty years, since I first began to study the rudiments of the Faith, may perhaps have been made as well informed upon this subject as one who has been numbered with the Church for some twenty years, I boldly declare that that opinion, as it lies in the *Schema* is not a doctrine of the faith, and it cannot become such by any definition whatsoever, even by the definition of a Council. We are the keepers of the Faith committed to us, not its master.[2]

Yet converts did not stand on one side of the infallibility question. John Henry Newman, while not a strident public opponent of the definition, lamented the controversy it provoked. In the early days of the council he described to Bishop Ullathorne his private reservations and distress—words which were later published to the world without his knowledge and to his chagrin. He observed:

What have we done to be treated, as the faithful never were treated before? When has definition of doctrine de fide been a luxury of devotion, and not a stern, painful necessity? Why should an aggressive insolent faction be allowed to 'make the heart of the just to mourn, whom the Lord hath not made sorrowful?' Why can't we be let alone, when we have pursued peace, and thought no evil? I assure you, my dear Lord, some of the truest are driven one way and another, and ... [some are] angry with the Holy See for listening to the flattery of a clique of Jesuits, Redemptorists, and converts.[3]

As much as Newman opposed the efforts of Oxford Movement converts like Henry Manning, William Ward, George Talbot, and others, he seemed equally distressed to find his theory of doctrinal development being used by council fathers to justify their acquiescence to a definition. With a touch of irony David Moriarty, Bishop of Kerry, observed to Newman in March 1870,

Strange to say, if ever this definition comes you will have contributed much towards it. Your treatise on development has given the key. A Cardinal said the other day—"We must give up the first ten centuries, but the infallibility is an

---

[2] Joannes Dominicus Mansi, ed., *Sacrorum conciliorum nova et amplissima collection*, 54 vols (Paris: H. Welter, 1901-1927), 52:469. English translation is found in: Raymond Clancy, "American Prelates in the Vatican Council," in *Historical Records and Studies*, Thomas Meehen, ed. (New York: United States Catholic Historical Society, 1937) 28:113-14.

[3] Newman to Ullathorne, 28 January 1870, *LD*, 25:18-19. Also see the exchange of correspondence after Newman's letter was made public on 14 March 1870. Ibid., 53-8.

obvious development of the supremacy." Of course development was ever at work in the Church, but you brought it out and placed it on a pedestal.[4]

Newman remonstrated that his understanding of development had been "attacked by various persons and praised by none—till at last it is used against me. However, I cannot be sorry for it, for without it I never should have been a Catholic."[5]

This catena of quotes is striking because it demonstrates that on both sides of the debate, issues and ideas that originated in the crucible of the Oxford Movement became inextricably bound up in events that resulted in the definition of papal infallibility. The quest for certainty in matters of faith, the longing for authentic apostolic authority—even anxiety over the interference of the state in church affairs—formed a bridge between the fervor found among the Oxford Movement members in their Anglican years, their reasons for becoming Roman Catholics, and their priorities and preoccupations in their Catholic years. This collection of essays is framed around three shared assumptions: first, that Oxford Movement converts brought into their Catholic experience preoccupations that had roots in their efforts to reform Anglicanism; second, that these shared concerns resulted in very different reasons for their conversions; and third, that their energy and theological creativity—that had changed the landscape of nineteenth-century Anglicanism—also transformed and refashioned Catholic theological discourse, particularly regarding papal authority. While these points appear self-evident once highlighted, this collection of essays is the first explicit exploration of this historical reality.

During the 1830s, members of the Oxford Movement—particularly those who would convert to Catholicism—idealized the apostolic and patristic eras of Christianity. The early church and its teachings were the paradigm of faith and practice given by Christ himself, and it was the standard against which later forms of Christianity should be judged. This line of reasoning, in turn, generated profound ecclesiological problems and raised the question: which Christian communion has most faithfully maintained the faith of the early church? While Newman and others sought to defend Anglicanism's claim to that patrimony, the rejection of certain fundamental principles of their argument by bishops and the British public ultimately led some to decide that the Church of England did not bear the marks of apostolicity. In their struggle to make Roman Catholicism their new spiritual home, Oxford Movement converts stumbled upon different

---

[4] David Moriarty to Newman, [no date], but Newman responds, 20 March 1870. *LD*, 25:58, n. 2.

[5] Newman to Moriarty, 20 March 1870. *LD*, 25:58.

paths to that common goal. Different theological assumptions provided the signposts that guided them on their journey to Rome.

The fact that Oxford Movement converts came to different conclusions about key Catholic concerns should not surprise us. The apodictic certainty of deductive reasoning, in an age that celebrated inductive analysis, appealed to some Oxford Movement converts. William Ward, Henry Manning, George Talbot and others found their spiritual home in this way. Manning took comfort in the dictum, *ubi Petrus, ibi ecclesia*. He stated in 1861, "the one truth which has saved me is the infallibility of the Vicar of Jesus Christ, as the only true and perfect form of the infallibility of the Church, and therefore of all divine faith, unity, and obedience."[6]

Yet other converts struggled to engage modernity's epistemological shift and embraced the cumulative weight of probability as the primary means to account for their faith. They justified their quest, in part, based Bishop Joseph Butler's philosophical works. John Henry Newman, Richard Simpson, G.J. Mivart and others found their way into the Catholic Church using this path. Integral to Newman's argument for the development of doctrine was the concept of "antecedent probability," which formed a convergent worldview of heart and mind. When used to analyze the Christian past, this implied a divinely directed continuity at work beneath the vicissitudes of history, and that later doctrinal definitions had their grounding in apostolic teaching. These developments could be ascertained through historical investigations and judged, partially, through a critical assessment of evidence.[7] Newman applied this principle in his response to Pusey's alarm after Vatican I defined papal infallibility. He insisted, "historical facts, which are objections to its definition, must ever be elements in its interpretation."[8]

Erastianism—state intervention in ecclesiastical affairs—had been a source of tension in the Church of England since the sixteenth century. Ironically, it was Erastian accommodations favoring disenfranchised Catholics in the late 1820s and early 1830s that sparked the Oxford Movement, and sent many of its members on a campaign to free Anglican ecclesial structures from state interference. They feared political subversion of cherished doctrines and values, because non-Anglican politicians in parliament exercised authority over the affairs of the Church of England. The Church Temporalities Act of 1833, which abolished eight Church of Ireland bishoprics and two archbishoprics, mandated

---

[6] Edmund Purcell, *Life of Cardinal Manning*, 2 vols (London: Macmillan and Co., 1895-96), 2:160.

[7] John Henry Newman, *An Essay on the Development of Christian Doctrine* (London: James Toovey, 1845), *passim*.

[8] Newman, *LD*, 25:198.

redistribution of more than fifty percent of the established church's revenues in Ireland, and eliminated a tax on the Catholic majority which had benefited the established Protestant church, proved the final blow for key Oxford men.[9] John Keble's sermon, "National Apostasy," which Newman marked as the beginning of the Oxford Movement, was motivated by this parliamentary intervention in church affairs.

When these passionate defenders of Anglicanism converted to Catholicism, some channeled this anxiety in defense of the Papal States, as the sole means to protect the pope's spiritual authority and shield him from the coercion of secular powers. Manning argued in 1863, "because it is the only spot of ground on which the Vicar of Christ can set the sole of his foot in freedom, therefore they who would drive the Incarnation off the face of the earth hover about it to wrest it from his hands."[10]

Other converts viewed the pope's temporal authority as an historical anomaly, the loss of which might even strengthen the pope's prestige and standing as the spiritual leader of all nations and peoples. Newman diplomatically refrained from attending a rally in support of the militarily embattled pope in February 1860, but noted on his newspaper clipping of the event, "I did not go to this meeting presided over by the Bishop [Ullathorne], because, tho' its ostensible object ... was to express sympathy for him [Pius IX] in his misfortunes, the *real* object was to be a demonstration in favour of the necessity of his *Temporal Power*."[11] On 7 June 1861, Newman wrote to John Acton, who had argued that the loss of the temporal power would be a benefit to the papacy and the Church. Newman stated, "your remarks on the Pope's temporal power in the last Number of the Rambler [May 1861, 132-40] were not only interesting and instructive, but such, I think, as no one ought to find fault with."[12]

From the revolutions of 1848 through the 1860s and beyond, these theological and political issues placed a spotlight on papal authority in conflict with temporal powers in Europe. As the pope's authority over the Papal States became more precarious, debates over the extent of his spiritual authority became more intense. The impact of Oxford Movement converts in the debates was disproportionate to their numbers. George Talbot, chamberlain to Pius IX, proved one of the pope's most trusted advisors. Talbot played a role in the definition of the Immaculate Conception in 1854, maneuvered Manning into the archbishop-

---

[9] Nigel Yates, *The Religious Condition of Ireland: 1770-1850* (New York: Oxford University Press, 2006), 48-50.

[10] Henry Manning, "Roma Æterna" (address delivered in 1863) in *Miscellanies*, 2 vols (London: Burns and Oates, 1877), 1:22-3.

[11] *LD*, 19:303, n. 3.

[12] Newman, *LD*, 19:506.

ric of Westminster, and served on the commission planning Vatican I before his confinement to an asylum outside of Paris. Manning was a major force at the council, and deeply involved in the political intrigue that determined the composition of conciliar commissions and the ordering of the council's agenda. While Newman refused to participate in the council, despite invitations from the pope, and English and French bishops, his surviving correspondence reveals the extent of his influence on council fathers. Talbot, Manning, and Newman are just three examples; yet dozens of Oxford Movement converts played roles in these developments during the 1860s and at Vatican I.

Life and history are never simple or drawn in straight lines. Because this collection of essays examines a *group* of converts rather than individuals, many factors come into play. Personal relationships, their life experiences and temperaments, their attraction to differing forms of theological analysis and devotional practices—these factors and more helped shape the Roman Catholic identities of the many dozens of well-educated and driven English men and women whose early lives had been devoted to Oxford Movement ideals.

Benjamin O'Connor's essay provides essential background to the Oxford Movement and its key figures. His account explores the major historical developments of the Oxford Movement, from its roots in the friendship of John Keble, Hurrell Froude, and John Henry Newman through its "disintegration" after the conversion of Newman and other members to Roman Catholicism. The essay focuses on the major points of conflict that arose during this time period, as well as the ecclesiological concerns that both influenced these conflicts and guided the participants of the movement.

Professor Jay Hammond's contribution considers how Newman's fascination with and close study of ancient heresies created a hermeneutical trap which ensnared him, as bishops and the British public turned against core principles of the Oxford Movement. He explains how this dilemma was resolved through the creation of his theory of development. Hammond's close reading of Newman's unpublished Apollonarian and Monophysite papers provides a unique perspective on this thorny and much examined topic.

Michael Shea's essay examines how Newman's theory of development came to be a catalyst for the definition of infallibility. While Newman had been a quiet opponent of the definition in the 1860s and during the council, his theory took on a life of its own after 1845, and was embraced or adapted by seemingly unlikely theologians—Giovanni Perrone chief among these. Shea argues that Newman's theory of development influenced the First Vatican Council both directly and indirectly.

Professor Kenneth Parker's essay traces out the anguished years and tortured path Henry Manning took on his way to Rome. Drawing extensively from his frank and revealing letters to Robert Wilberforce and others, Parker lays out Manning's logic and motives, which not only explain his conversion, but also his tenacious pursuit of an expansive definition of papal infallibility. He concludes that it is impossible to understand the Catholic Manning without a thorough understanding of his Anglican years.

Michael Pahls takes up Manning's story after his conversion, examines his meteoric rise to the archbishopric of Westminster just fourteen year later, and considers the interplay between Manning and his estranged Anglican friends, Edward Pusey and William Gladstone, over papal infallibility. While Pusey and Gladstone articulate different premises for their opposition to Manning's broad understanding of papal infallibility, Pahls argues that the Oxford Movement frames the contours of the arguments presented by these three men.

Hudson Davis's essay on William Ward moves beyond the caricature of the man, and considers how his mind and temperament influenced his approach to the Christian faith and church authority. Ward longed for mathematical precision in doctrine and practice. Davis explains how his yearning for objective certainty drew him toward an understanding of papal authority that outstripped traditional ultramontane ideals. Davis's essay sheds light on the complexity of this man, and demonstrates that Ward's Anglican background forms the necessary context for the infallibility cause he later championed in the *Dublin Review*.

Donna Reinhard considers the contributions made by Oxford Movement converts who are typically neglected in the standard narratives of the papal infallibility debates. In this essay—a unique guide to little known converts—Reinhard not only considers the contributions of converts who wrote or were involved in publishing periodicals, but also those who influenced the infallibility debates through relationships, as confidants and correspondents. Of the sixteen people highlighted in this essay, two Cambridge men and two women are included as members of the broader Oxford Movement who influenced the infallibility debates during their Catholic years.

Finally, Michael Pahls's essay on Newman's Anglican concept of the *schola theologorum*, and the role it played in his thought in the wake of the First Vatican Council. Newman's consoling words to the distressed and disaffected implied that the interpretive work of theologians—the *schola theologorum*—would remedy and correct aspects of *Pastor Aeternus* over time. In a suggestive conclusion, Pahls reflects on how Vatican II may be viewed as an example of Newman's *schola theologorum* at work in history.

Together these essays provide an introduction to a neglected aspect of Oxford Movement scholarship and highlights dimensions of the 1860s papal infallibility debates that have hitherto not been addressed explicitly. Because it opens a new and complex area of research, the collection has been as suggestive and broad as possible. The subject matter demands a multi-centered approach, one that honors the integrity of individual biography as well as the interplay of relationships, power struggles and a plurality of theological, political and historiographical ideas.The fact that authority, dogma, and history proved driving forces in their struggles as Anglicans during the Oxford Movement and resulted in differing motivations leading to their conversions should not surprise us. Nor should we be surprised to see these themes later providing fertile ground for their theological creativity and ecclesiastical activities as Roman Catholics. However, once we perceive the impact of these issues in the papal infallibility debates of the 1860s and understand the diverse roles played by Oxford Movement converts—like a *Gestalt* image—our vision of the papal infallibility debates and Vatican I is forever altered.

THE OXFORD MOVEMENT

BENJAMIN O'CONNOR

From the early 1830s, through the 1840s, and into the 1850s, the University of Oxford was the prime *locus belli* of an extraordinary controversy surrounding the Church of England. With the increase of secular influences on the Church during the first decades of the century, exemplified distinctly by the growing inclusion of non-Anglicans into the affairs of Parliament—and, thus, the affairs of Anglicanism itself—a groundswell of acute dissatisfaction arose among members of the Oxford community. This general sentiment eventually gave way to particular debates about the very nature of the English Church: its understanding of itself *qua* church; its proper relationship with the State; the importance of dogma and authority to its constitution; and its relationship to other Christian churches. These debates soon resonated outside the walls of Oxford, and led its proponents and adherents to quite unexpected results. This essay will provide a general overview of this unique amalgamation of ideas, people, place, and time, now known as the Oxford Movement, and will focus particularly on what is perhaps the most peculiar of its effects: the conversion of a large number of its participants to Roman Catholicism.

Historiography: Study of the Oxford Movement over the past two centuries

Study of the Oxford Movement—also called, among other things, the Tractarian Movement, after its central publication, *Tracts for the Times*—has been profoundly colored by these conversions to Catholicism. The first histories of the Movement lacked any kind of historical, theological, or personal distance from their subject(s), praising some figures, vilifying others, and portraying an either/or dichotomy that seemed to stem from the writer's own theological inclinations. More precisely, one's willingness to write at all on the subject can be seen as reflection of his or her personal stance. As Owen Chadwick states, the first reminiscences of the Oxford Movement reveal "a very striking thing—the people who resent it, or dislike it, or hate it, write their memoirs; the people who loved it and owed their soul to it and regarded it as the highest ideal of life they had ever known—are silent."[1] This partisanship, no doubt, has made the work of the scholar difficult, consistently impeding his or her quest for critical distance. But such apparent fervor has also provoked an increased methodological desire to define the line between subject and subjectivity, and between history and hagiography.

The first step in this definition, *vis-à-vis* the Oxford Movement, was a definition of the Movement itself. Whereas first-generation histories can be more accurately termed memoirs or reminiscences, second- and third-generation accounts can be called histories proper, in that they tried to account for the who, what, and where of the general happenings at Oxford in a somewhat systematic manner. These volumes, such as Bertram Windle's *Who's Who of the Oxford Movement*[2] or C.C.J. Webb's *Religious Thought in the Oxford Movement*,[3] are substantially less prone to the polemical or emotional tendency of first-generation works, began to mold the generally amorphous concept of "Tractarianism" into an entity that, while not definitive, was at least more recognizable and uniform.

With this scholarly groundwork laid, and the concept of the "Oxford Movement" more precisely understood, the most recent generation of Movement historians has examined the causes and effects of the Oxford Movement.[4] Indeed, the "how" and "to what end" of the Movement has been addressed in every stage of its historiography; but, in earlier generations, the points and persons of reference were too diverse, leaving a scholar unable to assess whether one explanation was more accurate than another. With the benefit of over one hundred years of literature on the subject, however, late twentieth-century historians were able to offer more insight than narrative.

Regarding the causes of the Movement, J.C.D. Clark's *English Society, 1688-1832*, a study of eighteenth- and nineteenth-century England, sees the Ox-

---

[1] "The Oxford Movement and its Reminiscencers," in *The Spirit of the Oxford Movement: Tractarian Essays* (Cambridge: Cambridge University Press, 1990), 137-138.

[2] Bertram Windle, *Who's Who of the Oxford Movement* (New York: Century, 1926).

[3] C.C.J. Webb, *Religious Thought in the Oxford Movement* (London: Society for Promoting Christian Knowledge, 1928). Webb was Oriel Professor of the Philosophy of Christian Religion at Oxford.

[4] This does not mean that historians have avoided general narratives. To the contrary, narrative histories have, in recent years, expanded their structural boundaries beyond the merely chronological or theological, to include multi-thematic exploration (e.g. C. Brad Faught, *The Oxford Movement: A Thematic History of Tractarians and Their Times*, [University Park, PA: Penn State Press, 2003]) and manuscript history (e.g. Rune Inberg, *In Quest for Authority*, [Lund, Sweden: Lund University, 1987]). See also James Pereiro's recent work, *"Ethos" and the Oxford Movement: At the Heart of Tractarianism*, (Oxford: Oxford University Press, 2008).

ford Movement as a direct consequence of the dissolution of the hierarchical political/theological system of the past, and the rise of modern-day political liberalism and egalitarianism.[5] Peter Nockles, claiming an "indebtedness" to Clark's work,[6] contends in *The Oxford Movement in Context* that the Oxford Movement was, additionally, a culmination of the general revival of High Church Anglicanism that had emerged in England in the aftermath of the French Revolution. Both works are considered seminal to present discussion of the Oxford Movement, and are widely believed to portray accurately the state of the question in current Oxford Movement studies.

Regarding the effects of the Movement, the scholarly implications extend beyond the discipline of history. The thoughts of many of the figures of the period have been unpacked and projected onto present times by many authors, academic or otherwise. In particular, John Henry Newman, one of the primaries of the Movement and its most celebrated (or infamous) convert to Catholicism, has become a *cause célèbre* within many theological, philosophical, and literary circles, and the ramifications of his participation in, and eventual defection from, the Oxford Movement have been the source of much academic work. Additionally, the branch of Christianity to which the Movement gave rise—Anglo-Catholicism—has been analyzed in light of its Tractarian origins, and assessed in terms of its twentieth- and twenty-first-century viability.[7] And these are only a few of the effects of the Oxford Movement being unpacked and explored.

This volume falls into the second category of present-day inquiry, that of the effects of the Oxford Movement. This introductory essay will provide a brief foray into its causes. As the book's overall goal is to explore the role of Oxford Movement converts in the later debate over papal infallibility, this essay will

---

[5] Clark writes: "Hereditary rule, primogeniture and religion were [had been] society's organising principles. ... What had changed was that, relatively suddenly, a particular description of a social nexus had been unseated from its intellectual and constitutional hegemony." *English Society, 1688-1832: Ideology, Social Structure, and Political Practice During the* Ancien Regime, (Cambridge: Cambridge University Press, 1985), 418.

[6] Nockles writes that Clark's book "was a source of intellectual inspiration to me," (xv), and that "Historians of Georgian Anglicanism are particularly indebted to J.C.D. Clark's ... study ... Clark has clothed the political debate of the period in a theological context which for too long had been denied it." *The Oxford Movement in Context: Anglican High Churchmanship, 1760-1857* (Cambridge: Cambridge University Press, 1997), 8.

[7] A fine example of such analytical/theological work is Sheridan Gilley, "The Ecclesiology of the Oxford Movement: A Reconsideration," in *From Oxford to the People: Reconsidering Newman and the Oxford Movement*, ed. Paul Vaiss (Leominster, UK: Gracewing, 1996), 60-75.

approach the Oxford Movement from a particular angle—that of conversion (or, just as importantly, lack thereof) to Roman Catholicism. Thus, more attention will be paid to some figures over others, though not in any valuative manner. Rather, this essay provides a narrative that will orient the reader towards the context of the infallibility debate, giving more precise reasons as to *why* certain figures held their respective position on papal infallibility during their "Catholic lives."[8]

The best manner in which to proceed, therefore, so as to incorporate general chronological narrative and particular conversion narratives, is to present the Oxford Movement as a "history of controversies." That is, the essay will illuminate some of the "trigger moments" for the figures of the Movement, which are almost entirely moments of conflict. Such an approach reflects the agonistic environment of Oxford and English academia in general during this period. Indeed, conflict was so prominent in this setting that Newman, later in life, denied the statement that he was a philosopher or theologian; rather, he believed himself to be a controversialist.[9] As the men of this period believed themselves to be engaged in battle, so it is apt to describe the Tractarian Movement on the whole as such. Specifically, this narrative will stretch from the controversy over dissolution of the Irish bishoprics in 1833 to the Gorham decision in 1850. Both of these events prove to be high watermarks of the conflict between the Anglican church and the English political state, and thus both serve as fine chronological and thematical bookends for the narrative.

The narrative will be divided in the following general order: first, the major events leading to the development of the Oxford Movement proper—that is, how the major figures discussed—Hurrell Froude, John Keble, John Henry Newman, and Edward Pusey—moved from grumbling to action; second, the major controversies within the context of the Movement itself; and third, the crucial factors and moments which convinced certain members of the Movement

---

[8] I recognize that this narrative approach truncates my ability to detail the profound pastoral and moral concerns of the Tractarians. Of course, pastoral issues are at the forefront of these men's arguments, as they were, almost without exception, Anglican clergy as much as they were scholars. Thus, the "battles" or "controversies" in which these men were engaged were on behalf of the constituencies they served. For a deeper treatment of this issue, see Owen Chadwick, *The Spirit of the Oxford Movement: Tractarian Essays* (Cambridge: Cambridge University Press, 1990) or Faught's aforementioned work.

[9] In an 1866 letter to W.G. Ward, on the topic of papal infallibility: "I am a controversialist, not a theologian, and I should have nothing to say about it [i.e., papal infallibility]." Quoted in E.P. Purcell, *Life of Cardinal Manning, Archbishop of Westminster* (Ann Arbor: University of Michigan, 1896), 2:322.

to leave the Church of England and join the Church of Rome.[10] This general framework, besides providing general thematic and chronological order, will offer opportunity to explore the three central elements of the Movement: the men themselves; their relationships to each other and the University of Oxford; and their understanding of the Church of England as a true Christian church.

Origins: Froude, Keble, Newman, and Pusey

While the formal beginning of the Oxford Movement is still a point of historical debate, its moment of definitive provocation does not share such ambiguity. Interestingly enough, though the movement is known primarily for its theology, its origins are decidedly political. As Chadwick writes, "It is safe to say that the Movement would not have taken the form which it took without the impetus of ecclesiastical and secular politics."[11] In February of 1833, Parliament passed a resolution designed to dissolve ten Anglican bishoprics in Ireland, the last in a series of legislative moves which revealed a trend of unwanted government control over the Church. In 1829, the Roman Catholic Emancipation Act had allowed non-Anglicans to sit in parliament for the first time. Three years later, the Reform Act of 1832 expanded parliamentary representation for industrialized regions, and increased franchise to Jews, Roman Catholics, and dissenting Protestants. The introduction in 1833 of the Church Temporalities Bill, was the veritable straw that broke the back of traditional high churchmen, as it confirmed the fears of these Oxford men about the new, heterogeneous parliament.

The dissolution of the Irish bishoprics reflected the sudden influence that these fledgling members of parliament (MPs) were having on the legislative body. The impact of Roman Catholics and "Dissenting" Protestants[12] inspired a fever pitch of reaction from conservative high churchmen. If parliament was now legislating against Anglican tradition on ecclesiastical and juridical matters, they asked, how long until it voted similarly on doctrinal matters? And even more fearfully, what would Anglicanism look like unless something drastic occurred? What was evident in the Irish bishoprics affair was an increase in

---

[10] There is the belief that there are two "Oxford Movements," so to speak; namely, the Tractarian Movement, led by Newman, Pusey, and Keble, and the post-Tractarian, or "Romeward Movement," led by William Ward, et al. Such an approach, while insightful, fails to account for Pusey's leadership role from 1841 forward.

[11] Chadwick, "The Mind of the Oxford Movement," in *The Spirit of the Oxford Movement*, 2.

[12] "Dissenters" were Protestants who did not conform to the established Church of England.

Erastianism: an increasingly inharmonious merging of church and state, to the detriment of the church and its doctrine.

At Oxford, the affair of the Irish bishoprics stirred high churchmen profoundly. The university had already been the scene of heated debate between more traditional and more liberal churchmen ever since 1829. In that year, the majority of Oxford fellows had voted against the election of the longtime MP Robert Peel, who had, after long defending the Church of England, planned upon his election to introduce the pro-Catholic legislation that would later become the Roman Catholic Emancipation Act. Peel's defeat had stemmed the tide of liberalism at Oxford, but the introduction of the Church Temporalities Bill had shown the dons that this defeat was only temporary.

With the Church Temporalities Bill of 1833, many high churchmen at Oxford now recognized that something needed to be done to restore the Anglican Church's dignity. Hurrell Froude (1803-1836), a fellow at Oriel College, later looked back at this resolution as the end of an era: "[T]he extinction of the Irish Protestant boroughs, and the great power accidentally given to Dissenters by the Reform Act, gave a concluding blow to the ancient system."[13] The fall of the "ancient system," though, did not necessarily have to mean the fall of the Church of England. The English church, Froude determined, deserved a fight. A man of exceptional force of character, Froude followed his rallying cry with action, moving with determination to find those of similar opinion.

Froude found a kindred spirit in his teacher, John Keble (1792-1866), a fellow at Oriel and professor of poetry, whose 1827 work *The Christian Year* had garnered him considerable fame and prominence. The two had known one another since Froude's arrival at Oxford in 1821, when Froude had come under Keble's tutelage. To Froude, it seemed provident that he had had Keble as his tutor. His friend and fellow Tractarian Isaac Williams wrote:

> He [Froude] was considered a very odd fellow at college, but clever and original: Keble alone was able to appreciate and value him. If he had not at this time fallen into such hands, his speculations might have taken a very dangerous turn; but ... from this time it was very much otherwise, he continued to throw out paradoxes, but always for good.[14]

---

[13] Richard Hurrell Froude, *The Remains of the Late Reverend Richard Hurrell Froude*, 4 vols (London: Rivington, 1838), 3:207.

[14] Isaac Williams, *The Autobiography of Isaac Williams, B.D* (London: Longmans, Green, and Co. 1892), 23.

Keble's steady guidance had tempered Froude's hyperbolic tendencies, and the relationship between the two soon blossomed into a deep friendship that was both intellectual and emotional.

As outgoing and extravagant as Froude was, Keble was reciprocally as quiet and reserved; an interpersonal dialectic that worked itself out in their response to the political stimuli of this period. Keble was diligent in his studies to the point of being, as some called him, "laborious."[15] In his personal religious opinions, he was equally severe. He was, like many other high churchmen, quite conservative, as he "abhorred innovation and indeed delighted in tradition for its own sake."[16] From Keble, R.W. Church writes, "Froude learned ... to be anti-Erastian, anti-methodistical, anti-sentimental and as strong in his hatred of the world, as contemptuous of popular approval, as any Methodist."[17] As interference from the government into Anglican affairs increased from 1829 forward, both men grew equally distraught. Yet it was Froude's impetus that moved their opinions beyond conversation. Church further observed that the religious opinions Keble instilled in Froude "might merely have made a strong impression, or formed one more marked school of doctrine, without the fierce energy which received it and which it inspired. But Froude, in accepting Keble's ideas, resolved to make them active, public, aggressive."[18] Thus, the student sought to motivate the teacher in much the same manner as the teacher had previously motivated the student.[19]

Keble did heed Froude's request, responding publicly to the Church Temporalities Bill on 14 July 1833, at the university's annual Assize Sermon in St. Mary's Church. In his sermon, entitled "National Apostasy," Keble condemned the Irish Church Bill, not merely in and of itself, but also for its broader implications. In his own words, Keble believed the bill to be a demonstration *par excellence* of "the growing indifference ... to other men's religious senti-

---

[15] Owen Chadwick, "The Limitations of Keble," in *The Spirit of the Oxford Movement*, 59.

[16] Faught, *The Oxford Movement*, 58.

[17] R.W. Church, *The Oxford Movement: Twelve Years: 1833-1845* (Archon, 1966), rpt. of 1892 ed., 32.

[18] Ibid.

[19] This does not mean that Keble was fearful of conflict, particularly when such conflict touched upon his personal beliefs. J.T. Coleridge, a first-generation biographer of Keble writes that "gentle as he was by nature, and loving-hearted to individuals ... it was not in his nature, nor according to his conscience, to be inactive when he felt deeply." J.T. Coleridge, *A Memoir of the Reverend John Keble* (Oxford: Parker, 1870), 221. For example, when he heard that one of the godparents of Queen Victoria's child was Lutheran, he led a public protest. Owen Chadwick, "The Limitations of Keble," 60.

ments."[20] Particularly disturbing to Keble was the insidiousness with which this attitude had emerged:

> Under the guise of charity and toleration we are come almost to this pass; that no difference, in matters of faith, is to disqualify for approbation and confidence, whether in public or domestic life. Can we conceal it from ourselves, that every year the practice is becoming more common, of trusting men unreservedly in the most delicate and important matters without one serious inquiry, whether they do not hold principles which make it impossible for them to be loyal to their Creator, Redeemer, and Sanctifier?[21]

At the core of Keble's argument was the claim that the Church of England was a truly apostolic successor, whose operations should not and could not be overtaken or controlled by the government.[22] Indeed, laws such as the Irish

---

[20] John Keble, "National Apostasy," Assize Sermon, (Steventon, UK: Rocke Press, 1983), 18.

[21] Ibid.

[22] See Michael Chandler, *An Introduction to the Oxford Movement,* (New York: Church Publishing, 2003), 19-20. The word "liberalism" was decidedly amorphous in this period, just as it is in our own times. Essentially, "to be liberal" meant to be liberal in the mind of the person making the claim. In this essay, liberalism means a tendency towards rationalistic thought. In the minds of Newman, Froude, Keble, et al., overuse of philosophy and rationalist method might qualify someone as liberal (see the Hampden controversy below). However, as will be seen in subsequent essays, Newman after his conversion was looked upon as a liberal by the neo-ultramontanes, who saw his unwillingness to embrace papal infallibility as decidedly anti-traditionalist. Yet many of those who sought to define papal infallibility were seen as liberal, as they were introducing new doctrine; the claim of the neo-ultramontanes, however, was that they were being conservative, identifying something that the Catholic Church had always believed. In the basic sense, "to be liberal" meant to embrace new or innovative thought or teaching. The reader should be alert to the semantical and cultural nuance of the term. For a general assessment of the rise of liberalism in Europe, see Owen Chadwick, *The Secularization of the European Mind in the Nineteenth Century,* (Cambridge: University of Cambridge Press, 1990); Jan Goldstein and John W. Boyer, *Nineteenth-Century Europe: Part Eight: Liberalism and Its Critics* (Chicago: University of Chicago Press, 1988). For an Anglican/Tractarian understanding of the term, see Gilley's "The Ecclesiology of the Oxford Movement" or William P. Haugaard, "A Myopic Curiosity: Martin Luther and English Tractarians," in *Anglican Theological Review* 66 (1984): 391-401. Josef Lewis Altholz offers an understanding of liberalism among some of the Anglican converts to Catholicism: *The Liberal Catholic Movement in England: The "Rambler" and Its Contributors, 1848-1864* (London: Burns and Oates, 1962). Marvin R. O'Connell provides a case study (Bishop Félix Dupanloup's interpretation of the *Syllabus of Errors*) in the self-understanding of Catholic liberalism vis-à-vis Catholic neo-ultramontanism in the 1850s

Church Bill belied the Christian identity of England, as "a nation which had for centuries acknowledged, as an essential part of its theory of government, that, *as a Christian nation, she is also part of Christ's Church, and bound, in all her legislation and policy, by the fundamental laws of that Church.*"[23] Thus, by abolishing the Irish bishoprics, parliament was not only undermining the church, but also the state itself.

While "National Apostasy" inspired very little controversy in the broader Oxford community upon its delivery and subsequent publication, it did attract the attention of John Henry Newman (1801-1890), another fellow of Oriel College. Considered one of the university's brightest minds, Newman had been a bulwark against liberalism at Oxford.[24] He had held Keble in high regard,[25] and saw the Assize Sermon as a moment of distinct importance. And so he drew himself closer to the message and implicit call to action of the sermon, in the hopes of continuing the work he believed started with Keble's address.[26]

Newman and Keble had become friends in 1828.[27] It was Froude who brought them together. Keble had originally been skeptical of Newman, as he thought Newman too liberal and too influenced by evangelicalism. But Froude had convinced Keble otherwise,[28] and the three men soon became a triumvirate that would launch the Tractarian Movement.

---

and 1860s: "Ultramontanism and Dupanloup," in *Church History* 53 (1984): 200-217. Finally, there are many fine sources on Newman and liberalism, most notably: Philip C. Rule, *Coleridge and Newman: The Centrality of Conscience*, (New York: Fordham University Press, 2004); Stephen Thomas, *Newman and Heresy: The Anglican Years*, (Cambridge, UK: University of Cambridge, 1991); and Paul Misner, "The 'Liberal' Legacy of John Henry Newman," in *Newman and the Modernists*, ed. Mary Jo Weaver, (Lanham, MD: University Press of America, 1985), 3-24.

[23] Church, *The Oxford Movement*, 92.

[24] See M.G. Brock, "The Oxford of Peel and Gladstone, 1800-1833," in *The History of the University of Oxford, Volume 6: Nineteenth-Century Oxford, Part I*, eds. M.G. Brock and M.C. Curthoys (Oxford: Clarendon Press, 1997), 7-71, especially 61.

[25] He writes in his *Apologia*, "When one day I was walking in High Street with my dear earliest friend [Froude] ... with what eagerness did he cry out, 'There's Keble!' and with what awe did I look at him!" *Apologia* 28 [147].

[26] Newman called Keble "[t]he true and primary author" of the Tractarian Movement, and marked the day of the Keble's Assize Sermon as the beginning of the movement. *Apologia* 28 [147].

[27] *Apologia*, 29 [148].

[28] As Chadwick writes, "It was Froude who persuaded Keble that he ought not to be suspicious of Newman, despite Newman's dialectic, despite his friendship with the liberal philosopher Whately, despite the Evangelical forces in his early life." Chadwick, "Mind of the Oxford Movement," 24.

It is impossible to divorce one's understanding of the Oxford Movement from one's understanding of the relationship between Froude, Keble, and Newman. As the eminent Newman biographer, Sheridan Gilley, writes, "The heart of the Oxford Movement was just this, the personal loyalty and affection between Newman, Froude, and Keble, and their love and affection for Oxford."[29] Each man cared deeply for the other, and learned from the other, bringing their own particular gifts and intellectual foci to bear upon their growing missions against Erastianism and Anglican liberalism. Dean R.W. Church, in his well-known memoir of the Movement, aptly describes the interplay between the three men: "Each acted on the other. Froude represented Keble's ideas, Keble's enthusiasm. Newman gave shape, foundation, consistency, elevation to the Anglican theology ... which Froude had learned from Keble."[30]

Even the men themselves understood the importance of their relationship to the Movement and its future; as Froude himself poignantly stated, "Do you know the story of the murderer who had done one good thing in his life? If I were asked what good deed I have ever done, I should say I had brought [Keble] and [Newman] to understand each other."[31] In these men and their relationship, Tractarianism found its initial impetus.

Tractarianism took form, however, in the publication of the *Tracts for the Times*. The idea for the tracts was one of a few that had emerged at a meeting of like-minded high churchmen at the country estate of Hadleigh, near Suffolk, on 25 July 1833. While others at the meeting had championed a league of defense for the Church of England, or the drafting of a declaration, Froude and Newman stood for stronger action. Talking to Isaac Williams, after the meeting, Froude implored, "[W]e must make a row in the world. Why should we not? ... Church principles forced on people's notice must do people good. ... We must try."[32] Newman, too, jumped on the idea, and, in the words of Chandler, "quickly made it his own."[33] In a given tract, the anonymous author could concisely and persuasively defend a theological issue close to his heart. Such an approach could simultaneously display the unity of those involved, and the diversity of their concerns.

The first three tracts, all authored by Newman, were published on 9 September 1833, and were addressed to clergy. In the very first tract, Newman set the

---

[29] Gilley, *Newman and His Age*, 111.
[30] Church, *The Oxford Movement*, 30.
[31] Froude, *Remains*, 1:438.
[32] Williams, *Autobiography*, 63.
[33] Chandler, *Introduction of the Oxford Movement*, 22.

tone for the future, sounding what George Herring dubbed the "clarion call" of Tractarianism:[34]

> But, if you will not adopt my view of the subject, which I offer to you, not doubtingly, yet (I hope) respectfully, at all events, *choose your side*. To remain neuter much longer will be itself to take a part. *Choose* your side; since side you shortly must, with one or other party, even though you do nothing. Fear to be of those, whose line is decided for them by chance circumstances, and who may perchance find themselves with the enemies of *Christ*, while they think but to remove themselves from worldly politics. Such abstinence is impossible in troublous times. *He that is not with me, is against me, and he that gathereth not with me scattereth abroad.*[35]

Soon, booksellers and clergy, encouraged by Newman, were selling the *Tracts for the Times*. Shrouded in mystery because of their anonymity, yet buttressed by the erudition and scholarship of their contributors, the Tracts grew in popularity.

Yet what did the Tractarians hope to accomplish in these publications? Primarily, they sought to defend the theological and historical tradition of the Church of England—as they understood it—so that it would not fold in the face of the Erastian challenge. The Tracts' vision coincided with what Chadwick called Keble's implicit command to Newman: "Don't be original."[36] This general principle, particularly in relation to doctrine, had more specific moral ramifications. In an 1834 edition of the first forty-six Tracts, such concerns are explicitly described:

> The Apostolic succession, the Holy Catholic Church, were principles of action in the minds of our predecessors of the seventeenth century; but, in proportion as the maintenance of the Church has been secured by law, her ministers have been under the temptation of leaning on an arm of flesh instead of her own divinely-provided discipline ... A lamentable increase of sectarianism has followed; being occasioned ... first, by the cold aspect which the new Church doctrines have presented to the religious sensibilities of the mind, next to their meagerness [sic] in suggesting motives to restrain it from out a more influential discipline.[37]

---

[34] George Herring, *What Was the Oxford Movement?* (London: Continuum, 2002), 27.

[35] *Tracts for the Times, Tract 1: Thoughts on the Ministerial Commission*, 4. Emphasis in original.

[36] Chadwick, "Mind of the Oxford Movement," 27.

[37] Members of the University of Oxford, *Tracts for the Times*, 4 vols (London: Rivington, 1834), 1: 7.

The Tractarians perceived the direct impact that the changes occurring in parliament would have on individual religious practice and moral living. The urgency with which they wrote, therefore, came from their concern for the day-to-day maintenance of the church, and its necessary effect on the salvation of the individual. "[I]n this modified sense," Chadwick wrote, "it is right to see the Oxford Movement as an impulse of the heart and the conscience, not an inquiry of the head."[38]

Other tracts soon followed Newman's first three. Keble wrote the fourth installation, on apostolic succession, and Froude wrote the seventh. Other contributors included: J.W. Bowden, another Oriel fellow; Thomas Keble, John's brother and fellow at Corpus Christi College; Alfred Menzies, fellow at Trinity College; and Benjamin Harrison, fellow at Christ Church. By 1835, seventy tracts had been written, of which Newman had written eighteen, and Keble had written seven.[39]

The other major contributor was Edward Bouverie Pusey (1800-1882), a former fellow at Oriel, and since 1828 Regius Professor of Hebrew. Pusey had known Newman since Pusey's arrival at Oriel in 1823—Newman had arrived in 1822—and both men shared a profound sense of reverence for the church and its doctrines. A political liberal earlier and a supporter of Peel in 1829, Pusey had grown more conservative in light of increasing parliamentarian influence on the Anglican church. Yet, he was initially reticent to advocate the Tractarian cause. He suspected the Tractarians of German tendencies that he detested. Having studied theology in Germany, Pusey was well aware of continental philosophy, and had disowned it intellectually upon his return to England. To him, the Tractarian mindset seemed an appropriation of the German theological method that he detested.[40] However, these fears were soon allayed by Newman, who informed Pusey that he could not read German and had not studied German theological method. Pusey joined the Tractarians, contributing five tracts by the end of 1835.[41]

Pusey's contribution soon became more than authorial, as leadership in the Movement was thrust upon him. In January 1834, Pusey wrote *Tract 18*, entitled

---

[38] Chadwick, "Mind of the Oxford Movement," 2.
[39] Chandler, *Introduction to the Oxford Movement*, 26.
[40] Faught, *The Oxford Movement*, 87.
[41] These tracts were: *Tract 18: Thoughts on the Benefits of the System of Fasting enjoined by our Church* (21 Dec. 1833); *Tract 66: On the Benefits of the System of Fasting prescribed by our Church. Supplement to Tract 18* (25 July 1835); *Tract 67: Scriptural Views of Holy Baptism* (24 August 1835); *Tract 68: Scriptural views of Holy Baptism (continued).* (29 September 1835); *Tract 69: Scriptural Views of Holy Baptism (concluded).* (18 October 1835).

"Thoughts on the Benefits of the System of Fasting Enjoined by our Church." The tract, while no more controversial than any of the others, bore Pusey's initials and became the first to break the seal of anonymity.[42] As a result, Pusey unintentionally became the face of the Oxford Movement. The Movement, which to this point had had no real nominal identity, save the occasionally-used "Tractarianism," began to be known (largely in a derogatory manner) as "Puseyism," and its adherents "Puseyites."[43]

Within the Movement, as well, people began to see Pusey as their head. Having the most sterling academic profile, he carried more gravitas than any other figure, and was comfortable in the public view. Newman, by most accounts the prime intellectual force behind the movement, accepted Pusey's leadership as necessary; as Chadwick explained, "He [Newman] allowed that Pusey had imported into it a weight of scholarship, a sobriety and a gravity which might otherwise have been lacking."[44] In his own words, Newman credits Pusey with giving a definitive shape and identity to the Tractarian cause: "[H]e was able to give a name, a form, and a personality, to what was without him sort of a mob."[45] With Pusey at the public helm, the movement bearing his name gained a self-sustaining force that would maintain it through future conflicts.

---

[42] This was not a gaffe on Pusey's part. As Williams described it: "He said, smiling to Newman, wrapping his gown round him as he used to do, 'I think you are too hard on the peculiars, as you call them (i.e., the Low Church party); you should conciliate them; I am thinking of writing a letter myself with that purpose' .... 'Well,' said Newman, 'suppose you let us have it for one of the Tracts!' 'Oh, no,' said Pusey, 'I will not be one of you!' This was said in a playful manner; and before we parted Newman said: 'Suppose you let us have that letter of yours which you intend writing, and attach your own name or signature to it. You would then not be mixed up with us, nor in any way responsible for the Tracts!' 'Well,' Pusey said, at last, 'if you will let me do that, I will.'" Williams, *Autobiography*, 71-72.

[43] There were many other names for the Tractarians, which Owen Chadwick enumerates in his essay "The Oxford Movement: and its Reminiscencers": Tractites, Apostolicals, Keble-ites, Malignants, Newmanites, Tractators (1842), Newmanians, Neomanians, Newmaniacs. "If the phrase 'Oxford Movement' was used," Chadwick adds, "the writer put it into inverted commas." *Spirit of the Oxford Movement*, 135.

[44] Chadwick, "Mind of the Oxford Movement," 37.

[45] *Apologia*, 65 [184]. Newman continues, "He [Pusey] was a man of large designs; he had a hopeful, sanguine mind; he had no fear of others; he was haunted by no intellectual perplexities." Ibid., 65 [184].

Controversies: Hampden, Froude's Remains, the Via Media, and Tract 90

The first of these conflicts erupted in February 1836, when Renn Dickson Hampden (1793-1868), principal of St. Mary Hall, was appointed Regius Professor of Divinity at Oxford. This appointment drew the ire of the Tractarians, who saw Hampden as too liberal.[46] The general disapproval with Hampden's theology stemmed from his presentation at Oxford's 1832 Bampden Lectures, which had, as William Palmer wrote, "a tendency [that was] decidedly Rationalistic; that they went to the extent of representing our article of faith, and our creeds, as based on merely human and uncertain theories."[47] Two years later, in 1834, Hampden had promoted the admission of dissenting Protestants to Oxford, a stance that, in the sight of many, unnecessarily relaxed the *Thirty-nine Articles*. Evangelicals joined the Tractarians in the opposition to Hampden,[48] as his actions were seen as an affront both to the Church of England and the University of Oxford.[49] The Tractarians feared Hampden's influence on the education of

---

[46] Hampden's opponents believed that he drank too deeply of philosophical method. As Church wrote, "Dr. Hampden, the man in Oxford best acquainted with Aristotle's works and with the scholastic philosophy, had thrown Christian doctrines into a philosophical calculus which seemed to leave them little better than the inventions of men." Church, *The Oxford Movement*, 74.

[47] William Palmer, *Narrative of Events connected with the publication of the Tracts for the Times* (London: Rivington, 1883), 128.

[48] S.L. Ollard, *A Short History of the Oxford Movement* (London: Faith Press Reprints, 1963), 51. Ollard noted that this affiliation was known as the "Broad Church school," and that "a few years later, it would have been impossible." Ibid. For Evangelicals, Hampden's theology was too reliant on philosophy, and not enough on Scripture. With his appointment, complained one of the Evangelical journals, "Protestantism was stabbed to its very vitals." *The Watchman*, reported in a letter by James Mozley to his sister Maria, dated February 20, 1836. See J.B. Mozley, *Letters of the Rev. J.B. Mozley*, ed. Maria Mozley (London: Rivington, 1885), 54.

[49] Hampden's challenge to the traditions of the university must not be underestimated. As Church, himself intimately acquainted with Oxford and its ways, wrote: "Oxford was as proud and jealous of its own ways as Athens or Florence; and like them it had its quaint fashions of polity; its democratic Convocation and its oligarchy; its social ranks; its discipline, severe in theory and usually lax in fact; its self-governed bodies and corporations within itself; its faculties and colleges, like the guilds and 'arts' of Florence; its internal rivalries and discords; its 'sets' and factions." Church, *Oxford Movement*, 160.

undergraduates:[50] according to Peter Nockles, appointing Hampden was seen by many as "a deliberate blow against the University."[51]

Response to the appointment was swift and vociferous. While many engaged Hampden's character, a more practical form of opposition also emerged. Newman and Pusey, in company with the high churchman W.F. Hook, developed a petition to the Archbishop of Canterbury, and collected the signatures of 76 members of the university. The petition stated that Hampden lacked the approval of the university as a whole and charged that he "orally and in printed publications [held] doctrines and principles fundamentally opposed to the Church of England."[52] The Archbishop of Canterbury, in turn, petitioned the King, William IV, and the Prime Minister, Lord Melbourne.

The Tractarians also mounted their attack on the scholarly front. In addition to his role in developing the petition, Newman wrote a pamphlet against Hampden, entitled *Elucidations of Dr. Hampden's Theological Statements*. In the pamphlet, Newman delineated the danger of Hampden's theology. As George Herring stated:

> The central issue for Newman was the creeds, the classic statements of faith by the undivided Church; Newman saw them as of divine inspiration and authority. Hampden, he argued, merely interpreted them as historical documents of human derivation and cast in the language of their times, and thus effectively denied that doctrines such as the Trinity and Incarnation were revealed by God.[53]

Newman's assertions reflected the wider beliefs of high churchmen, specifically that Hampden undervalued the church fathers and the apostolic magisterium in general.[54] With this emphasis on the tradition of the church, the Tractarians began to turn more to the teachings of the church fathers as the justification for their own understanding of doctrine. Hampden, on the other hand, divorced the-

---

[50] Chandler, *Introduction to the Oxford* Movement, 34.

[51] Peter Nockles, "'Lost Causes ... and Impossible Loyalties': The Oxford Movement and the University," in *The History of the University of Oxford*, vol. 6: *Nineteenth-Century Oxford, Part I* (Oxford: Clarendon, 1997), 222.

[52] E. Cardwell to Archbishop Wellington, 15 February 1836. Cited in Nockles, "'Lost Causes,'" 223.

[53] George Herring, *What Was the Oxford Movement?* (London: Continuum, 2002), 57.

[54] Nockles, "'Lost Causes,'" 230.

ology from church history, and was thus separating the church proper from its primitive roots.[55]

When it became clear that the appointment of Hampden would, in fact, go through as planned,[56] the opponents sought avenues of limiting his powers. The Tractarians and their allies put forward a motion to strip Hampden of his ability to vote on the committee that selected speakers for formal university sermons. The Regius Professor of Divinity was an important member of this board, and depriving Hampden of this privilege would cause great embarrassment.

From March to May of 1836, the movement to remove Hampden from the Speakers Committee took legislative form. The first manifestation of the motion, brought forward in March 1836, had enough votes to remove Hampden, but was vetoed by the proctor, E.G. Bayly. However, Bayly's term as proctor ended after Easter and he was replaced by proctors more sympathetic to the anti-Hampden sentiment. In April, the heads of the colleges voted, 14 to 11, to bring the statute before Convocation, or the formal gathering of the general Oxford community. On 5 May, the measure passed 484 to 94, with no veto by the proctors. Hampden was formally relieved of his duties to the Speakers Committee, a moment which Windle called "the zenith of the Oxford Movement."[57] The Tractarians had won their first formal battle against Erastianism, and asserted, as Nockles concluded, "the independence of Church and University against the pretensions of a reforming ministry."[58] For the Tractarians, the Hampden Affair represented a defeat for Erastianism and a victory for tradition and orthodoxy.

This profound Tractarian regard for tradition came into stark focus two years later with the publication of Hurrell Froude's letters and diaries, entitled *Remains of the Late Reverend Richard Hurrell Froude* in 1838. Froude had died

---

[55] Nockes continues by discussing Pusey: "Significantly, in his second edition of his *Dr. Hampden's Past and Present Statements Compared* [1836], Pusey added sections on tradition and the Church that bolstered the 'Tractarian' emphasis. The scriptures themselves, he claimed were to be interpreted 'as expanded by the consent of catholic antiquity, or the agreement of the universal church.' Hampden, he argued, was attacking the Anglican position, and not the Roman." Ibid., 231. Hampden himself did not believe that he was devaluing church doctrine or that he was guilty of heresy. As Herring notes, "[I]n 1847, when he was created Bishop of Hereford, [Hampden's] fellow bishop Samuel Wilberforce of Oxford, finally read Hampden's Bampton Lectures for himself and discovered no heresy in them!" Herring, *What Was the Oxford Movement?*, 57.

[56] Windle comments that "Melbourne ... paid no attention to all this disturbance." Windle, *Who's Who of the Oxford Movement*, 27.

[57] Ibid. Windle noted, however, that "it must be remembered that, in this case, they [the Tractarians] and their opponents within the camp of the Establishment made common cause." Ibid., 27-28.

[58] Nockles, "'Lost Causes,'" 228.

tragically of consumption in 1836, at the age of 32, and Newman and Keble took it upon themselves to edit and annotate their friend's voluminous writings. The first of four volumes was released in 1838, to no small controversy, separating the Tractarians from their anti-Erastian sympathizers.

Froude's work revealed conservative theological tendencies. He condemned the Protestant reformers, writing in a December 1835 letter that, "I hate the Reformation and the Reformers more and more."[59] Furthermore, he displayed an affinity for the church of antiquity and the Middle Ages,[60] praising saints like Thomas Becket, and using the Roman breviary in his devotional practices. Froude admitted to subverting the teachings of the Church of England. "Since I have been at home," he wrote upon returning from an 1832-1833 abroad with Newman and his father, "I have been doing what I can to proselytize in an underhanded way."[61] The work of Protestant reformers, for Froude, seemed to have been inadequate. "I am every day," he confessed in an 1834 letter, "becoming a less and less loyal son to the Reformation."[62]

The perceived "Romish" character of the *Remains* caused enormous scandal, and threw the entire Tractarian cause into shadow. Non-Tractarian high churchmen and low church evangelicals, who had united with the Tractarians against Hampden, now abandoned the movement entirely. The high churchman Edward Churton told Pusey, "[T]here are sentences and even pages of that book which I could wish almost to have lost my right hand sooner than seen published,"[63] while the evangelical paper *Christian Observer* editorialized that "[t]he battle of the Reformation must be fought once more."[64] Even within the Tractarian Movement itself, the work was divisive; Yngve Brilioth noted that the book "was a wedge which split the Tractarian block."[65] The support, both academic and popular, which the Tractarians had enjoyed two years earlier, had vanished, and had, more accurately, mutated into grave opposition.

---

[59] Froude, *Remains*, 1:389 (Dec. 1835).

[60] Piers Brendon notes that the *Remains* displayed Froude's "romantic vision of the medieval [sic] Church." *Hurrell Froude and the Oxford Movement* (London: Elek, 1974), 185).

[61] Froude, *Remains*, 1:322.

[62] Ibid., 326.

[63] *LD*, 6:222.

[64] "The Rev. C. Dodgson on the Ripon Ordination Questions; With Remarks in Reply," *The Christian Observer Conducted by Members of the Established Church* 38 (August 1838), 507.

[65] Yngve Brilioth, *The Anglican Revival: Studies in the Oxford Movement* (New York: Longmans, Green and Co., 1933), 158.

Why then did Newman and Keble decide to publish such a controversial work? It appears that they felt it necessary. As Herring noted, "Part of the *ethos* of Tractarianism was its aggression and provocation, to attack as the best form of defense [sic], to shock deliberately, so to polarize issues that people would be forced to take sides."[66] The entire tone of the *Remains* recalled Newman's first tract, which exhorted its readers to "*choose your side*," and displayed the very fervor that Froude himself had displayed in life.[67] Piers Brendon noted that the publication of the *Remains* "jolted the Movement forward in the direction in which Newman and Keble wanted it to go,"[68] that is, towards radical reform of the Church's political, moral, and ecclesiological priorities.

Newman knew that the publication would stir controversy. Indeed, he saw such controversy as necessary. Nockles noted, "He was quite prepared to alienate the large 'orthodox body' of the Church of England whose early support had proved the Movement's life blood, if the Movement's hold over the rising generation at Oxford could thereby be assured."[69] The movement was not for the lukewarm or semi-interested, but rather for those wholly devoted to the re-envisioning of the Church of England. For Newman and Keble, one's reaction to the *Remains* would gauge one's commitment to the Tractarian cause.

The condemnation of Froude's beliefs and practices led to continuing questions about the theology, and specifically the ecclesiology, of the Tractarians. Were they Catholic or Protestant? The answer, crafted by Newman, was that they were neither; rather, the Church of England was an ecclesiological entity unique in itself, and separate from Catholicism and Protestantism. Indeed, the Anglican Communion was what Newman called a "*via media*" of orthodoxy between the two factions, properly orienting the Church Universal towards the truths of the faith given by Christ to the Apostles.[70] As Christopher Dawson described, Newman believed that this apostolic "deposit of faith" was,

> The essential note of the true Church and that it was there to be found most perfectly in the Anglican Church. Rome had added to it, Protestantism had

---

[66] Herring, *What Was the Oxford Movement?*, 58.

[67] Brendon writes that Newman and Keble believed that "Froude represented the true, uncompromising spirit of the Movement." Brendon, *Hurrell Froude*, 184.

[68] Ibid.

[69] Nockles, *The Oxford Movement in Context*, 282.

[70] Chandler notes that Newman borrowed the term "via media" from the English divines of the seventeenth century. Chandler, *Introduction to the Oxford Movement*, 31. The position goes as far back as Matthew Parker (1504-1575), the first Elizabethan archbishop of Canterbury, who sought a "golden mediocrity" whereby peace between Catholics and Calvinists could develop. See Chadwick, "The Mind of the Oxford Movement," 6.

subtracted from it, only in the Church of England was to be found the safe middle way of Catholic orthodoxy—the Apostolic Church and the Faith of the Fathers.[71]

In light of the failure of the other two "branches," as they were called, of the Church, it was of even greater importance that the Church of England know itself and understand its mission.

Newman formally presented his theory in 1836, the same year as the Hampden controversy, in his *Lectures on the Prophetical Office of the Church viewed Relatively to Romanism and Popular Protestantism.*[72] The work was essentially a combination of his *Tract 38: Via Media, Vol. 1* and *Tract 41: Via Media, Vol. 2*, which he had written in the summer of 1834. In this work, Newman explained the proper understanding of church tradition. As George Herring observed:

> Newman makes the distinction between two Traditions in the Church, the Apostolic and the Prophetic. The first is the unchanging deposit of the faith, and the second is the vast literature effectively constituting a commentary on that deposit; but the latter is not fundamental and contains different levels or degrees of credit.[73]

According to Newman, the goal of a proper church was twofold: to conserve the given truth; and to contain the orthodoxy of the "vast literature" of the post-apostolic era. During their period of encroaching Erastianism, it was especially necessary for the Anglican Church to recall its theological roots, and eradicate teachings contrary to these.

In order for the Church of England to respond to the challenges of the times, it needed to define itself *qua* church. For Newman, the Anglican Church was a valid institution, because it had remained faithful to Catholic teachings. As he noted in his *Apologia*, he had believed that the Church was divided into Greek, Latin, and Anglican branches, each of which "inherited the early undivided Church *in solido* as its own possession."[74] These three branches were "identical"

---

[71] Christopher Dawson, *The Spirit of the Oxford Movement*, (New York: Sheed and Ward, 1933), 103.

[72] Dawson noted that William Palmer, non-Tractarian high churchman who was at one time quite close to Newman, produced his own *via media* theory in 1838, called the "Branch Theory," the same year as Newman's second edition. The book, though, was not a highly-regarded work, and certainly does not carry the scholarly weight of Newman's work. Yngve Brilioth called it "one of the most narrow-minded productions of Anglican theology." *The Anglican Revival: Studies in Oxford Movement*, (London: Longmans, Green, and Co., 1933), quoted in Dawson, *Spirit of the Oxford Movement*, 103.

[73] Herring, *What was the Oxford Movement?*, 35.

[74] *Apologia*, 72 [191].

with the early church, agreeing in all things "but their later accidental errors."[75] The Church of England was *not* a reforming Protestantism in the same way as the Lutheran and Reformed traditions. Instead, Newman insisted:

> [T]he English Church did *not* revolt from those who in that day had authority by succession of the Apostles ... The Church then by its rulers and officers reformed itself. There was no new Church founded among us, but the rights and the true doctrines of the Ancient existing Church were asserted and established.[76]

Newman believed that Anglicanism's claim to catholicity gave heft to the entire Tractarian argument. From this *ontologia ecclesiae*, arguments for reform could substantively and validly flow.[77]

Criticism of the *via media* theory spurred the further study of patristics as a means of establishing the Church of England's ancient credentials. R.W. Church noted that the overall criticism of Newman's theory was that it was a "paper theory," separated from actual and potential reality.[78] Newman was convinced that his theory could work and "wanted to bring out in a substantive form a living Church of England, in a position proper to herself, and founded on distinct principles."[79] These principles, he claimed, were found in the early church. His study of the fathers had convinced him of this, and his interest was echoed by other like-minded Tractarians such as Pusey and high churchmen like Hook.[80] Without appeal to the ancient church, Nockles noted, Newman and other Tractarians

---

[75] Ibid. For example, as Nockles noted, "Rome may have been a true church but she was deemed to have abandoned Antiquity by adding to as well as corrupting the faith with tenets such as Transubstantiation, Purgatory, the Invocation of Saints, devotion to the Blessed Virgin Mary, Indulgences, and obligatory private confession. Peter Nockles, "Sources of English Conversions to Roman Catholicism in the Era of the Oxford Movement," in *By Whose Authority?: Newman, Manning, and the Magisterium*, ed. V. Alan McClelland (Bath: Downside Abbey, 1996), 13.

[76] *Tract 15: On the Apostolical Sucession in the English Church*, (Oxford: Oxford University, 1840), 3.

[77] Faught noted that this "three-pronged position" of "dogma, definite religious teaching, and his view of the Church of Rome," allowed Newman "to attack almost fearlessly his enemies and at the same time draw to himself and to the Movement supporters whose ardor for the position enunciated eventually, in many cases, outdid his own." Faught, *The Oxford Movement*, 64.

[78] Church, *The Oxford Movement*, 212. He continued, in the voice of an opponent to the theory: "There may be an ideal halting-place, there is neither a logical nor an actual one, between Romanism and the ordinary negations of Protestantism."

[79] *Apologia*, 73 [192].

[80] Viz., Church, *The Oxford Movement*, 222.

were convinced that "moral certainty was impossible."[81] Such scholarship solidified the Tractarian effort, particularly in light of the vociferous attacks levelled against it since the publication of Froude's *Remains*.

Yet Newman began to question his theory in 1839, when Nicholas Wiseman (1802-1865), who would in 1850 become Cardinal Archbishop of Westminster, asserted that the Anglican Church was not grounded in antiquity. In "The Anglican Claim to Apostolical Succession," published in the *Dublin Review*, Wiseman drew comparisons between the Donatists of Augustine's time, and the Anglicans of the present day. In this parallel analysis, both groups—the Donatists and the Anglicans—were seen to be a small sect compared to the rest of Christianity, and both made claims to patristic roots and, thus, doctrinal authority. In response to the Donatists, Augustine had stated "*securus judicat orbis terrarum*," that is, "the world judges securely" over and above the ruling of a minority sect. The same statement, Wiseman concluded, could be made against the Anglicans of his time.[82]

The effect of this article on Newman was profound, and led him to reevaluate his theory of the *via media*. Newman was stunned to find that early church teachings, which he had utilized to validate his religious opinions, seemed now to condemn them. As he stated in his *Apologia, securus judicat orbis terrarum* "were words that went beyond the occasion of the Donatists," and that gave "cogency" not only to Wiseman's article, but also the entire controversial history of the church.[83] He continued:

> What a light was hereby thrown upon every controversy in the Church! not [sic] that, for the moment, the multitude may not falter in their judgment ... not that the crowd of Oriental Bishops did not need to be sustained during the contest by the voice and the eye of St. Leo; but that the deliberate judgment, in which the

---

[81] Nockles, "Conversions and the Oxford Movement," 18.

[82] Wiseman wrote, "If the case, therefore, of the Anglican Church had to be decided by the principles and voice of antiquity, we do not see how any verdict but that of schism can be pronounced against it. It is in a state of separation from the aggregate of churches dispersed against the world. It cannot make an excuse; it cannot raise a point either of fact or of right, in bar of judgment, which has not been already met by the judicious sagacity of the great supporter of the unity of the Church [i.e., Augustine], when combating the cavils of the Donatists." Nicholas Wiseman, "'Tracts for the Times' Part III: The Catholic and Anglican Churches" *The Dublin Review*, 7 (Aug-Sep 1839), 163. Quoted in *Apologia,* 110 [228].

[83] *Apologia,* 110 [228].

whole Church at length rests and acquiesces, is an infallible prescription and a final sentence against such portions of it as protest and secede.[84]

Augustine's phrase had condemned Newman 1400 years later, and had, in Newman's words, "absolutely pulverized" the concept of the *via media* as he understood it.[85] The Church of England could not stand on its own against the rest of the Church, and Newman's doubts were beginning to emerge as to whether Anglicanism was a true church or an errant sect.

The writings of the other Tractarians expressed some of Newman's same concerns. From 1836 to 1841, twenty more *Tracts for the Times* were published, which delineated opinions that both distanced the writers from Protestantism and seemed to draw them closer to Roman teaching. In their concerted effort to validate the Church of England as an authentic branch of the Church Catholic, these writers—including new writers such as Henry Edward Manning (1808-1892), Archdeacon of Chichester; Charles Marriott, fellow at Balliol College; and Isaac Williams, fellow at Trinity College and close friend of the late Froude—came into increasing conflict with the Protestant mentality of the country. Of particular note is Williams's *Tract 80* and *Tract 87*—both entitled "On Reserve in Communicating Religious Knowledge"—which, as Nockles stated, "struck at the root of the Evangelical tenet of individual conversion and understanding of the doctrine of Atonement."[86] By so joining themselves to the church of antiquity, the Tractarians were also divorcing themselves from the church of the present.

This conflict climaxed in February 1841, with the publication of Newman's *Tract 90*, which called for an interpretation of the *Thirty-nine Articles* less antagonistic towards Catholics. In the tract, entitled "Remarks on Certain Passages in the *Thirty-nine Articles*," Newman noted problems with teachings in twelve of the articles, addressing issues such as purgatory and transubstantiation. Newman recognized that his work was controversially anti-Protestant, and did not hide from the implication. As he stated in the conclusion:

> It may be objected that the tenor of the above explanations is anti-Protestant, whereas it is notorious that the Articles were drawn up by Protestants, and intended for the establishment of Protestantism; accordingly, that it is an evasion of

---

[84] Ibid., 110 [228].
[85] Ibid., 111 [229].
[86] Nockles, "'Lost Causes,'" 244.

their meaning to give them any other than a Protestant drift, possible as it may be to do so grammatically, or in each separate part.[87]

Simply put, Newman believed that the Catholic case had to be made, whatever the consequences might be.

In *Tract 90*, three specific ecclesiological issues emerged: the role of the church in authoritatively interpreting Scripture; Anglicanism's claim to be the unifier of the one church; and finally the preoccupation with opposing the authority of the Bishop of Rome.[88] To the first issue, Newman responded that the church "*expounds and enforces the faith ... that it derives ... wholly from Scripture.*"[89] The teaching office of the church, therefore, should not be in conflict with the Bible, but should rather "educe an *harmonious interpretation* of Scripture."[90] Both tradition and Scripture were therefore necessary, both as complements to one another, and as purveyors of the Christian truth.

This understanding of balance between Scripture and tradition played heavily into Newman's vision of the Church of England as the middleway between Rome and Protestantism. For Newman, the *Thirty-nine Articles* were "drawn up with the purpose of including Catholics; and Catholics now will not be excluded. What was an economy in the reformers, is a protection to us."[91] As he would later write in his *Apologia*, his own tone was meant to be conciliatory, inasmuch as reconciliation was necessary for the protection of Anglicanism in general.[92]

This "acceptance of reconciliation" extended to the most controversial issue between Catholics and Protestants, that of the papacy. Newman believed the papacy to be a development of men—not a revelation of God—and, as he noted, "what man can make, man can destroy."[93] Yet, God had given authority to bishops and as a result, the Church Universal consists, as Imberg stated, "of a number of independent Churches, each ruled by its own Bishop."[94] The office of

---

[87] *Tract 90*, 80.

[88] An excellent summary of the argument in *Tract 90* can be found in Rune Imberg, *In Quest of Authority: The "Tracts for the Times" and the Development of the Tractarian Leaders, 1833-1847*, (Lund, Sweden: Lund University Press, 1987), 129-134. I am indebted to Imberg's work.

[89] *Tract 90*, 7. Emphasis in original.

[90] Ibid.

[91] Ibid., 23.

[92] Newman wrote, "My tone was, 'This is necessary for us, and have it [i.e., his own interpretation of the Articles] we must and will, and, if it tends to bring men to look less bitterly on the Church of Rome so much the better.'" *Apologia*, 123 [238].

[93] *Tract 90*, 77.

[94] Imberg, *In Quest of Authority*, 133.

a universal leader, such as the pope, is thus unnecessary,[95] but only insofar as a Christian is not under the pope's direct authority. "We find ourselves, as a Church," he wrote, "under the King now, and we obey him; we were under the pope formerly, and we obeyed him."[96] Indeed the pope *had* been the authority over England once, and had been duly respected. Times and new authorities had changed the circumstances, and thus Anglican priorities.

Though Newman's tract ultimately defended the Church of England, the outcry against its sympathies for Rome was swift and vicious. As R.W. Church noted, "Unhappily, *Tract 90* was met at Oxford, not with argument, but with panic and wrath."[97] High churchmen and liberals alike condemned Newman as a "crypto-papist,"[98] and the bishop of Exeter, Henry Phillpotts, found the approach of Newman's work "utterly irreconcilable" with orthodox Anglican beliefs.[99] On 8 March 1841, four tutors protested the tract, and a week later, on 15 March, the Hebdomanal Board at Oxford condemned the tract as "evading rather than explaining the sense of the *Thirty-nine Articles*."[100] The vociferous reaction against Newman's tract called the *Tracts for the Times* into question, and warranted critical response from both the University and the local bishop, Richard Bagot. Soon, the university officially disassociated itself with the *Tracts*, and Bagot asked that the publication be shut down. In response, Newman agreed to terminate the *Tracts*, provided that the English bishops would not condemn *Tract 90*, and that he would be allowed to publish it elsewhere.

The entire ordeal of *Tract 90* took a great toll on Newman emotionally. He retired to the country parish of Littlemore at the end of 1841, having been "denounced as a traitor who had laid his train and was detected in the very act of firing it."[101] There, he began to contemplate his place in the Anglican Church, and slowly began to realize that his proper place in the Church of England was not to be in it at all. "From the end of 1841," he recalled in his *Apologia*, "I was

---

[95] "Mutual intercourse [between bishoprics] is but an *accident* of the Church, not of its essence." *Tract 90*, 78. Emphasis in original.

[96] Ibid., 79.

[97] Church, *The Oxford Movement*, 290.

[98] Ironically enough, R.D. Hampden took the opportunity to reassert his own orthodoxy. As Nockles noted, Hampden "seized his moment and preached a conservative defense of the Articles against Tractarian casuistry, insisting, in sharp contrast to the ambivalent language of his earlier works, on the Articles' literal and dogmatic nature." "'Lost Causes,'" 242.

[99] Henry Phillpots, *A Charge to the Clergy of the Diocese of Exeter* (London: John Murray, 1842), 28.

[100] This is the language from the board's official condemnation (15 March 1841). A facsimile of the pronouncement can be found in Nockles, "'Lost Causes,'" 241.

[101] *Apologia*, 88 [205].

on my death-bed, as regards my membership with the Anglican Church, though at the time I became aware of it only by degrees."[102]

"Catastrophes": Newman, Ward, Manning, and other conversions to Rome

Newman would remain at Littlemore for four years, engaged in a profound spiritual struggle. His "semi-monastic life of study and prayer," as Vincent Ferrer Blehl called it,[103] separated Newman from his duties and brothers at Oxford, and afforded him the opportunity to explore his questions without distractions. He began his retreat in the hopes of further studying the early church; as he stated, "I had determined to put aside all controversy, and I set myself down to my translation of St. Athanasius."[104]

Controversy followed Newman nevertheless, as during the summer of 1841 he "received three blows," which in his words "broke" his spirit.[105] The first "blow" came from his study of Athanasius, which demonstrated to him the error of Anglicanism. He wrote, "I saw clearly, that in the history of Arianism, the pure Arians were the Protestants, the semi-Arians were the Anglicans, and that Rome now was what it was then."[106] As with Wiseman's article, Newman saw that the parallels between the Church of England and the church of antiquity were not encouraging. Rather, they were quite condemnatory. He began to see that the *via media* would never work, as the only "branch" of the church that had maintained the fullness of the truth since antiquity was Rome.

The second blow proved to be the attacks levelled against Newman on account of *Tract 90*. "The Bishops," he noted, "one after another began to charge against me. It was a formal, determinative movement."[107] The weight of the original attack had driven him to Littlemore in the first place, but the general episcopal condemnation drove Newman to a state of ecclesiological despair. It seemed as though his church had rejected him, when he by his lights had not rejected the church.

The final and most powerful strike against Newman's Anglican conscience was the establishment of the Jerusalem bishopric in July 1841. The Prussian and

---

[102] Ibid., 137 [252].

[103] Blehl, "Newman's Conversion of 1845: A Fresh Approach," in *By Whose Authority?: Newman, Manning, and the Magisterium*, ed. V. Alan McClelland (Bath, UK: Downside Abbey, 1996), 131.

[104] *Apologia*, 130 [245].

[105] Ibid.

[106] Ibid., 130 [245].

[107] Ibid. He later wrote, "It [Tract 90] was addressed to one set of persons, and has been used and commented on by another." Ibid., 142 [257].

British governments, in collaboration with their state churches, had agreed to establish this new see, for the sake of protecting the Protestants living in the Holy Land. The move was mainly political, and meant to counter similar actions taken by the Russians and the French to protect their respective Orthodox and Roman Catholic constituencies in the Middle East. The problem with the establishment of this bishopric, however, was that the only Protestants in Jerusalem were Lutherans, not Anglicans. For Newman, this turn of events was appalling. He voiced his opinion in print during July 1841, stating that such a move put the Church of England in league with heretics and infidels.[108] Parliament, though, did not heed Newman's call to episcopal isolationism, and passed the bishopric measure on 5 October 1841. The decision confounded and disturbed Newman in its lack of religiosity. Writing to a friend, he stated, "We have not a single Anglican in Jerusalem; so we are sending a Bishop to *make* a communion."[109] He believed this to be Erastianism at its most perverse.

These seemingly irreconcilable faults of the Anglican Church haunted Newman for two years. In September 1843, he resigned his post at St. Mary the Virgin, ending his public Anglican ministry.[110] Because a large number of dons, particularly younger ones, had recently taken these steps, and then converted to Roman Catholicism, many saw Newman's actions as a definitive step towards Rome. However, Newman did not acknowledge his announcement as the first sign of defection, but rather a reflection of his discontent with Anglicanism's

---

[108] Newman wrote in the *British Critic*: "When our thoughts turn to the East, instead of recollecting that there are Christian Churches there, we leave it to the Russians to take care of the Greeks, and the French to take care of the Romans, and we content ourselves with erecting a Protestant Church at Jerusalem, or with helping the Jews to rebuild their Temple there, or with becoming the august protectors of Nestorians, Monophysites, and all the heretics we can hear of, or with forming a league with the Mussulman against Greeks and Romans together." "Private Judgment," in *Essays Critical and Historical*, 2 vols (London: Longmans Green, 1910), 2:365-66.

[109] In a letter to Mr. Bowden, 12 Oct. 1841 he continued, "[T]here are converted Anglican Jews there who require a Bishop; I am told there are not a half-a-dozen." Elsewhere, he wrote, "We are now to be joined with a schismatic and heretical body [Lutheranism] to set up a joint bishopric in a place, by the way, where neither of us has any claim to jurisdiction." *Apologia*, 133 [249]. Cf. *LD*, 8:294-96.

[110] He also had published, in February of that same year, a retraction of the highly anti-Catholic opinions of his past. Mainly, he had broken himself of the opinion of "Mariolatry" in Roman Catholicism, under the tutelage of Dr. Charles William Russell of Maynooth. He noted in his *Apologia* that he had been trained to believe that Rome "suffered honours to be paid to the Blessed Virgin ... incompatible with the Supreme, incommunicable Glory of the One Infinite and Eternal." *Apologia*, 138 [253].

current state of affairs.[111] Though he still thought himself a loyal son of the Church of England, he did struggle with doublemindedness. As he told his friend, J.B. Mozley, "The truth is ... I love the Church of Rome too well."[112] To assuage his tormented conscience, he began to write. His theological reflections, particularly on the nature of doctrine in the church, became the basis for his *Essay on the Development of Christian Doctrine*.

During his writing, Newman began to realize that he could not be a man with a foot in two doors; he would either have to choose Anglicanism—and thus reject Rome—or vice versa.[113] But he could not reject Rome, with its patristic roots and firm hold on both doctrine and tradition. The Church of England's hold on Christian truth, on the other hand, seemed to be at best tenuous. Conversion to Rome appeared to be the best option:

> On the one hand I came gradually to see that the Anglican Church was formally in the wrong, on the other that the Church of Rome was formally in the right; then, that no valid reasons could be assigned for continuing in the Anglican, again no valid objections could be taken to joining the Roman.[114]

For Newman, the Roman Catholic church offered the definitive moral and theological certainty that the Church of England lacked.[115]

Newman still battled internally until 1845, when he completed his break with the Church of England.[116] In November of that year, he completed and had pub-

---

[111] Yet some in higher positions thought Newman was being dishonest with himself and with them. As Newman himself indicated in his *Apologia*, "Such fidelity ... was taken *in malam partem*, by the high Anglican authorities; they thought it insidious." *Apologia*, 165 [278].

[112] Newman to the Rev. J.B. Mozley, 1 September, 1843. *LD*, 9:494.

[113] Newman wrote: "It was impossible to let it alone: the Anglican position could not be satisfactorily maintained, without assailing the Roman." *Apologia*, 183 [293].

[114] Ibid., 181 [292].

[115] Newman stated: "I am far more certain (according to the Fathers) that we [Anglicans] are in a state of culpable separation, than that developments do not exist under the Gospel, and that the Roman developments are not the true ones. I am far more certain that our (modern) doctrines are wrong than that of the Roman (modern) doctrines are wrong." Ibid., 179 [290].

[116] The question often asked about Newman's entire conversion process is: why it did take so long? Blehl's answer to the question is quite insightful: "First, he did not feel a clear call in conscience to do so [i.e, convert sooner]. Secondly, if he were in error in entering the Catholic Church, he would lead others into error, or despairing of truth, into scepticism. Thirdly, he thought he might be suffering from 'judicial blindness,' a punishment for some secret fault, and so he revealed his conscience to Keble. Fourthly, he had a dread of going by feelings and not by reason and conscience. ... He also recognized

lished his *Essay on the Development of Christian Doctrine*, and felt compelled to convert.[117] On 25 September 1845, he gave his final sermon as an Anglican, entitled "The Parting of Friends," in the presence of Pusey and Keble. On 3 October, he resigned from his fellowship at Oriel College, a position he had held for over twenty years. The following week, on 9 October 1845, John Henry Newman was received into the Roman Catholic Church. He remained at Littlemore until 23 February 1846, when he left behind both his retreat and Oxford. He would not return to the university until 1878, for the purpose of visiting Keble.

The effect of Newman's conversion on the Oxford community, particularly the Tractarians, cannot be overstated. The reactions to the event ranged from surprise to complete devastation. Mark Pattison, a former student of Newman at Oriel and fellow of Lincoln College, stated, "The sensation to us was as of a sudden end of all things and without a new beginning."[118] John William Burgon's description was not so much despair as anger: "We felt that we had been betrayed, and we resented the wrong which had been done to us."[119] Even Benjamin Disraeli, future Prime Minister of Britain recognized Newman's importance to the Church of England, writing later that "[t]he secession of Mr. Newman dealt a blow to the Anglican Church under which it still reels."[120]

---

the price he would have to pay: for in joining a despised minority he would become ostracized from relatives and friends." Blehl, "Newman's Conversion," 132.

This discussion offers an opportunity to consider briefly the question of "insight into conversion." One of the great endeavors of Oxford Movement scholarship, throughout its history, has been the quest to uncover the reasons—personal, psychological, theological—behind the conversion of so many Tractarians, particularly Newman. Newman, more than any other, left scholars his own self-reflective notes, books, and diaries, which are copious and easily accessible. For this reason, a scholarly industry has coalesced around his experience. Two examples: Jeffrey Marlett, "Conversion Methodology and the Case of Cardinal Newman," *Theological Studies* 56 (1997): 669-685; Kenneth Parker, "The Role of Estrangement in Conversion: The Case of John Henry Newman," in *Christianity and the Stranger: Historical Essays*, ed. Francis Nichols (Atlanta: Scholars Press, 1995), 169-201.

[117] "Newman's Conversion," 132. Newman's angst centered itself on the question of salvation. As he writes in his diary entry for 8 January: "The simple question is, Can *I* ... be saved in the English Church? am *I* in safety, were I to die to-night? Is it a mortal sin to *me*, not joining another communion?" *Apologia*, 208 [315].

[118] Mark Pattison, *Memoirs* (London: Macmillan, 1885), 235.

[119] John William Burgon, *Lives of Twelve Good Men*, 2 vols (London: Scribner & Welford, 1888), 1: 235.

[120] Benjamin Disraeli, *The Works of Benjamin Disraeli, Earl of Beaconsfield*, eds. Edmund Gosse and Robe Arnot, (London: M.W. Dunne, 1904), xxv.

Church concluded his memoir with Newman's conversion, calling the event "The Catastrophe." According to Church, the Oxford Movement "ceased to be strongly and prominently Academical."[121] The Oxford Movement had lost its great intellectual titan, and thus its great scholarly foundation.[122]

Yet Newman's conversion was the last in a series of blows which had befallen the Tractarian cause during the first half of the 1840s. In 1842, Keble resigned his position as Professor of Poetry at Oxford after eleven years, and the university held an election for the vacant appointment. Isaac Williams (1802-1865), close friend of Keble and Froude, and fellow tract writer, as well as an accomplished poet, appeared well-situated to be his successor.[123] His membership in the Tractarian cause, however, cast a dark pall over his candidacy. Indeed, as Herring noted, "everything had become so 'politicized' in the university that anything a known Tractarian did or stood for would be opposed on purely theological grounds."[124]

Williams's opponent was a relatively obscure poet named James Garbutt, of Brasenose College, whose poetry was of little acclaim, but whose non-Tractarianism was notable. In the election, Garbutt won handily, 921 to 623, and was awarded the professorship. S.L. Ollard observed that this election "was the first open defeat" of the Tractarian party.[125] Also in 1842, Pusey was suspended from preaching by the Hebdominal Board for the sermon *The Holy Eucharist, A Comfort to the Penitent*, which was deemed theologically in error.[126] "The Trac-

---

[121] Church, *The Oxford Movement*, 406-407. He explains: "No one indeed held such a position as Dr. Pusey's and Mr. Keble's; but though Dr. Pusey continued to be a great power at Oxford, he now became every day a much greater power outside of it; while Mr. Keble was now less than ever and Academic, and became more and more closely connected with men out of Oxford, his friends in London, and his neighbors at Hursley and Winchester." Ibid., 407.

[122] This is in no way meant to demean Pusey's influence on the movement, both before and after Newman's conversion. However, Pusey's power was more in his leadership skills, as well as his academic reputation. To say that Newman was the great intellectual force behind the movement is to assert nothing new in scholarship, nor to impugn the facts of the period.

[123] Windle, *Who's Who of the Oxford Movement*, 34. As Windle writes, Williams "was the best man available at the time."

[124] Herring, *What Was the Oxford Movement?*, 63.

[125] Ollard, *Short History of the Oxford Movement*, 62.

[126] Pusey himself had intervened on behalf of Williams and Tractarianism during the campaign for the poetry professorship, a move that made the campaign, in the words of Chandler, "almost entirely a theological contest." Chandler, *Introduction to the Oxford Movement*, 78. Chandler observed that Pusey believed Williams's victory in the election would be a victory for the Tractarians. This led Pusey to circulate a letter saying as much,

tarians," Herring stated, "were now becoming the victims of that very tactic of university condemnation which they had sought to employ against Hampden."[127]

Such "university condemnation" reached a frenzied high point with the punishment of William G. Ward (1812-1882) in early 1845. Ward, a fellow and tutor at Balliol, had published during the summer of 1844 *The Ideal of a Christian Church*. Nockles described it as, "a provocative, unashamedly Romanizing treatise."[128] The book took up the argument of Newman's *Tract 90*, arguing for a more Catholic reading of the *Thirty-nine Articles*. Yet Ward's assertions were far less nuanced than Newman's, and his claims were much broader. For him, the "ideal" of the Christian Church was Roman, not Anglican, and the doctrines delineated in the Articles were "in their natural meaning ... Catholic."[129] Church explained that Ward "admitted that he *did* evade the spirit, but accepted the 'statements of the Articles,' maintaining that this was the intention of their original sanctioners. ... [H]e showed that Evangelicals, high church Anglicans, and Latitudinarians were equally obliged to have recourse to explanations, which to all but themselves were unsatisfactory."[130] The Church of England was, therefore, a kind of hybrid church, and, in this way, secondary to Rome in its importance.[131]

Ward's bold assertions, scandalous on their own terms, were magnified by the fact that he still considered himself an Anglican. This "slander" of the fathers of the Articles, coupled with Ward's somewhat gleeful obstinancy, incurred powerful measures of censure from the Hebdominal Board. In December 1844, it was proposed that Ward's book be condemned and that he be deprived of his degrees. The measure was passed two months later, on 13 February 1845, at a raucous meeting of the board, and Ward was remanded to the level of an undergraduate. As R.W. Church put it, Ward's punishment was "a shattering blow" to the Tractarians.[132] Ward himself would not remain in the

---

in which "he was rather blunt," and which "sharpened the party element in the election." Ibid. Williams himself believed, in retrospect, that Pusey's involvement—particularly this letter—did more harm than good, contributing greatly to Garbutt's resounding victory.

[127] Herring, *What Was the Oxford Movement?*, 63-64.

[128] Nockles, "'Lost Causes,'" 259.

[129] W.G. Ward, *The Ideal of a Christian Church Church Considered in Comparison with Existing Practice* (London: James Toovey, 1844), 478.

[130] Church, *The Oxford Movement*, 351.

[131] Church wrote that Ward's book "assumes that the Roman Church, and only the Roman Church, satisfies the conditions of what a Church ought to be," Ibid., 373-374.

[132] Ibid., 388. He further explained, "It was more than a defeat, it was a rout, in which they were driven and chased headlong from the field; a wreck in which their boasts and hopes of the last few years met the fate which wise men had always anticipated. Ox-

Church of England, marrying later that year, and preceding Newman into the Roman Catholic Church by a few months.

The events of 1845, punctuated by Newman's defection to Rome, sent the Tractarian Movement into a tailspin. Without the institutional clout that it had exerted during the Hampden affair, and without the powerful presence of the deceased Froude and the converted Newman, the movement wandered through a kind of extended depression. Keble, in partial retirement following his resignation of his poetry professorship, sunk from the public spotlight, and provided more support and guidance than genuine leadership. It was Pusey, despite the losses to Tractarianism, as well as the deaths of his wife and daughter, in 1839 and 1844 respectively, who provided a reluctant but steadying force throughout this time. He believed that the Tractarian cause still burned bright, and that the recent developments were not a cause to give up hope. As he wrote in his open letter of response to Newman's conversion, God "will surely not forsake us now."[133] This optimistic attitude, coupled with his irenic approach to those who had "gone over" to Rome, was a beacon of hope and comfort for those faithful Tractarians who had been scandalized by the recent events. Now Pusey's hope for reform lay in the clergy that Oxford would produce, rather than tracts. Tractarianism's public pulpit had vanished.

The Tractarians, though, endured one last great trial in 1850, with the occasion of the Gorham decision. Three years earlier, in 1847, the Reverend George Cornelius Gorham (1787-1857), a divine in the diocese of Exeter, had been nominated to a parochial living at Bampford Speke. Though involving a relatively obscure parish, Gorham's nomination became controversial. He did not hold to the doctrine of baptismal regeneration, refusing to admit that the baptized person experiences "new birth" through the sacrament. Bishop Phillpotts, whom Ollard called "an old-fashioned High Churchman,"[134] and who had previously condemned Newman's *Tract 90*, held this doctrine to be one of the most

---

ford repudiated them." Ibid., 388. Nockles put the actions of, and reactions to, the Hebdominal Board in perspective: "Dean Church suggested that the heads were motivated by an ignorant, old-fashioned belief that the appeal of Romanism for Oxford graduates and MAs lay in 'a silly hankering after the pomp or the frippery of Roman Catholic worship, and at best a craving after the romantic and sentimental.' Yet it can be argued that the heads took the steps which they did in the Ward affair precisely because they recognized the reality and depth of the appeal of Romanism in the junior university, and acted according to their duty as guardians of the faith of the young." "'Lost Causes,'" 261.

[133] Pusey to the *English Churchman*, 16 October 1845. The full text appears in H.P. Liddon, *The Life of Edward Bouverie Pusey*, 4 vols (London: Longmans Green & Co, 1897), 3:462.

[134] Ollard, *Short History of the Oxford Movement* , 88.

fundamental in Anglicanism, and explicitly laid out in the *Book of Common Prayer*. He refused to appoint Gorham to the living. This case became one of great interest to Tractarians, especially Pusey, who had written much on baptism during the previous two decades.[135]

In June of the next year, Gorham appealed Phillpotts's decision, asking the Court of Arches, the highest ecclesiastical court in England, to override the bishop. The court ruled in favor of Gorham, saying that he should be instituted. Phillpotts again refused, and Gorham went to the Judicial Committee of the Privy Council, a move well within his legal rights. Yet for Tractarians, it was another example of the doctrinally corrosive effect of Erastianism. In March 1850, the Privy Council, comprised of persons of varying levels of religious belief,[136] declared Gorham eligible for the position of the living, stating that his beliefs were "not contrary or repugnant to the doctrine of the Church of England as established."[137] As with the Church Temporalities Bill of 1833, and the establishment of the Jerusalem Bishopric in 1841, English political and legal authorities had superceded ecclesiastical and doctrinal concerns.

The effects of the decision were swift and powerful, as a large number clergymen abdicated not only their ministerial positions, but the Church of England entirely. "Here," wrote Herring, "was a secular court upholding heresy, and as a result there was a further hemorrhage of clergy from Tractarianism to Rome."[138]

---

[135] Chandler noted that the case interested divines of all ideological backgrounds: "Many High Churchmen feared that their position would become impossible if Phillpotts were to be defeated. Conversely, evangelicals who thought that Gorham was right feared that they would not be able to stay in the Church of England if their views were held to be inadmissible. The liberals were ... anxious that definitions should be avoided." Chandler, *Introduction to the Oxford Movement*, 98.

[136] Windle described the council's constituency: "It must be noted ... that that body is recruited from persons of all forms and no forms of belief, and that there might not, in a given case, be a single adherent of the Anglican Church assisting as a judge at the hearing; secondly, that the *Book of Common Prayer*, being a schedule to an Act of Parliament, the meaning of its words is susceptible of judicial determination, just as the phraseology of any other act is." Windle, *Who's Who of the Oxford Movement*, 58.

[137] *The Judgment of the Judicial Committee of Privy Council, Delivered March 8, 1850, Reversing the Decision of Sir H.J. Fust* (London: Seeleys, 1850), 16.

[138] Herring, *What Was the Oxford Movement?*, 71. As Webb put it, "There were not a few ... who thought that the toleration of Gorham by a court which, though they questioned its competence, was *de facto* the supreme tribunal of the Church of England, gravely compromised the position of that Church as an orthodox branch of the Catholic Church." Webb, *Religious Thought in the Oxford Movement*, 102-103. Herring asserted that those who left were "assistant curates, not rectors and vicars, thus arguably limiting the potential damage to the Movement." Herring, *What Was the Oxford Movement?*, 71.

Among the most prominent Tractarian converts were Archdeacon Robert I. Wilberforce, of the prominent, strongly Anglican Wilberforce family; James Hope, fellow at Merton College; Thomas Allies, fellow at Eton and Wadham College; William Maskell, chaplain to Bishop Phillpotts; and Henry Edward Manning, archdeacon of Chichester. Yet Manning—who would himself, fourteen years after his 1851 conversion, succeed Cardinal Wiseman as Archbishop of Westminster and *de facto* primate of England—best summarized the general dissatisfaction with the Church of England following the Gorham decision: "The violation of the doctrine of Baptism," he wrote in a later journal entry, "was of less gravity to me than the violation of the divine office of the Church by the supremacy of the Crown in council."[139] This loss of discipline, for Manning and other converts, reflected the loss of teaching authority; secular forces now had such a grasp on the workings of the Anglican Church, that the true religious powers of the Church were unsalvageable.[140]

Despite the great number of such conversions to Roman Catholicism, as well as the continuing shadow cast by Erastianism, Tractarians such as Pusey, Keble, Dean Church, Charles Marriott, and James Mozley remained firm in the Anglican faith. Their steadfastness in the face of many controversies was surprising, as many thought that their own conversions to Rome would soon occur. Newman wrote, "When I became a Catholic, I was often asked, 'What of Dr. Pusey?'"[141] Indeed, as the Tractarian cause had seemingly crumbled around them, so too it seemed that these men's paths would eventually lead to Rome. Yet this was not so, and the men continued to strive toward reunion with their now departed brethren, as well as toward the further purification of Anglicanism from Erastianism.[142] By the time that Keble and Pusey died, in 1866 and 1882 respectively, they had become quietly tragic figures, condemned by public opinion, abandoned by former compatriots—yet ever hopeful in their quest for the betterment of the Church of England.

Yet Manning and Robert Wilberforce stand out as striking examples of major defections from the Movement because of the Gorham case.

[139] Journal entry, Dec. 1887, in Purcell, *Life of Cardinal Manning*, 1:558.

[140] See Nockles, "Sources of English Conversions to Roman Catholicism in the Era of the Oxford Movement," 22.

[141] *Apologia*, 65 [185].

[142] The trials, though, continued—quite literally—as George Anthony Denison, Archdeacon of Taunton, was prosecuted for teaching the Real Presence in 1854. He was first convicted, but eventually exonerated, and his trial served as a rallying point of a revival of high church ritualism among the Tractarians and their followers. See Ollard, *Short History of the Oxford Movement*, 90-92.

Conclusion

This narrative of the Oxford Movement has outlined the major controversies, behind the conversion of many Tractarians to Roman Catholicism. While many details were sacrificed for the sake of brevity and scope, such omissions should stimulate further questions about the Oxford Movement and its participants. This account—stretching in this narrative from the introduction of the Church Temporalities Bill in 1833 to the Gorham decision in 1850—sets the stage for the later controversy over papal infallibility which will be discussed in the rest of this volume.

At the root of the entire movement was the issue of ecclesiology, namely how a church—in this case the Church of England—exists as an entity unto itself, separate from secular politics. The Tractarians explored how the church understood itself on its own terms, outside of the influence of the English state. As the Movement progressed, many Tractarians still held firm to the belief that Anglicanism was a true branch or division of Christianity, and that its apparent corruptions were only temporary. Others, namely those who converted to Catholicism, thought these secular intrusions more than temporary, and came to believe that the Church of England was inherently flawed by its ties to the state. They came to believe that the only true Christian church was the Roman Catholic Church. In Catholicism, these converts perceived the true presence of the Holy Spirit: its magisterial lineage uninterrupted since the apostolic era, and its teachings consistent throughout its history. It is fair to say that the men never could have envisioned the end result of the movement begun in 1833.

Indeed, just as an anxiety to protect the Church of England from the dangerous forces of Erastianism spurred Tractarianism to develop, and led some Tractarians to convert to Roman Catholicism, so too did an anxiety to protect the Roman Catholic Church from the forces of secularization drive these converts to choose a particular side in the papal infallibility debate of the 1860s. The subsequent essays in this volume will follow along the theme of ecclesiology, delineating how Tractarian converts to Catholicism understood the role of the papacy in their newfound ecclesiastical community.

Dr. Jay Hammond analyzes Newman's conversion in light of the relationship between Newman's hermeneutics and his study of early church heresies. C. Michael Shea then delineates the reception history of Newman's theory of development of doctrine from 1845 to 1870, and contends that the theory played a more prominent role in the First Vatican Council than is commonly thought. Dr. Kenneth Parker, in the third essay, describes Manning's neo-ultramontane vision of the Catholic Church as a continuation of the ecclesiological vision of his Anglican years. This is followed by Rev. Michael Pahls's discussion of how

Manning's neoultramontane approach to the papacy varied from Pusey's irenicism and Prime Minister William Gladstone's pragmatism. Hudson Davis's essay, discussing William G. Ward, is a spiritual biography in nature, and analyzes how Ward transformed from a man devoted to Tractarianism to a man devoted to the Catholic Church and eventually the pope. Donna Reinhard, in her essay, describes a number of the less prominent, even forgotten converts of the Oxford Movement, focusing on those who influenced the First Vatican Council more indirectly, with either their writing, insider access to the council, or moral support. Finally, Rev. Pahls takes up Newman's theology of the *schola theologorum*. He considers how this theological vision influenced the Second Vatican Council's reception of *Pastor Aeternus*.

In each of the converts which the volume examines, one can see the roots of his thought in the Oxford Movement, specifically how earlier involvement in Tractarianism shaped his understanding of the Roman Catholic Church as both a human and divine institution. Once the Anglican roots of their Catholic thought are brought into clear focus, the roles of converts in the papal infallibility debates of the 1860s take on a new shape and meaning. A surprising conclusion emerges—that one of the defining events in modern Roman Catholic history drew much of its energy from developments originating in the ecclesiastical foment of the Church of England.

THE INTERPLAY OF HERMENEUTICS AND HERESY IN THE PROCESS OF NEWMAN'S CONVERSION FROM 1830 TO 1845

JAY M. HAMMOND

Much has been written about Newman's conversion.[1] Although various authors interpret his conversion differently, all agree that it was a process. For example, Ian Ker, following the *Apologia*'s chronology, interprets the process by reading Newman's Anglican years through the lens of his Catholic years, which insinuates that his conversion was inevitable.[2] He tends to read the process backward from his Catholic conversion of 1845. In contrast, Gilley deviates from the *Apologia*'s temporal structure and interprets the process of Newman's conversion as a product of his evangelical formation as an adolescent.[3] He tends to read the process forward from his evangelical conversion of 1816. Turner too rejects the *Apologia*'s narrative, but focuses on Newman's virulent attacks against evangelicalism rather than his spiritual development from it.[4] He tends to read the process as reflecting Newman's engagement in religious warfare beginning in 1833 and ending in 1845 with the "disruptive and confused schismatic" being forced out of the English church. All agree that Newman's conversion was a complex and fascinating process.

Conversion as process also corresponds with Newman's own understanding of the term. In 1828 he described conversion as "the process, not the com-

---

[1] Ian Ker, ed., *Newman and Conversion* (Notre Dame: University of Notre Dame Press, 1997); Jeffrey Marlett, "Conversion Methodology and the Case of Cardinal Newman," *Theological Studies* 58 (1997): 669-85; Avery Dulles, "Newman Conversion, and Ecumenism," *Theological Studies* 51 (1990): 717-31; Paul Schmidt, "Newman's Conversion: Loss and Elegiac Longing," *Renascence* 36.4 (1984): 203-18; John Griffin, "The Anglican Response to Newman's Conversion," *Faith and Reason* 3 (1977): 17-34; John Thirlwall, "John Henry Newman: His Poetry and Conversion," *Dublin Review* 242 (1968): 75-88; John Vitello, "The Conversion of John Henry Newman," *Review for the Religious* 36.5 (1977): 715-28; Kenneth Parker, "The Role of Estrangement in Conversion: The Case of John Henry Newman," in *Christianity and the Stranger: Historical Essays*, ed. Francis Nichols (Atlanta: Scholars Press, 1995), 169-201.

[2] Ian Ker, *John Henry Newman: A Biography* (Notre Dame: University of Notre Dame, 1990), vii-ix.

[3] Sheridan Gilley, *Newman and His Age* (London: Darton, Longman and Todd, 1990), 321-34.

[4] Frank Turner, *John Henry Newman: The Challenge to Evangelical Religion* (New Haven, CT: Yale University Press, 2002), 1-23; also see *Apologia Pro Vita Sua and Six Sermons*, ed. Frank Turner (New Haven: Yale University Press, 2008), 1-115.

mencement of a religious course—the gradual changing, not an initial change."[5] In January 1832 he commented:

> When men change their religious opinions really and truly, it is not merely their opinions that they change, but their hearts; and this evidently is not done in a moment–it is slow work; nevertheless, though gradual, the change is often not uniform, but proceeds, so to say, by fits and starts, being influenced by external events, and other circumstances.[6]

He was more succinct in the *Apologia*: "Great acts take time."[7]

My thesis is that the process of Newman's conversion involved the interplay of two things: his hermeneutical principles and his historical-dogmatic studies of heresy. While the principles of Newman's hermeneutic guided his interpretation of heresy,[8] the contextualization of that interpretation reflects more the history of the nineteenth century than the fourth century.[9] In other words, Newman's investigations into heresy were historical, but his own theological preoccupations against liberalism were the primary impetus for his historical study. He looked into the past to help him discern the theo-political events of the present. In effect, Newman conducted his historical studies of heresy so he could construct a rhetorical strategy against his adversaries, and he assembled that strategy according to his underlying hermeneutical principles. Accordingly, analysis of the shifts within that rhetorical strategy during its construction, col-

---

[5] Birmingham, BOA, Newman, MS A.91, "Remarks on the Covenant of Grace in Connection with the Doctrines of Election, Baptism and the Church."

[6] John Henry Newman, "Sudden Conversions," in *Parochial and Plain Sermons*, 8 vols (London: Rivingtons, 1878), 8:225.

[7] *Apologia*, 156.6 [270]. Elsewhere in the *Apologia* Newman provides a concise ten year chronology of his conversion; see 169.35-170.14 [282]. For an alternative read that questions the *Apologia*, see Turner's introductory sketch in *John Henry Newman*, 1-23.

[8] For the purpose of this essay, a hermeneutic is defined as a group of principles, either implicit or explicit, governing the interpretation of any statement or experience thus yielding a particular meaning.

[9] It is safe to say that Newman's patristic research merged with his public struggle against liberalism. Hence, in his heresy research, we find Newman having one eye on the heresies of the past and another on the liberalism of the present. However, the problems of simultaneity within historical chronology are critical. Because of the complexity of the historical background, it is difficult to determine whether Newman applied to his contemporary polemics principles discovered during his patristic research, or if the historical context first affected his method of research. My argument assumes that the circumstances of Newman's opposition to liberalism conditioned his patristic research regarding the rise and refutation of heresy.

lapse and reconstruction from 1830-1845 provides a lens through which the process of his conversion may be perceived.

To demonstrate the interplay of Newman's hermeneutical principles and his historical-dogmatic studies of heresy, the essay has two main parts. Part one identifies the four principles of Newman's hermeneutic: the principles of conscience, dogma, probability, and imagination. The interaction of these four principles forms a hermeneutical dialectic of *belief* and *development*. The struggle of Newman's conversion records the process of explaining this dialectic as a cogent system of thought.[10]

Part two applies the principles of Newman's hermeneutical dialectic of *belief* and *development* to his historical-dogmatic studies of heresy. I primarily base my analysis upon five works written during the period: first, *The Arians of the Fourth Century* (1830-32),[11] in which he produced the rhetorical strategy that could be used against Christian liberals; second, his unpublished Apollinarian papers (1835), in which he more explicitly explored implicating liberals with his rhetorical strategy; third, his unpublished Monophysite papers (1839), where his rhetorical strategy backfired, resulting in his famous self-identification as a Monophysite; fourth, his *Tract 90* (1841) and the ensuing collapse of the *via media,* which increasingly alienated Newman from Anglicanism; and fifth, his *An Essay on the Development of Christian Doctrine* (1845), where Newman rearticulated his dialectical hermeneutic as the test-case for converting to Roman Catholicism. In the first three works Newman studied past heresies so as to incriminate his contemporaries. With the last two studies Newman turned to reassess the "heretical" developments of Anglicanism and Roman Catholicism so he could decide whether to convert.[12] Throughout the process, Newman's un-

---

[10] I derive these four principles from the *Apologia*. This is not to say that Newman was fully aware of these principles within the process of his conversion. Rather, the four principles simply represent Newman's *understanding* of his religious opinions. Nevertheless, utilizing information from the *Apologia* to explain the process of Newman's conversion will demonstrate a high degree of correlation between the historical events and Newman's recollection of those events. However, the validation of such a method ultimately hinges upon whether one believes these same principles could be identified in Newman's works from the 1820s and 1830s. I assume that they can, but such a study exceeds the parameters of the present topic. Thus, I proceed with a healthy skepticism and check the *Apologia*'s evidence against Newman's study of heresy in the 1830s.

[11] Newman reported that he began the work in 1830. *Apologia*, 35.25 [153]. It was ready for press in July 1832, and published in 1833. *Apologia*, 41.1-2 [158-9]. Thus, it was complete before Newman left for his Mediterranean vacation in December 1832.

[12] On the one hand, Newman, until 1843, viewed Roman Catholicism as heretical. He "thought the Pope to be Antichrist." *Apologia*, 57.18 [176]. Newman commented that his anti-Roman Catholicism formed a "false conscience" that left a stain on his imagina-

derlying hermeneutic never substantially changed; rather, his conversion of 1845 was a nuanced reordering of the fundamental principles within his hermeneutic of *belief* and *development*.

Belief/Faith and Development/Church: The Two Poles of Newman's Hermeneutic

In the *Apologia Pro Vita Sua* (1864), Newman confessed that his conversion rested upon the relationship between the faith and the church. He noted, "This was my issue of the controversy from the beginning to the end. There was a contrariety of claims between the Roman and Anglican religions, and the history of my conversion is simply the process of working it out to a solution."[13] From 1830 to 1839, Newman paralleled the faith with his idea of Anglicanism, and the church with Roman Catholicism.[14] In delineating the dynamics involved in his conversion, Newman declared:

> These then were the *parties* on the controversy:—the Anglican *Via media* and the popular religion of Rome. And next, as to the *issue*, to which the controversy between them was to be brought, it was this:—the Anglican disputant took his stand upon Antiquity or Apostolicity, the Roman upon Catholicity. The Anglican said to the Roman: 'There is but One Faith, the Ancient, and you have not kept to it'; the Roman retorted: 'There is but One Church, the Catholic, and you are out of it.[15]

The tension between "Apostolicity *versus* Catholicity"[16] brought fundamental shifts in his religious hermeneutic throughout the process of his conversion.[17]

---

tion. *Apologia*, 20.9-13 [137]. See also *Apologia* 57.33-38 [177] and 59.20 [178]. Note the connection Newman made between the imagination and conscience.

[13] *Apologia*, 106.16 [224].
[14] *Apologia*, 102.2 [220].
[15] *Apologia*, 101.29 [220]; also see 138.29 [254].
[16] *Apologia*, 102.6 [22], 103.13 [221]. Newman explained the difference with additional terms: "Antiquity argues according to 'Primitiveness' while catholicity follows 'Universality.' In the eyes of the opposite position, strict primitiveness, on one side, seems susceptible to schism because England is estranged from the ancient ecclesial Catholicity, while, on the other side, rigid universality succumbs to idolatry because Rome has added to the Creed." *Apologia*, 106.35-107.18 [224].

[17] It is important to note that Newman's understanding of apostolicity was dependent upon the assumed principle of antiquity; specifically, that the apostles handed on the true deposit of the faith without any changes or alterations. Thus Newman's principle of antiquity was derived from his understanding of the nature of revelation. All was given to the apostles, and they handed the truths of dogma onto subsequent generations. Apostoli-

Newman's understanding of the relationship between faith and church can be considered in two ways. On one level, the above quote can be interpreted as revealing the historical *context* by which the process of Newman's conversion unfolded. Nineteenth-century England, specifically Oxford, provided the polemical milieu within which Newman vigorously reacted against liberalism. Thus, one can analyze the historical conditions that influenced his understanding of the relationship between the faith and the church. However, *what* Newman thought about that relationship depended on *how* he interpreted the relationship. Consequently, on another level, the same statement may be viewed as revealing the *content* of the hermeneutic operative within the historical context. Thus, one can also examine the process of Newman's attempt to reconcile the antagonism he envisioned between the faith and the church which culminated in his intellectual conversion in 1839 and subsequent re-appropriation of his hermeneutic from 1840-1845. A passing comment in the *Apologia* correlates with the linked dimensions of *context* and *content*: "My opinions in religion were ... the birth of my own mind and the circumstances in which I had been placed."[18] In short, the *content* of Newman's hermeneutic, operative within the historical *context*, caused shifts in how he interpreted both.

Fundamentally, these shifts stem from Newman's conceptual organization of faith and church according to the ideas of *belief* and *development*. Belief parallels his articulation of the faith that is rooted in apostolicity, and development parallels his concept of the church, which emerges from catholicity. In effect, the conflict concerning the faith and the church was mirrored by a dissonance within his hermeneutic, namely, the relationship between *belief* and *development*.

As mentioned, four principles were operative within Newman's dialectical hermeneutic of *belief* and *development*: conscience, dogma, probability and imagination.[19] The first two shape Newman's idea of *belief* (i.e., faith or apostolicity), while the other two structure his idea of *development* (i.e., church or

---

city was the guarantee of true doctrine. Hence, Newman considered apostolicity as necessarily prior to catholicity. In short, apostolicity defined catholicity, not vice versa.

[18] *Apologia*, 91.17 [209].

[19] These four principles are not simply notional; rather, Newman was preoccupied with a concrete and real hermeneutic. This is confirmed if one considers Newman's "autocentrism" by which he referred all things to the self, and he definitely considered himself as real. Thus, for Newman, a dictate of conscience necessarily led to conduct. It was the person who acted; yet, Newman thought belief preceded action. Thus it was imperative that a person possess proper belief. He keenly recognized the fundamental importance of the interpreter, and concomitantly the fundamental role the hermeneutic plays in the process of coming to certitude of belief.

catholicity). In effect, the process of Newman's conversion was a consequence of his deepening understanding of the inter-relations among these four principles.[20] The interrelated dimensions of Newman's conversion can be summarized accordingly:

Table 1: The Dimensions and Dissonances of Newman's Conversion Process

The Parties	Apostolicity of Anglicanism	vs	Catholicity of Catholicism
The Issue	Faith	vs	Church
Dialectic Hermeneutic	Belief	vs	Development
The Principles	Conscience and Dogma	vs	Probability and Imagination

To elucidate the dissonances that caused shifts in his hermeneutic, the principles comprising that hermeneutic must be further explained.

The Four Principles of Newman's Hermeneutic

First, the principle of conscience is primary to Newman's understanding of belief. In the *locus classicus* at the beginning of the *Apologia,* Newman conveyed the powerful impression that formed his conscience. He recorded that his intellect rested "in the thought of two and two only absolute and luminously self-evident beings, myself and my Creator."[21] He elaborated on the seminal

---

[20] It exceeds the scope of this essay, but the synthesis of Newman's dialectical hermeneutic can be understood as paralleling the Illative Sense. It is through the synthetic power of the Illative Sense that the apparent contradictions within the hermeneutical dialectic were worked out into a more integrated system. Thus the four principles were convergent probabilities which were unified by the power of the Illative Sense. See John Henry Newman, *An Essay in Aid of a Grammar of Assent*, ed. Ian Ker (Oxford: Clarendon, 1985), 222-247.

[21] *Apologia*, 18.5 [134].

event three times: "From a boy I had been led to consider that my Maker and I, His creature, were the two beings, luminously such, *in rerum natur* ... It is face to face, 'solus cum solo', in all matters between man and his God."[22] And again, "If I am asked why I believe in a God, I answer that it is because I believe in myself, for I feel it impossible to believe in my own existence (and of that fact I am quite sure) without believing also in the existence of Him, who lives as a Personal, All-seeing, All-judging Being in my conscience."[23] And even more forcefully, "Were it not for this voice [of the absolute primary truth of God's existence], speaking so clearly in my conscience and my heart, I should be an atheist ... ."[24] It was from the foundational experience of *solus cum solo* that Newman's emphasis on conscience throughout his works can be traced.[25] Conscience was the compass that guided Newman's actions; to act against his conscience was simply inconceivable.[26] Specifically, conscience was what compelled Newman's sense of duty.[27] More generally, it was the centripetal principle that provided cohesion to the other three principles of his hermeneutic.

Second, the principle of dogma was the other aspect to Newman's idea of belief. He wrote:

> When I was fifteen (in the autumn of 1816) a great change of thought took place in me. I fell under the influences of a definite Creed, and received into my intellect impressions of dogma, which, through God's mercy, have never been effaced or obscured.[28]

---

[22] *Apologia*, 177.4, 11 [288].

[23] *Apologia*, 180.2 [291].

[24] *Apologia*, 216.23-38 [322].

[25] For an article that discusses this experience recorded in the *Apologia* and Newman's idea of conscience see: Terrence Merrigan, "*Numquam Minus Solus, Quam Cum Solus*—Newman's First Conversion: Its Significance for His Life and Thought," *The Downside Review* 103 (1985): 110-113. Also see, Jan Walgrave, *Newman the Theologian* (New York, Sheed & Ward, 1960), 201-240 and 342-363.

[26] For example, in relation to the Jerusalem Bishopric Newman comments, "I had no right, I had no leave, to act against my conscience. That was a higher rule than any argument about the Notes of the Church." *Apologia*, 139.33 [255]; also see 134.14 [249].

[27] For example, while explaining the relation of probability to certitude, Newman boldly stated, "This was the region of Private Judgment in religion; that is, of a Private Judgment, not formed arbitrarily and according to one's fancy or liking, but conscientiously, and under a sense of duty." *Apologia*, 32.3 [151]. Note the connection that Newman makes between probability and conscience. Thus, throughout the *Apologia*, Newman emphasizes that his sense of duty drove his decision making process. *Apologia*, 59.20-32 [178], 111.8 [229], 134.17 [249], 137.27-138.22 [253-4], 208.27-29 [253].

[28] *Apologia*, 17.20 [133].

Referring to the same event, Newman reemphasized the importance of dogma:

> From the age of fifteen, dogma has been the fundamental principle of my religion: I know no other religion; I cannot enter into the idea of any other sort of religion. ... What I held in 1816, I held in 1833, and I hold it in 1864. Please God, I shall hold it to the end.[29]

These quotations reveal two things: first, dogma registered a deep and enduring influence upon Newman's hermeneutic, which second, served as the fundamental principle of his religion.[30] Undergirding Newman's principle of dogma was his strong affinity for antiquity, which he recognized as being synonymous with apostolicity.[31] Thus Newman linked dogma, antiquity and apostolicity altogether; one implied the others.[32] Yet of the three, it seems that Newman favored antiquity as the litmus test for truth.[33] For belief to be true, it had to be ancient.[34]

Third, the principle of probability is the first aspect to Newman's concept of development. He had a unique understanding of probability, derived from Bishop Butler's writings, which Newman attempted to explain several times in the first part of the *Apologia*.[35] Probability played a central role in Newman's epistemology which naturally impacted his hermeneutic. His clearest explanation of probability is found in the following quotation:

> My argument is in outline as follows: that the absolute certitude which we were able to possess, whether as to the truths of natural theology, or as to the fact of a revelation, was the result of an *assemblage* of concurring and converging probabilities, and that, both according to the constitution of the human mind and the will of its Maker; that certitude was a habit of mind, that certainty was a quality of propositions; that probabilities which did not reach to logical cer-

---

[29] *Apologia*, 54.30 [174]; also see 57.8 [176].

[30] Newman echoed his identification of dogma as "the fundamental principle of my religion" when he described the beginning of the Oxford Movement, *Apologia*, 55.3 [174]; also see 71.12 [190].

[31] *Apologia*, 101.33 [220].

[32] Specifically, Newman linked antiquity with dogma in *Apologia* 35.37-36.1 [154], and antiquity with apostolicity in 101.33 [220]; also compare 102.5 [220] and 103.13 [221].

[33] For example, antiquity was the basis of the *via media*. *Apologia*, 97.27 [216].

[34] This claim holds true for *An Essay on the Development of Christian Doctrine* (London: Longmans, Green, & Co.; reprint, 1878), 159-164, wherein Newman asserted that the first note of genuine development is the "Preservation of Type."

[35] *Apologia*, 23.9 [141], 29.35 [148], and 31.10 [150].

tainty, might suffice for a mental certitude; that the certitude thus brought about might equal in measure and strength which was created by the strictest scientific demonstration; and that to possess such certitude might in given cases and to given individuals be a plain duty, though not to others in other circumstances.[36]

Fourth, the principle of imagination is the second aspect to Newman's understanding of development:

> my imagination ran on unknown influences, on magical powers, and talismans ... I thought life might be a dream, or I an Angel, and all this world a deception, my fellow-angels by playful device concealing themselves from me, and deceiving me with the semblance of a material world.[37]

Further on in the *Apologia*, Newman mentioned the role the imagination plays in the formation of ideas and one's religious opinions:

> Now I come to two other works, which produced a deep impression on me in the same Autumn of 1816, when I was fifteen years old, each contrary to each, and planting in me the seeds of an intellectual inconsistency which disabled me for a long course of years. I read Joseph Milner's Church History ... [and] I read Newton on the Prophecies ... . My imagination was stained by the effects of this doctrine up to the year 1843; it had been obliterated from my reason and judgment at an earlier date; but the thought remained upon me as a sort of false conscience.[38]

I include the second quote to demonstrate the role the imagination had in formulating images and ideas which influenced Newman's belief.

To summarize, four principles form Newman's dialectical hermeneutic of *belief* and *development*: conscience, dogma, probability and imagination. On one side, conscience and dogma shaped Newman's understanding of *belief*. On the other side, probability and imagination formed his understanding of *development*. The inter-relations among these four hermeneutical principles informed Newman's research on fourth-century heresies so as to identify and condemn the heresies of nineteenth-century England. Thus, Newman derived his rhetorical

---

[36] *Apologia*, 31.10 [150].

[37] *Apologia*, 16.25 [132].

[38] *Apologia*, 19.35 [136]. In his later writings, especially the *Grammar of Assent*, Newman further articulated the role of imagination within the epistemological process. For an article which analyzes Newman's use of imagination in his theological method see David Hammond, "Imagination and Hermeneutical Theology: Newman's Contribution to Theological Method," *The Downside Review* 106 (1988): 29-31.

strategy from his theory of heresy, first articulated in *The Arians of the Fourth Century*, but the background of his polemics against liberalism provided him with the need for the rhetorical strategy.

The Second Reformation: Liberalism vs. Anglicanism (1830-1833)

In 1831 Newman was commissioned to write a history of the early councils. In his hands, this became a history of the Arian controversy.[39] However, Newman's historical research was conditioned by his own context, specifically the challenges of modernity. He acknowledged the link between the content and context of his research in the *Apologia*: "While I was engaged in writing my work upon the Arians, great events were happening at home and abroad, which brought out into form and passionate expression the various beliefs which had so gradually been winning their way into my mind."[40] The great events included: the repeal of the Test and Corporation Acts of 1828, the Catholic Emancipation Act of 1829, the Reform Act of 1832, and the Church Temporalities Act of 1833. These political events had religious repercussions that greatly troubled Newman because he saw them as representing a progressive agenda that eroded the authority of the Church of England. Thus, within this heated context, Newman wrote *The Arians of the Fourth Century* according to an historiographical method of analogical association that paralleled the various parties of the fourth century with those of the nineteenth.[41] With such a typology, Newman vilified the Arians of the fourth century so he could attack Christian liberals, evangelicals, moderate Protestants, Dissenters, Unitarians, and Roman Catholics.[42] For

---

[39] Stephen Thomas, *Newman and Heresy: The Anglican Years* (New York: Cambridge University Press, 1991), 34-49.

[40] *Apologia*, 39.17 [157].

[41] Newman's analogous historiography most likely derived from his patristic research, which he began in the long vacation of 1828. *Apologia*, 35.20 [153]. Alexandrian typology, especially the "idea of pagan history as a preparation for the Gospel," taught Neman to read history analogously. See Charles Frederick Harrold, "John Henry Newman and the Alexandrian Platonists," *Modern Philology* 37 (1940): 279-91, especially 282 and 287. For the influence of Joseph Milner's historiography, see Thomas, *Newman and Heresy*, 46-49.

[42] I agree with Frank Turner that by the time Newman wrote the *Apologia*, "Newman transformed the liberalism of the 1830s into something to be deplored in 1864 by both Roman Catholic and Protestant audiences." Turner, *Newman*, 15. In the *Apologia* "evangelical Dissenters, churchmen willing to accommodate modestly their grievances, moderate Protestants, and establishment evangelicals were all reduced to *liberals* whose goals and values embodied *liberalism*, terms that meant one thing from 1830 to 1845 and

Newman, "the enemies of Christianity are, in fact, *anything at all* which is *not* the established Church."[43]

In Part I of *The Arians*, Newman constructed his ancient/modern link by contrasting the two great centers of pre-Nicene Christianity: Antioch and Alexandria. Likewise, his history of the controversy between these two "schools and their parties" presupposed that first, a primitive deposit of revealed truth predated the doctrinal creeds of Nicaea, and that second, the refutation of heretical developments helped produce the orthodox creeds. In other words, condemning heresy is what connected the root of revelation with the fruit of orthodoxy. The interplay of these two elements formed the basis of Newman's understanding of antiquity,[44] especially "the ancient maxim that heresy is *novelty* and novelty is always wrong."[45] Newman concluded *The Arians* by describing the process and its relationship to the church of his day:

> Such is the general course of religious error; which rises within the sacred precincts, but in vain endeavors to take root in a soil uncongenial to it. The domination of heresy, however prolonged, is but one stage in its existence; it ever hastens to an end, and that end is the triumph of the Truth ... And so of the present perils, with which our branch of the Church is beset, as they bear a marked resemblance to those of the fourth century, so are the lessons, which we gain from that ancient time, especially cheering and edifying to Christians of the present day. Then as now, there was the prospect, and partly the presence in the Church, of an Heretical Power enthralling it, exerting a varied influence and a usurped claim in the appointment of her functionaries, and interfering with the management of her internal affairs.[46]

Newman's historical parallelism achieved three things that wed Newman's age with that of Arius: first, the struggle of heresy and orthodoxy ultimately ends with the triumph of Truth and the defeat of false beliefs caused by false developments; second, the analogous deficiency of the Antiochian "Aristotelico-

---

another in 1864." Ibid., 23. This essay assumes the earlier meaning of *liberalism* when it uses the term to describe Newman's opponents.

[43] Thomas, *Newman and Heresy*, 23.

[44] Newman commented that his Arian studies provided him an opportunity to examine the principle of Antiquity as "the true exponent of the doctrines of Christianity ... The course of reading, which I pursued in the composition of my [Arian] volume, was directly adapted to develop it in my mind." *Apologia*, 35.37-36.6 [154]. Also see: Turner, *Newman*, 142-143.

[45] Thomas, *Newman and Heresy*, 33.

[46] John Henry Newman, *The Arians of the Fourth Century* (Notre Dame: University of Notre Dame Press, 2001), 393.

Judaic" school and the rationalism of liberalism;[47] and third, the corresponding deceit of the Alexandrian "Eclectic sect" and eclectic character of Christian liberalism: evangelicals, moderate Protestants, and Unitarians. A brief examination of the last two will clarify the contours of Newman's ancient/modern typology.

First, the Antiochean traits of Judaism and Sophism parallel the characteristics of liberalism. On the one hand, Newman identified Antioch's judaizing as the birthplace of heresy. Newman's rhetoric was harsh:

> I will not say that Arian doctrine is the direct result of a judaizing practice; but it deserves consideration whether a tendency to derogate from the honour due to Christ, was not created by an observance of the Jewish rites, and much more, by that carnal, self-indulgent religion, which seems at that time to have prevailed in the rejected nation.[48]

Antioch's Judaism led to "doctrinal opinions, which are grossly humanitarian."[49] With the mischievous linking of judiazing and humanitarianism, Newman subtly connected the Arians with the liberal Christians of his day who were willing to tolerate Christian diversity (i.e., latitudinarianism).

On the other hand, Antioch's sophistry provided a theoretical framework for the articulation and dissemination of Arianism.[50] Although the Antiocheans falsely claimed apostolic authority, their syllogistic reasoning actually brought innovation,[51] which "naturally led them on to disparage, rather than to appeal to their predecessors."[52] Such innovation also led to intellectual arrogance that tended toward infidelity because the Arians "put themselves above the ancients, and the teachers of our youth, and the prelates of the day; considering themselves alone to be wise, and to have discovered truths, which had never been revealed to man before them."[53]

For Newman, Antioch's Judaism degraded Christ and its Sophism destroyed Christ's apostolic church. Accordingly, his criticism of the Arians was the same as his complaint against the liberals who, in his eyes, were jettisoning traditional Christian authority for modern modes of reasoning in the areas of

---

[47] Ibid., 109.
[48] Ibid., 18.
[49] Ibid., 22.
[50] Ibid., 25-26.
[51] Ibid., 26-34.
[52] Ibid., 35-36.
[53] Ibid., 36. Later Newman elaborated, "And from the first, it has been the error of heretics to neglect the information thus provided for them, and to attempt of themselves a work to which they are unequal, the eliciting a systematic doctrine from the scattered notices of the truth which Scripture contains." Ibid., 52.

politics, religious belief, and church identity.[54] In short, both the Arians and liberals were guilty of trying to reform the creeds they had received.[55]

Second, Newman exonerated Alexandria from any taint of heresy. He stated, "in the following pages, I hope to clear the illustrious Church in question of the grave imputation thus directed against her from opposite quarters."[56] While Newman acknowledged that Arius was from Alexandra, his heretical teachings arose because "Arius was educated at Antioch."[57] Thus, the Alexandrian Church in no way contributed to the rise of Arianism. Rather, its catechetical school, founded by St. Mark, was the "Missionary and Polemical Church of Antiquity."[58] Its authority derived from the *disciplina arcani* of the apostolic tradition, that is, the "secret" oral tradition of the apostles that complimented the written scriptures.[59] This *disciplina arcani* did not supersede scripture, but worked in conjunction with scripture "to refute the self-authorized, arbitrary doctrines of the heretics."[60] The secret tradition of the *disciplina arcani* ceased to exist once the creeds of the early councils were divulged.[61] With the Alexandrian *disciplina arcani*, Newman accomplished two things: first, he posited apostolic tradition as an authority in conjunction with scripture, and second, he claimed that this "secret" tradition was prior to all heretical innovation. With the first, Newman could argue against the evangelicals of his day. For example speaking of his own time, Newman observed:

> We have some difficulty in putting ourselves into the situation of the Christians in those times, from the circumstances that the Holy Scriptures are now our sole means of satisfying ourselves on points of doctrine. Thus, every one who comes to the Church considers himself entitled to judge and decide individually upon its creed. But in that primitive age, the Apostolical Tradition, that is, the Creed, was practically the chief source of instruction, especially considering the obscurities of Scripture.[62]

---

[54] Thomas, *Newman and Heresy*, 37-38.
[55] Ibid., 39.
[56] Newman, *Arians*, 40.
[57] Ibid., 39.
[58] Ibid., 41.
[59] Ibid., 50-51, 55, 89, 134.
[60] Ibid., 55.
[61] Ibid., 55.
[62] Ibid., 134-135. Newman is even more explicit later when he asserts that Scripture alone can not provide sufficient protection to revealed dogma. Ibid., 143-150. He uses the dogma of the Trinity as an example: while Scripture provides the seminal evidence for the Trinity (ibid., 151-155), the dogma of the Trinity needed support and clarification provided by ecclesiastical teachings on the Trinity inspired by the Apostolic Tradition.

For Newman, the creeds, which made the *disciplina arcani* public, "were facts, not opinions,"[63] that guided the interpretation of scripture. Moreover, the *disciplina arcani* ensured correct allegorical interpretation of scripture[64] and its economy,[65] as well as, the use of pagan concepts[66] and platonic teachings.[67] In short, the *disciplina arcani*/creeds ensured orthodox dogma. With the second, he could claim, "the ante-Nicene heresies were in many instances the innovations of those who had never been in the Church, or who had already been expelled from it."[68] Thus, Newman could boldly state, "the heretical spirit is ever one and the same in its various forms":[69] subjective innovation away from the objective truth of the creeds and the *disciplina arcani*, which preceded them. In sum, the *disciplina arcani* providentially controlled correct interpretation and authentic integration while excluding all erroneous innovation.

In contrast, to the Alexandrian *disciplina arcani*, the eclectic sect of Antioch reveled in subjective innovation. Again Newman pointed to the Jews as the probable culprits,[70] and with the eventual support of the imperial court, especially Julian the Apostate, the eclectic philosophy spread and "state polytheism" prospered.[71] The distant echo between the "state religion" of the fourth-century and that of Newman's own time quickly reverberates into a thundering accusation. The central heresy of the eclectic sect was "*Neologism*, a heresy which, even more than others, has shown itself desirous and able to conceal itself under the garb of sound religion, and to keep the form, while it destroys the spirit, of Christianity."[72] In "the rationalism of the Eclectics" Newman saw the rationalism of his own day.[73] So the reader would not miss his analogical comparison, Newman made the association explicit:

Ibid., 156-178. Likewise, the eclectics' *neologism* "interpret[s] the Scriptures in the place of the Church" (ibid., 142), which enabled them to join forces with the Antiochian sophists.

[63] Ibid., 134.
[64] Ibid., 57-63.
[65] Ibid., 64-78.
[66] Ibid., 79-88.
[67] Ibid.89-87.
[68] Ibid., 134.
[69] Ibid., 139.
[70] Ibid., 101.
[71] Ibid., 102.
[72] Ibid., 103.
[73] Ibid., 104-106.

Who does not recognize in this old philosophy the chief features of that recent school of liberalism and false illumination, political and moral, which is now Satan's instrument in deluding the nations, but which is worse and more earthly than it, inasmuch as his former artifice, affecting a religious ceremonial, could not but leave so much of substantial truth mixed in the system as to impress its disciples with somewhat of a lofty and serious character, utterly foreign to the cold, scoffing spirit of modern rationalism?[74]

With the ancient/modern typologies, Newman attempted to denounce all forms of liberalism, whether secular or Christian, which he saw eroding the foundation of 'traditional' religion in England.

The four principles within Newman's hermeneutic were integral to his emerging theory of heresy and its accompanying rhetorical strategy. First, Newman tended to typecast heretics as harboring a bad conscience, while the orthodox theologians adhered to the apostolic tradition with a good conscience, thereby squelching any temptation for curious innovation. Second, the principle of dogma, based upon the *disciplina arcani* and later expressed in the creeds, represented the *a priori*, revealed truth over against the subjective innovation of the various heretics. Thus, Newman perceived heretical development as always *a posteriori* to the immutable rule of faith. Third, the principle of probability enabled Newman to group all heretics together: "the heretical spirit is ever one and the same in its various forms."[75] Ironically, with an innovative use of probability, Newman reasoned that all heresy shared the same errant spirit of innovation. Fourth, the principle of imagination allowed Newman to make analogical comparisons with the "heretics" of the fourth century and the "liberals" of the nineteenth century. From the controversial context of the former, Newman devised a rhetorical strategy that he could wield against the latter. Armed with the new rhetorical strategy devised in his Arian studies, Newman was ready to embark on a "second reformation":[76] the *via media* and the birth of the Tractarian Movement.[77] The hope for a "second reformation" reverberated in the conclusion to *The Arians:*

---

[74] Ibid., 106.

[75] Ibid., 139.

[76] *Apologia*, 40.33 [158]; also see 50.14 [169], where Newman commented, "It would be in fact a second Reformation," as he describes the start of the Oxford Movement.

[77] As Thomas Ferguson rightly points out that Newman published *The Arians* prior to the start of the Oxford Movement. Thus, Newman's historical work influenced his Tractarianism and was not an apologetic for it. Thomas Ferguson, "The Enthralling Power: History and Heresy in John Henry Newman," *Anglican Theological Review* 85.4 (2003): 643-644.

Meanwhile, we may take comfort in reflecting, that, though the present tyranny has more of insult, it has hitherto had less of scandal, than attended the ascendancy of Arianism; we may rejoice in the piety, prudence and varied graces of our Spiritual Rulers; and may rest in the confidence, that, should the hand of Satan press us sore, our Athanasius and Basil will be given us in their destined season, to break the bonds of the Oppressor, and let the captives go free.[78]

In a final figurative association Newman fashions himself and his fellow Tractarians as contemporary manifestations of Athanasius and Basil who will free the Church of England from their "heretical" oppressors. Yet, Newman's "second reformation" would undo the first by replacing *sola scriptura* with scripture interpreted by the apostolic tradition, which upheld the faith of the creeds and prevented unwarranted development.

Controversy at Oxford: Anglicanism vs. Liberalism (1833-1836)

Newman's dialectical hermeneutic fueled his rhetoric during the Oxford Movement.[79] From 1833 to 1836 he immersed himself in a continuous controversy against liberalism which he viewed as the great apostasy of his age.[80] Throughout this period, Renn Dickson Hampden "was Newman's ever present rival."[81] Newman identified Hampden's theological opinions as personifying the pervasive influence of liberalism.[82] Newman was also deeply disturbed by the

---

[78] *Arians*, 394.

[79] In the *Apologia*, Newman declares that the Oxford Movement was based on three principles: Dogma, which was against the Liberals; the visible Church, which was against the Evangelicals who minimized its authority; and Anti-Romanism, which was against Roman Catholicism. *Apologia*, 54.17-58.6 [173-7]. Thus, as Newman set out to create the *via media*, he did so against these three groups. All of his theoretical principles had concrete targets.

[80] See Robert Pattison, *The Great Dissent: John Henry Newman and the Liberal Heresy* (New York: Oxford University Press, 1991), 54-64.

[81] See Thomas, *Newman and Heresy*, 71; Pattison, *The Great Dissent*, 61; and *Apologia*, 61.11ff [180ff].

[82] In 1834 Hampden, rather than Newman, was elected professor of moral philosophy. Later that year, Hampden published his *Observations on Religious Dissent* in which he challenged the requirement that students subscribe to the *Thirty-nine Articles*, thus allowing dissenters to matriculate at Oxford. However, the conflict became a feud in 1836, when, Hampden was elected Regius professor of divinity. Newman saw Hampden as manifesting the spirit of liberalism which was overcoming the theology of Oxford. Not only was the subscription to the *Thirty-nine Articles* challenged, but the Regius profes-

apostasy of his friend Blanco White.[83] Newman considered White's apostasy as a manifestation of the true spirit of liberalism.[84] The liberalism at Oxford, the Hampden controversy, and Blanco White's apostasy all conditioned Newman's patristic research[85] leading to his Apollinarian papers of 1835.[86]

Within this controversial context, Newman employed his rhetorical strategy against liberalism.[87] He believed there was a three-fold character to liberalism: first, it chronically suffered from an anti-dogmatic tendency; second, it ultimately depended on the authority of private judgment; and third, it inadvertently reduced theology to mere rationalism.[88] In the Apollinarian papers, Newman again employed his rhetorical strategy to find an authoritative basis in antiquity for combating his contemporaries, via an illustration of how their tacit liberalism ultimately led to apostasy. Again, the interplay between his theory of heresy and the principles of his dialectical hermeneutic framed his emerging understanding of the relationship between belief and development.

In August 1835, Newman was hard at work on his theory of heresy.[89] Picking up from *The Arains*, he assumed that the underlying identity of all heresy was essentially the same.[90] In the opening paragraph of his unpublished essay *Apollinarianism* this position is evident:

---

sorship had been filled with the worst of liberals at Oxford. See Gilley, *Newman and His Age*, 137ff; and Ker, *John Henry Newman*, 106ff.

[83] See Thomas, *Newman and Heresy*, 80; and Pattison, *The Great Dissent*, 64.

[84] For Newman, the event of White becoming a Unitarian in 1835, at the height of Newman's confrontations with Hampden, concretely demonstrated the pervasive power of the liberal heresy. See Ker, *John Henry Newman*, 119.

[85] Ibid., 123.

[86] In August 1835, Newman wrote about 30 pages of notes on Apollinarianism and four papers on the subject. The four papers are: Birmingham, BOA, MS B.2.8.c, "Defection of Apollinarius," 15 August 1835; "Apollinarius History," 19 Augustine 1835; "Apollinarianism," 22 August 1835; [untitled Apollinarianism MS], [undated].

[87] From 1834 to 1836, Newman thought himself surrounded by opposing positions. He had to contend with the Anglo-Protestants, the Romanists, the evangelical Protestants, the liberals, and the atheists. Thus his analysis of the heresies of the early church were equally as complex as his contemporary identification of the various manifestations of liberalism. Newman's theory of heresy—which interpreted the heresies of Arianism, Apollinarianism, Nestorianism, Sabellianism, Docetism, and Socinianism as having the same underlying identity—provided a theoretical basis for his rhetorical strategy which would also identify the numerous liberal groups as having the same underlying identity, i.e., heresy.

[88] *Apologia*, 254-262 [359-369].

[89] Thomas, *Newman and Heresy*, 88.

[90] Birmingham, BOA, MS B.2.8.c, Newman, "Apollinarianism," 2.

... not forgetful the while, that all heresies may be made upon paper to look contrary to each other, while in fact, when analyzed, all will rather be found to run together into one, for they are all really opposed to the Truth and the Truth alone, which seems at first sight merely to lie in the middle between them.[91]

Although Newman understood the underlying identity of all heresies to be identical,[92] the identity is twofold. On the one hand, he perceived heresy as a deviation from the Truth. On the other, heresy had logical consequences regardless of the heretic's good intentions. Throughout the Apollinarian papers, Newman consistently assumed that the apostolic deposit of the faith was anterior to the corrupting influence of heretical interpretations.[93] An analysis of the heresy's development eventually revealed the hidden, errant principles inherent in its system. In short, the argument of the Apollinarian papers was that orthodox *belief* was always anterior to heretical *development*. Thus Newman's theory of heresy was an implicit manifestation of his dialectical hermeneutic between his ideas of *belief* and *development*.

The four principles within Newman's hermeneutic were integral to his evolving theory of heresy. First, he considered the principle of conscience as it related to the heretic. Newman now separated the heretic's intention from the underlying principles of the heretical system itself. At length, Newman demonstrated how good men, zealous for the faith, could foster fatal theological principles that unsuspectingly led them down the path of heresy. Second, was the principle of dogma which he maintained was an immutable *a priori* revealed Truth. Consequently, he again measured heretical development against the orthodox rule of faith. Third, Newman utilized the principle of probability to examine the inner logic of heretical systems. He dissected the inner constitution of heresy to expose its diseased presuppositions. Via inference, Newman took a heterodox system to its logical conclusions, revealing the formal principles from

---

[91] Ibid., 1. One should note Newman's comment that heresy is "opposed to the Truth and the Truth alone, which seems at first sight merely to lie in the middle between them." Already in 1835 one can see that Newman was inadvertently defining Heresy as a *"via media."* In 1839, Newman realized the similarity between this characteristic of heresy and his own *via media*.

[92] Thomas, *Newman and Heresy*, 103.

[93] Here Newman continued the argument he proposed in *The Arians of the Fourth Century* (1832). The influence of Bishop Butler's arguments are evident in Newman's chronological presentation of the relationship between orthodoxy and heresy. For Newman, the truth of orthodoxy always preceded the inset of heretical developments. Again, Newman's understanding of the "deposit of faith" defined heresy as being a distorted development of the pre-existing revealed truth; see BOA, MS B.2.8.c, Newman "Apollinarianism," 8-9.

which it developed.[94] Fourth, Newman applied the principle of imagination to explain how the heretic was misled by new ideas constructed by his innovative imagination. Hence, Newman's theory of heresy was an expression of the four principles within his dialectical hermeneutic.

Newman concluded the unpublished manuscript *Apollinarius' History* by comparing ancient heresy to liberalism.[95] He considered his theory of heresy as equally applicable to all heresies, ancient as well as modern. Newman's analogies between the controversy in the fourth century and the liberal spirit confronting the contemporary church were poignant and calculated. Just like Apollinarius of the fourth century, men of the nineteenth century were being led away from the faith because of logical errors perpetuated by the spirit of liberalism. Newman's intention was explicit. He compared Apollinarius to the tendencies of liberal thought to reveal the one root of both heresies.[96] Newman's theory of heresy proved a powerful rhetorical strategy,[97] and he used it against contemporary adversaries.[98]

---

[94] At the same time Newman began his work in the Apollinarian papers, he read Blanco White's book *Observations on Heresy and Orthodoxy* (1835). Newman was particularly intrigued by White's thesis that "Sabellianism is but Unitarianism in disguise." Newman perceived the importance of White's thesis, and it influenced Newman's investigation of the theory of heresy in the Apollinarian papers. For Newman, White's statement was a confession that all heresies are essentially the same in that they all are contrary to the Truth which is contained in the doctrines of the church. See Thomas, *Newman and Heresy*, 81 and 88.

[95] BOA, MS B.8.2.c, Newman, "Apollinarius' History," 17-19.

[96] For an example of how Newman applied his theory of heresy to his contemporary situation see John Henry Newman, *Historical Sketches*, 3 vols, 6th ed. (London: Longmans, 1886), 1:392-396.

[97] With his theory of heresy, Newman could attack liberalism from a double front. He could critique all contemporary liberal ideas within his theory of heresy. Moreover, he could also use his theory of heresy to elucidate how a specific individual moved away from the eternal Truth. Newman's rhetorical trap was set and he was eager to lure opponents into it in an attempt to reveal liberalism as a modern heresy that was co-extensive with the heresies of the early Church.

[98] Of course, obvious targets were Hampden and White. Yet Newman did not limit the applicability of his rhetorical strategy to them. Other individuals Newman critiqued within his rhetorical strategy included: Nicholas Wiseman, Henry Hart Milman, Thomas Erkine, Jacob Abbot, Thomas Chambers, and Freidrich Schleiermacher. See Thomas, *Newman and Heresy*, 108-163. Newman also employed his rhetorical strategy in his *Elucidations on Dr. Hampden's Theological Statements* (Oxford: Baxter, 1836), in which he unsuccessfully attempted to prevent Hampden from becoming Regius Professor of Divinity. Likewise, he applied his rhetorical strategy in Letter XVI of the "Letters on the

An excellent example of this was *Tract 73* (September 1835), published just one month after completing his Apollinarian papers.[99] Stephen Thomas argues that this tract was Newman's most significant theological work of the period.[100] The three aspects of liberalism: anti-dogmatism, abuse of private judgment, and rationalism were all articulated in the argument of *Tract 73*, yet the method Newman used reflected the rhetorical strategy he had developed in his Apollinarian papers. Thus Newman's dialectical hermeneutic was essential to his argument within the *Tract 73*. However, his new interpretive construct was actually a rhetorical trap in which, in the summer of 1839, he himself would become ensnared.

Construction of the Via Media: *Anglo-Catholicism vs. Romanism (1837-1839)*

From 1837 to 1839, each of Newman's major published works reflected his developing theory of the *via media*. In the *Lectures on the Prophetical Office* (1837),[101] Newman's distinction between the apostolic tradition and the prophetical tradition was a *via media* which attempted to demonstrate that the *Thirty-nine Articles* did not contradict the early Creeds, yet were distinct from the doctrinal developments of Romanism. Likewise, in the *Lectures on Justification* (1838),[102] Newman presented a *via media* between the Protestant position of *sola fides* and the Romanist insistence on works by arguing for the patristic doctrine of the indwelling presence of God within the soul. And, in the *Oxford University Sermons* (1839),[103] Newman masterfully presented the idea that convergent probabilities explain the relationship between faith and reason; thus side-stepping both the evangelical Protestants' position of an irrational faith, and the Romanists' excessive dependence upon syllogistic reasoning. In the same vein, Newman attempted to navigate a position between the emotionalism of internal evidencing and the rationalism of external evidencing.

Church of the Fathers" in the *British Magazine and Monthly Register of Religious and Ecclesiastical Information* (London: Rivingtons, 1836), 148-154.

[99] John Henry Newman, "On the Introduction of Rational Principles into Revealed Religion," in *Tracts for the Times*, vol. 3 (London: Rivington, 1837).

[100] See Thomas, *Newman and Heresy*, 71.

[101] John Henry Newman, *Lectures on the Prophetical Office of the Church Viewed Relatively to Romanism and Popular Protestantism*, 2 vols (London: Longmans, 1885).

[102] John Henry Newman, *Lectures on the Doctrine of Justification*, 3rd ed. (London: Rivingtons, 1874).

[103] John Henry Newman, *University Sermons: Fifteen Sermons Preached Before the University of Oxford, 1826-1836*, eds. D. M. MacKinnon and D. Holmes (London: SPCK, 1970).

The *University Sermons* were Newman's last major works prior to his Monophysite papers. In the sermons he argued that it is necessary both to examine and to know one's first principles if the real meaning of one's own system is to be understood. Thus, it is probable that Newman entered the long vacation of 1839 intending to define with greater precision the principles upon which the *via media* rested. Like his Apollinarian papers, Newman naturally turned to his patristic research seeking arguments in antiquity to support his position. Again, his present context provided a lens through which he interpreted history.

In this context, Newman commenced his Monophysite papers in July of 1839.[104] By August he had re-acquainted himself fully with his theory of heresy.[105] In surveying the parties of the Monophysite controversy, Newman carefully distinguished the radical Monophysite Eutyches from the moderate Monophysites, and the orthodox position of Chalcedon. Newman analyzed these three parties in a dual manner.

First, in the unpublished manuscript "The Monophysite Heresy," Newman identified the Monophysites as an overly zealous reaction against Arianism. Newman concentrated on the theological distinctions and arguments of the three opposing Christological formulations, applying his method of logical inference to uncover the hidden principles of the two heretical systems. However, Newman was perplexed because the moderate Monophysite position was not innovative; rather, it was conservative. The Monophysites, arguing from the Nicene Creed, stated that the "two nature" doctrine was not in Scripture, and that Athanasius himself had not expounded such a position. Thus their conception of the nature of the faith was similar to Newman's own static belief in antiquity.

Second, in the unpublished manuscript, "On Monophysitism", Newman showed a particular interest in the political and rhetorical dimensions of the Monophysite conflict. He examined the ecclesiological positions within the Monophysite debate by investigating the differing attitudes regarding the introduction of the two nature doctrine into the orthodox definition of the faith.

---

[104] Newman wrote three papers on the Monophysites during August 1839, all of which are unpublished. They are: Birmingham, BOA, MS B.2.8.c, "The Monophysite Heresy," 23 August 1839, which primarily analyzed the various doctrinal positions within the Christological controversies prior to the Council of Chalcedon; Birmingham, BOA, MS B.2.8.c, untitled MS, August 1839, which explored the ecclesiological positions of the various Churches involved in the Christological debates of the fourth century; Birmingham, BOA, MS B.2.8.c, "On Monophysitism," 23 August 1839, which contains polished notes on doctrine.

[105] In the long vacation of 1839 Newman wished to return to his "own line of reading, the early controversies of the Church," which he had suspended since 1835. Letter to Isaac Williams, 18 July 1839. See *LD*, 7:110.

Newman perceived that the Chalcedonian definition hinged on the formal acceptance amongst the churches of this development in the articulation of the apostolic faith. The Monophysite controversy proved to Newman the importance of ecclesiastical authority in developing the Orthodox expression of the faith.

Newman's twofold analysis of the Monophysite controversy again paralleled his dialectical hermeneutic upon which his own understanding of the relationship between the faith (belief) and the church (development) stood. His examination of the theological beliefs and respective ecclesiological arguments of the moderate Monophysites closely mirrored his own private use of antiquity and the accompanying rhetoric of the *via media*. The analogy between the past and the present pierced Newman's consciousness. Eutyches, like the Protestants, held an extreme position; the Council of Chalcedon, like Rome, held another; and the moderate Monophysites held a *via media* between the two. Newman looked into his own interpretive construct and saw his "face in that mirror, and [he] was a Monophysite."[106] His interpretive construct was no longer a protective wall. It became the best argument against himself.

He was thunderstruck. This flash of insight blinded his previous understanding of the *via media,* reflecting throughout the relationships between the faith and the church, Anglicanism and Roman Catholicism, and particularly his dialectic of belief and development. Newman became a casualty of his own rhetorical trap; his *intellectual* conversion soon followed.

Within a week after finishing his Monophysite papers, and before reading Dr. Wiseman's article, Newman wrote a cryptic letter to Thomas Mozley on 6 September 1839 alluding to something which deeply vexed him:

> I have been reading and writing hard all week—and my hand aches so now, I can hardly get on with this. I hope I have broken the neck of my job—but I have a good deal to do. ... *Supposing* by any chance you heard of me suddenly running off in spite of this, not to you, but elsewhere, you must not be surprised or tax me with double dealing. A call of very urgent duty which I have no right, nor is it pleasant to talk about, might suddenly carry me away against my will; but it is not likely. Things have happened lately which have shocked me a great deal—do not say anything about this.[107]

Newman was already shaken by the discovery he made in his Monophysite research, when soon after he read Dr. Wiseman's article[108] which used Newman's own method of arguing analogically from antiquity. This article touched a

---

[106] *Apologia*, 108.24 [226].

[107] *LD,* 7:136.

[108] Nicholas Wiseman, "The Anglican Claim of Apostolic Succession," *Dublin Review*, 7 September 1839.

nerve which had already been exposed a week earlier. Newman confessed to Frederick Rogers on 22 September 1839:

> I have had the first real hit from Romanism. ...You see the whole history of the Monophysites has been a sort of alterative, and now comes this dose at the end of it. It does certainly come upon one that we are not at the bottom of things. At this moment we have sprung a leak. ... [A]n uncomfortable vista opened which was closed before.[109]

The new uncomfortable vista was Newman's mental view of the relationship between the faith and the church. In his Monophysite papers, he discovered that the church did not settle matters simply by referring to an immutable deposit of Truth; rather, the church itself was the authority that defined the orthodox rule of faith. Apostolicity and catholicity were inextricably intertwined. This intellectual conversion necessitated a fundamental shift in Newman's dialectical hermeneutic of belief and development because Newman's beloved principle of antiquity was undercut by the dynamics of the early councils, which "decided ecclesiastical questions on a simpler rule than that of Antiquity ... here then Antiquity was deciding against itself."[110] Far from being antagonistic, apostolicity-faith-belief and catholicity-church-development were intrinsically interconnected. Afterward, Newman would continually refer to his Monophysite research as the impetus for changing his religious opinions.[111]

Newman was profoundly disturbed by the analogy of the Monophysite heresy because it made him recognize the unconscious "heretical" tendencies that he possessed. He had claimed that the Monophysites' private judgment and rationalism led to their anti-dogmatic refusal to accept the Chalcedonian definition of faith. Then, after reflecting upon Dr. Wiseman's article, he saw with greater clarity that the ancient heresy of Monophysitism foreshadowed the heresy of his day—liberalism.

---

[109] *LD*, 7:154.

[110] *Apologia*, 110.18 [228].

[111] This critical point is evidenced by his letters to: Frederick Rogers, 22 September 1839, *LD,* 7:154 and 3 October 1839, *LD*, 7:159-160, Robert Wilberforce, 26 January 1842, *LD*, 8:440, John Keble, 4 May 1843, *LD*, 9:328, Henry Manning, 25 October 1843, *LD*, 9:585, and Edward Pusey. 19 February 1844, *LD*, 10:126, and John Keble, 30 October 1844, *LD,* 10:376. Thus Newman himself, before the *Apologia* of 1864, considered his Monophysite research as effecting a great change in his thought. Newman's metaphorical identification of himself as a Monophysite was not simply a rhetorical device used to defend his honesty. In contrast, see the comments from Turner, *John Henry Newman*, 335-337 and 603-613, who finds little evidence from 1839 to support Newman's self-identification as a Monophysite.

To his distress, Newman detected the three aspects of liberalism in his own thought. First, he recognized that the *via media* was an intellectual compromise culpable of rationalism. Second, he realized that his individualistic use of antiquity in constructing the *via media* was an abuse of private judgment. Third, Augustine's phrase *"securus judicat orbis terrarum,"* revealed to Newman that he was guilty of ecclesiological error because he was cut off from the ancient Catholic church.[112] He believed his *via media* suffered the same anti-dogmatic tendency as did the moderate Monophysites.

Such an intellectual revolution forced Newman to view the function of the four principles within his dialectical hermeneutic from a new perspective. First, Newman's conscience motivated him to explore the principles of the *via media*, but his conscience would not allow him to ignore what he discovered; he had to determine "its bearing on [his] duty."[113] Second, Newman's static conception of dogma shifted to an idea of the dynamic role the church played in defining Christian doctrine. Third, Newman sought to discern the converging probabilities pointing to the *via media*'s authenticity. But his Monophysite research identified the *via media* as a divergent probability that prompted him to revisit "its logical value." Fourth, in Newman's imagination the *via media* was firmly rooted in the faith of the early church, but his analogical association identified the *via media* as heretical. For Newman, Augustine's fifth-century claim of *securus judicat orbis terrarum* destroyed his nineteenth-century claim of a *via media*.

These shifts in Newman's four principles radically altered the meaning of his dialectical hermeneutic. The impact of his intellectual conversion made him stagger. Yet he was to receive three more blows that buckled him.

Collapse of the Via Media: *Anglicanism vs. Anglo-Catholicism (1840-1842)*

For Newman, belief was prior to and guided his actions; a shift in his belief necessarily warranted a corresponding action. Thus, Newman's quasi-monastic retreat to Littlemore in 1840 was his response to his intellectual conversion the previous year.[114] Newman needed time to clear his conscience by critically examining the logical consequences and possible theological repercussions of his new understanding of the relationship between belief and development.

---

[112] Wiseman constructed his entire argument upon Augustine's phrase *securus judicat orbis terrarum*. Newman interpreted Augustine's phase as identifying the *via media* as being culpable of ecclesiastical heresy. See: *Apologia*, 110.13-25 [228].

[113] Ibid., 111.8 [229].

[114] Ibid., 157.29-162.30 [271-6] and 168.35 [281].

From 1840 to 1842 Newman's enduring doubts concerning the validity of his principles progressively weakened his faith in the vitality of the *via media*. In 1841 Newman was on his "death-bed" regarding his membership in the Anglican Church.[115] The *via media* became a *via mortis* for Newman's faith in Anglicanism.

Newman had identified antiquity as the font of proper belief, while his anti-Roman rhetoric flowed from his accusation that Rome had developed beyond the primitive deposit of the faith. However, his intellectual conversion moved him to conclude that the faith and the church necessarily co-exist within a synergetic dynamic. A living faith must exist within a living church, and a living church implied development. This critical realization resulted in the ensuing collapse of the *via media*. The reconfiguration of his dialectical hermeneutic brought a fresh understanding of the relationship between the faith/belief and the church/development.[116]

Tract 90 was the fruit of Newman's intellectual crisis, the offspring of his dialectical hermeneutic and his desperate attempt to find a way to remain Anglican.[117] For the past six years, the *Thirty-nine Articles* had been a stumbling block for Newman.[118] They seemed to preclude a Catholic interpretation. He needed to demonstrate that this was more apparent than real. Newman's intellectual conversion led him to pit antiquity against Anglicanism. Thus he put Anglicanism on trial.

---

[115] Ibid., 137.5-8 [252].

[116] The analogy of ancient heresy weighed heavily upon Newman's concept of orthodoxy. The *via media* actually destroyed Newman's immutable concept of orthodoxy and subsequently his view of the relation between the faith and the church. Newman's analogical method identified the *via media* as heretical, but it also revealed that orthodox belief is not simply static; rather, it develops. Since the *via media* was derived from the principle of antiquity, and it was the *via media* which destroyed Newman's concept of orthodoxy, his understanding of the relationship between the faith and the church drastically changed. Two fundamental principles to the *via media* were Newman's dependence on Antiquity and his anti-Roman rhetoric. Again this is an incipient expression of his dialectical hermeneutic.

[117] John Henry Newman, "Remarks in Certain Passages in the Thirty-nine Articles," in *Tracts for the Times*, vol. 6 (London: Rivington, 1841).

[118] In the Hampden controversy Newman awkwardly defended the *Thirty-nine Articles*. In the *Lectures on the Prophetical Office* he skillfully attempted to mend the apparent differences between the *Thirty-nine Articles* and the creeds; and in the *Lectures on Justification* he interpreted the articles on justification by seeking shelter in the patristic theology of God's indwelling presence.

Tract 90 was an *experimentum crucis* in which his dialectical hermeneutic acted as the independent variable.[119] In the tract Newman argued that the *Thirty-nine Articles* were not to be interpreted according to the meaning of the authors, but according to the Catholic sense of the church.[120] The argument was an expression of his dialectical hermeneutic; *belief* in the *Thirty-nine Articles* could be according to the *developed* Catholic interpretation of them. However, such an interpretation contradicted the obvious meaning of some articles.[121] In his defense of the *Tract 90*, Newman went so far as to make a critical distinction between Romanism and Roman Catholicism,[122] which moved him further from mainline Anglicanism and closer to Roman Catholicism.

Then, from July to November of 1841, Newman received three blows which shattered his confidence in Anglicanism.[123] The first blow came in July when he returned to his patristic research. In studying Athanasius and Arianism, the analogy between the *via media* and heresy again flooded his mind. A second time he identified the *via media* as existing *in loco hereticum*.[124] Soon thereafter, he received another blow: the onslaught of episcopal condemnations of *Tract 90*.[125]

---

[119] *Apologia*, 122.29 [238].

[120] Ibid., 128.20 [244]. Here Newman cited a letter dated 15 March 1841. Also see: 138.3 [253].

[121] By interpreting the *Thirty-nine Articles* with a developmental lens, Newman undercut their obvious meaning. By softening the distinction between the *Thirty-nine Articles* and the Roman position, he opened the door for liberalism to apply the same principle in its favor. Newman's *Tract 90* fatefully played into the hands of the liberals—a position which he had recently reiterated in the scathing satire, *The Tamworth Reading Room*. See: Gilley, *Newman and His Age*, 195.

[122] In Newman's response to Bishop Baggot and the *Letter to Jelf* he repeated that there was no obligation to interpret the *Thirty-nine Articles* according to the sense of its authors. Yet he also stressed the distinction between his use of anti-Romanism and the Roman Catholic Church proper. Newman claimed that the popish system was not synonymous with the Roman Church, which had its roots authentically planted in antiquity. Newman's distinction between Roman Catholicism and the corruptions of Romanism was also softened by Dr. Charles Russell, who provided Newman with Catholic seminary textbooks showing him that his perceptions of the corruptions of Roman doctrine were false. See: Ker, *John Henry Newman*, 225-226.

[123] *Apologia*, 130.6 to 136.17 [245-251].

[124] "I saw clearly, that in the history of Arianism, the pure Arians were Protestants, the semi-Arians were the Anglicans, and that Rome now was what it was then." Ibid., 130.15 [245].

[125] Ibid., 87.13-89.34 [204-207], 130.23-131.28 [246] and 141.29 [256]. Interestingly, the last twelve pages of Part I of the *Apologia* (78-89 [196-207]), which covers from 1833 to 1839, describe the reasons for and responses to *Tract 90*, which occurred in 1841.

One by one, the bishops denounced Newman's Catholic interpretation of the *Thirty-nine Articles* as logically leading to Romanism. In October 1841, Newman claimed that if the bishops suppressed his interpretation, he would be unable to remain in the Church of England.[126] He could only assent to the *Thirty-nine Articles* with a Catholic interpretation. The third blow was the Jerusalem Bishopric Controversy which confirmed for Newman that Anglicanism was in schism.[127] He was astounded by the political intrigue and the religious farce of the Jerusalem bishopric that the British and German governments engineered as a joint Anglican/Lutheran venture. He experienced this as blatant evidence of Erastian abuse and Anglican complicity with heretics.

As a response to these three blows, Newman moved to Littlemore in 1842, actively seeking a monastic setting. He no longer believed in the *via media*, and now considered Anglicanism to be cut off from the ancient Catholic faith.[128] At Littlemore, he was hard at work reorganizing his dialectical hermeneutic. Late in 1842 he began to prepare notes concerning the development of doctrine.

The four principles were instrumental to Newman's emerging awareness of his dialectical hermeneutic and ensuing estrangement from Anglicanism. First, in good conscience, Newman could not assent to the *Thirty-nine Articles* except with a Catholic interpretation. His conscience would not allow him to compromise or pursue another middle course. Second, Newman believed that the meaning of dogma was at issue. He saw the meaning of the creeds as opposing the popular Protestant meaning of the *Thirty-nine Articles*. Third, the converging probabilities of the three blows increasingly convinced Newman that he could not remain in the Anglican Church. Once he tested Anglicanism against his dialectical hermeneutic, the convergent probabilities pointed him toward Roman Catholicism. Fourth, Newman's hermeneutic preoccupied his imagination. His intellectual conversion directed him to make new analogies, to ask new questions, and to seek new answers. Because of these critical shifts, Newman could no longer consider Anglicanism his home. He set out for Rome, using his dialectical hermeneutic as a guide.

---

[126] Letter to Maria Giberne on 17 October 1841. *LD*, 8:299. Also see the earlier letters of 1 April 1841 (148) and 9 May 1841 (189); and the later letter to Mrs. John Mozley on 19 January 1842 (429-430).

[127] *Apologia*, 131.29-133.26 [246-8] and 139.15 [254]. Also see: 549 [cf. 246, n. 55]. The protest against the affair that Newman reproduced in the *Apologia* highlights his dismay. Ibid., 135.1-37 [250-1]. Moreover, he repeatedly mentioned the scandal of the "Jerusalem Bishoprick" in his letters from the summer of 1841 to the spring of 1842.

[128] See the letters to Samuel Rickards on 1 December 1841, *LD*, 8:359-360; William Dodsworth on 2 January 1842, ibid., 405; and Robert Wilberforce on 26 January 1842, ibid., 440-441.

Reconstructing the Hermeneutic: Anglicanism vs Roman Catholicism (1843-1845)

By Newman's own admission, it was not until 1843 that he turned towards Rome.[129] This is evidenced by his retraction of his anti-Roman rhetoric in January of 1843 and resignation from St. Mary's in September of the same year.[130] However, Newman still had to work out his hermeneutic into a coherent system.

In his last university sermon, Newman explored the epistemological dimensions of his hermeneutic.[131] This analysis contained seminal ideas which would be fundamental to the *Essay on the Development of Christian Doctrine* (1845). Newman's epistemological analysis in the *Essay on Development* was a scholarly presentation of his own mental development since his intellectual conversion three years before.[132] Understandably, this analysis revolved around his dialectical hermeneutic.[133] Thus, Newman's own growth in understanding his hermeneutic was analogously applied to the whole of Christian history.[134]

---

[129] *Apologia*, 196.32 [304].

[130] Ibid., 181.29-182.3ff [292] and 195.18-196.6 [304].

[131] John Henry Newman, *Fifteen Sermons Preached Before the University of Oxford Between A.D. 1826 and 1843* (Notre Dame, IN: University of Notre Dame Press, 1998), 319-20. The full title of the last Oxford University Sermon is, "The Theory of Developments in Religious Doctrine." Therein Newman argued that the mind may be impressed with an idea which is only tacitly known. Yet, the person can develop to a greater awareness the implicit idea. The emergence of the tacit idea into awareness provides convergent probabilities resulting in the mind's reflective assent to the idea. The process of coming to awareness takes time. Thus, Newman argued that time is the handmaiden of truth. This argument was expanded in the first chapter of *An Essay on the Development of Christian Doctrine*, and was essential to the overall argument of the *Essay*.

[132] Newman's epistemological analysis of his idea of development is primarily found in chapter one "On the Development of Ideas." Ibid., 31-50.

[133] In the *Grammar of Assent* (1870), Newman re-articulated the principle/idea distinction of the *Essay on Development* into his "notional" and "real" modes of apprehension. These two modes of apprehending generate two forms of propositions which the mind interprets as differing forms of inference leading to the two types of assent—notional and real. Via the relationship of these types of assent, Newman explored the difference between simple and complex assent. However, critical to Newman's analysis was his understanding of the relationship between belief and development. His epistemology focused on assent which is the formal object of a hermeneutical system.

[134] Newman would never abandon his method of analogical reasoning. Such analogical reasoning was instrumental in his theory of heresy, rhetorical strategy, intellectual conversion, estrangement from Anglicanism, idea of convergent probabilities, and his description of the synthetic power of the Illative Sense.

Just as Newman wrote *Tract 90* as a test for Anglicanism, he wrote the *Essay on Development* as a test case for Roman Catholicism.[135] Naturally, the instrument for the experiment was his dialectical hermeneutic. The thesis of the *Essay* was that Christianity is a revealed idea that develops. Accordingly, Newman argued that there were antecedent probabilities in favor of historical developments in doctrine.[136] He did not attempt to prove logically the truth of Roman Catholicism; rather, he only wanted to demonstrate that the converging probabilities of his historical analysis pointed to Rome as the true church.[137] In short, Newman argued that the aspects of a proposition can not exhaust the meaning of the idea of doctrine, and no idea can fully manifest the mystery of the revealed principles from which the doctrine emerged.[138] In other words, the principle (revelation) is inherent in the product (dogma), while the formulation of the product is dependent on the process (church tradition). Since the converging probabilities indicated that his idea of the development was correct, it was also probable that Rome was the true church. It became imperative for Newman to become Roman Catholic.

The four principles were essential to Newman's *Essay on the Development of Christian Doctrine*. First, Newman's conscience provided the purpose for the *Essay*. He had to decide whether or not to convert. Second, the thesis of the *Essay* proposed a developmental understanding of dogma. Revelation is not dogma per se; rather, dogma is a developed idea of revealed principles. Third, the argument of the *Essay* depended on antecedent probability. Fourth, the method of

---

[135] Newman states that *Tract 90* and the *Essay on Development* both proceeded according to the "principle of doctrinal Development." The earlier work applied it to Anglo-Catholicism, the latter, Roman Catholicism. See *Apologia*, 80.8-24 [199].

[136] For Newman, the Church must have an inner power of development because growth is the only evidence of life in the Church. Thus, he historically argued, via antecedent probability, God's revelation was not only in the scriptures and the apostolic tradition, but continued in the doctrinal development of the church which was guided by the presence of God's Spirit to an ever increasing understanding of the revelation. There was growth in the church, because there was a development in the church's understanding of God's revelation.

[137] Newman employed an organic metaphor to demonstrate that the converging probabilities indicated that the early church was analogous to the modern Church of Rome. Thus, Roman Catholicism was an authentic development of the apostolic church.

[138] In a basic way, Newman's dialectical hermeneutic in the *Essay on the Development of Christian Doctrine* can be seen as functioning in a two-fold manner: 1) belief is based on revealed principles which are invariant and provide the content of the faith; 2) development is an articulation of the revealed principles within doctrine, which are relative to the demands of particular historical contexts and specific questions raised by human reason.

the *Essay* depended on Newman's imaginative articulation of his dialectical hermeneutic. His imagination synthesized his hermeneutic into a coherent interpretation of Christian history.

Throughout the process of Newman's conversion, the four principles remained intact, his dialectical hermeneutic never substantially changed; thus, the *Essay on Development* closely resembled the idea of development in his heresy research that he had begun fifteen years earlier. Yet his intellectual conversion necessitated nuanced changes in his understanding of the four principles which, in turn, occasioned a fundamental shift in the meaning of his hermeneutic. Concomitant with this shift was the new meaning of the relationship between the faith and the church. This was key to Newman's religious conversion because it involved a new understanding of revelation, antiquity, history, and the development of doctrine. Newman's dialectical hermeneutic united all these into one comprehensive vision.[139] Hence, the *Essay on Development* was the vehicle for Newman's conversion. Before he completed it, he resolved to be received into the Roman Catholic Church.

Conclusion

When commenting on his religious conversion, Newman reflected, "Catholics did not make us Catholics; Oxford made us Catholics."[140] Indeed, Oxford did provide the context for Newman's conversion, but the content of his dialectical hermeneutic spawned his conversion. The four principles upon which he interpreted history and judged the evidence of his contemporary situation played a primary role in his embracing Roman Catholicism. Newman's hermeneutic not only resulted in his assent,[141] but in a wider sense, it was the underlying impetus to the genius of his theological thought.[142]

---

[139] Newman's position in the *Essay* concerning the dynamic relationship between faith and church was a manifestation of his own dialectic of belief and development. The principle/idea distinction of the *Essay* paralleled the dialectic of his ideas of belief and development within his hermeneutic. It could be argued that Newman applied the epistemology of his hermeneutic to his formulation of ecclesiology.

[140] Letter to Edgar Estcourt on 2 June 1860, *LD*, 19:352.

[141] Knowledge, or simple belief, is derived from assent (truth of a proposition). On the other hand, understanding, or certitude, is an act of reflex assent, to assent to an assent (meaning of a proposition). Both are dependent upon the hermeneutic, but the former is properly related to the interpretive method of one of the four principles, while the latter emerges from the hermeneutic circle itself within which the four principles generate meaning.

[142] This was especially evidenced by Newman's utilization of his hermeneutic as he articulated an epistemology in *An Essay in Aid of a Grammar of Assent*.

Newman's understanding of his idea of development in the *Essay on Development* was a nuanced reordering of his use of development in his theory of heresy that he first devised in *The Arians of the Fourth Century*, fifteen years earlier. Newman had made a fatal distinction between the authority of the creeds and the authority of the church which shaped the creeds. Newman had appealed to the static standard of antiquity, yet his Apollinarian and Monophysite research revealed to him that antiquity itself demonstrated development. He recognized the importance of the church's role in defining, protecting, and propagating the faith.[143] Such responsibilities implied that the church had a power to develop. By this it served and preserved the faith. Therefore, instead of arguing that dogma was always anterior to heresy, he became convinced that revealed principles were always prior to heretical interpretations. Newman replaced the word/thing distinction of his heresy research with the principle/idea distinction of the *Essay on Development*. Ultimately, the interplay between hermeneutics and heresy within the process of Newman's conversion provided him with a new "rule of faith and development," which would play a significant role in the questions over the development of dogma surrounding Vatican I and its aftermath.

---

[143] Newman's seven point criteria for the historical development of doctrine: 1) true development must be of the same form as early Christianity; 2) it must show conformity with early Christianity; 3) it must have the power to assimilate new ideas; 4) it must flow logically from the principles of the apostolic faith; 5) it must be true to the past, yet anticipate the future; 6) it must have a vitality and life, being able to adapt and overcome; and 7) it must demonstrate an organic ability of overcoming false interpretations.

NEWMAN'S THEORY OF DEVELOPMENT AND THE DEFINITION OF PAPAL INFALLIBILITY

C. MICHAEL SHEA

"Now at the end of twenty years," Newman wrote to his friend after the close of the Vatican Council, "I am told from Rome that I am guilty of the late Definition by my work on Development, so orthodox has it been found in principle."[1]

When considering the Oxford Movement and its impact upon the definition of papal infallibility, figures such as Henry Manning, William Ward, or George Talbot are usually the first to come to mind. More commonly passed over, however, is John Henry Newman, who remained in England during the council and thought the new definition inopportune.[2] Without intending it, this most famous of Oxford converts nevertheless had a considerable impact upon the event through his celebrated theory of the development of doctrine.

The purpose of this essay is to explore the reception of Newman's theory, so as to better tell the story of its role in the definition of papal infallibility at the First Vatican Council in 1870. By virtue of the theory's impact upon events and people associated with the new dogma, I build a case for its influence in three ways: I first argue that the theory indirectly influenced the 1870 definition through its role in defining the dogma of Immaculate Conception of Mary in 1854 and also the precedent that this definition established for the later event.

---

[1] Letter to Fr. Coleridge, S. J. (1822-1893) dated 5 February 1871, *LD*, 25:279; cited in: Stephen Dessain, "The Reception Among Catholics of Newman's Doctrine of Development, Newman's own Impressions," *Newman Studien* 4 (Nürnberg: Glock und Lutz, 1964): 189.

[2] J. Derek Holmes shows how Newman came to understand the new teaching before and after its definition. See: "Cardinal Newman and the First Vatican Council," *Annuarum Historiae Conciliorum* 1 (1969): 374-398. Holmes earlier article illustrates Newman's views on the issue of infallibility before Vatican I. See: "How Newman Blunted the Edge of Ultramontanism," *Clergy Review* 53 (1968): 353-62. Although this study presents Newman's stance on the question in a nuanced fashion, the article's title is somewhat misleading, since Holmes never argues for Newman's opinions having an effect on the Church at large.

Secondly, I suggest that the theory conditioned conciliar deliberations through general awareness of the notion among those involved, as well as its association with the earlier definition of 1854. Connected to this is the third manner of influence, namely, that the theory appealed to two important leaders within the dissenting party of bishops at the council and may have played a role in the strategy of the opposition. Taking these facts as a whole, I conclude that the theory of development assumed a significant and multifaceted role in the definition of 1870.

This is not to say that the theory was generally accepted by bishops or adopted in the official documents of the Church. Most churchmen were in fact guarded about the theory and perceived it to downplay or even threaten the unchanging character of Christian truth. In order to draw out my thesis in tandem with this important counterpoint, the material I present here is organized chronologically. I begin with the publication of the theory in its fully developed form in November of 1845 and end with testimonies reflecting perceptions of the dogma after its adoption in July of 1870.

Early Reception and Establishment (1845-1850)

The genesis of Newman's theory partially explains why it often met with ambivalence. The drafting of the *Essay on the Development of Christian Doctrine* occurred in 1844 and 1845,[3] when Newman was still an Anglican. The work was presented as justification for his decision to join the Roman Church. This was a fact known to those who read it,[4] or had an interest in its impact.[5] The manner in which the theory was received, however, varied greatly. Newman's anglophone context provides a helpful starting point for observing this variation. The *Essay* quickly sparked interest among those who paid attention to the Oxford Movement, but questions were also raised concerning its orthodoxy. Less

---

[3] Specifically, the *Essay* had been written between March of 1844 and September of 1845. Owen Chadwick, *From Bossuet to Newman,* 2nd ed. (London: Cambridge University Press, 1987), 160.

[4] The fact was made clear by Newman himself in the preface to the first edition. See: John Henry Newman, *An Essay on the Development of Christian Doctrine* (London: W. Blanchard and Sons, 1845), iii-xi.

[5] Many of the events in England were made known to the rest of the world through the French reports of Jules Gondon. See: *Du movement religieux en Angleterre: ou les progress du catholicisme et le retour de l'église anglicaine à l'unité* (Paris: Signier et Bray, 1844); and his subsequent work, *Conversion de soixante ministres Anglicans ou membres des universites anglaises, et de cinquante personnes de distinction, avec une notice sur mm. Newman, Ward, Oakeley* (Tournai, Belgium: Casterman, 1846).

than a month after the *Essay*'s publication, James Hope (1812-1873), an acquaintance of Newman, asked him about the reception of his theory among Catholics. "My experience," Hope stated, "would lead me to believe that many of them would be startled by it."[6] It was openly attacked in America by the Catholic convert, Orestes Brownson (1803-1876), who considered it heretical and essentially Protestant;[7] and in Rome, the theory brought on considerable suspicion.[8] Fortunately for Newman, his new bishop, Nicholas Wiseman (r. 1840-1865), was supportive of the theory of development. Between 1846 and 1849, Wiseman's sympathy helped to keep the theory safe from ecclesiastical censure. The theory was also aided by the praise of influential figures in France, such as Georges Darboy, later Archbishop of Paris (r.1863-1871),[9] and also Bishop Clément Villecourt (r. 1836-1867), who confessed to being "ravished by [the] book."[10]

These and other personal connections had a continuing impact on the role of the theory of development through the 1850s and 1860s, affording it not only a certain resistance to condemnation but also a measure of respectability. A key figure in establishing this respectability was Giovanni Perrone (1794-1876), the Jesuit Chair of Dogmatic Theology at the Roman College.[11] Perrone worked on many of the most influential congregations in the Curia during the period between the publication of the *Essay* and Vatican I.[12] He had served under the two popes prior to Pius IX, often in the capacity of defining correct doctrine and assuring condemnations of suspect views.[13] In addition to Perrone's great

---

[6] *LD*, 11:240. Cited in, Dessain, 180.

[7] Ibid., 182.

[8] Newman's diary entries indicate that Brownson's attacks were also known in Rome. *LD*, 11:274. Other reactions can be found in: Chadwick, *From Bossuet to Newman*, 164-184.

[9] Dessain, 187-8. Darboy became archbishop of Paris in 1864, and was an inopportunist at the council. See: Klaus Schatz, *Vaticanum I (1869-1870)*, 3 vols (Paderborn: Ferdinand Schöningh, 1993), 1:34-36 (hereafter, *Vaticanum*).

[10] "Je suis ravi de ce livre ... Après avoir lu cet ouvrage, on connait mieux l'Eglise et on l'aime plus tendrement." Dessain, 188.

[11] For biographical information on Perrone, see: Walter Kasper, *Die Lehre von Tradition in der Römische Schule* (Freiburg im Breisgau: Herder, 1962), 16-18. Also see: A. Vacant, E. Mangenot, and É. Amann, eds., *Dictionnaire de théologie catholique* (Paris: Librairie Letouzey et Ané, 1933), 12:1255-1256.

[12] Christoph Weber. *Kardinäle und Prälaten in den letzten Jahrzehnten des Kirchenstaats. Päpste und Papsttum*, 2 vols (Stuttgart: Anton Hiersmann, 1978), 1:256, 335.

[13] For information on Perrone's involvement in the Roman College and theological controversies, see: Roger Aubert, *Le pontificat de Pie IX (1846-1878)*, Histoire de

immediate influence in Roman theology and curial business, his theological textbooks were read in a number of seminaries. His masterwork, the *Praelectiones theologicae*, went through thirty-four printings, and his *Compendium*, forty-seven.[14] Many of the students of Perrone's School also became important leaders in the theological discourse of this period. For example, W. Maier and Fr. Hettinger, J. Hergenröther, and C. Schrader all took part in the First Vatican Council's preparatory commission.[15] M. J. Scheeben (1835-1888) became one of the most voluminous tract writers for the ultramontane cause during the 1860s.[16] Newman's association with a man practically synonymous with orthodoxy would have diminished suspicion concerning Newman's ideas by a considerable measure.

Newman became acquainted with Perrone in 1847 while training for the priesthood in Rome. During this time the perception of his *Essay* among curial authorities weighed heavily on his mind.[17] His meeting and subsequent friendship with the Roman professor was thus a fortuitous event for Catholic perceptions of the theory.[18] Sometime during the summer of that year, Newman

---

l'église depuis les origins jusqu'à nos jours, vol. 21 (Paris: Bloud & Gay, 1952), 192-195. For a more detailed account of the theological controversies, see: Edgar Hocedez, S.J., *Histoire de la théologie au XIXe siècle*, 3 vols (Paris, Édition Universelle, 1952), 2:93-4, 2:354-5. For Perrone's considerable influence over bishop's synods during the 1860s, see: Paul Hennessy, "Infallibility in the Ecclesiology of Peter Richard Kenrick," *Theological Studies* 45 (1984): 702-703.

[14] *Dictionnaire de théologie catholique*, 12:1255-1256. See also: Hermann Joseph Pottmeyer, *Unfehlbarkeit und Souveränität: die Päpstliche Unfehlbarkeit im System der Ultramontanen Ekklesiologie des 19. Jahrhunderts* (Mainz: Mattias Grünwald Verlag, 1975), 280, 283-297.

[15] Ibid., 279; Schrader's contribution found in: Schatz, *Vaticanum*, 1:24.

[16] Pottmeyer, *Unfehlbarkeit und Souveränität*, 265, 372.

[17] *LD*, 11:274.

[18] Perrone's recollection of the relationship he and Newman shared is referenced in an 1867 letter written to Newman, see: John Henry Newman, *John Henry Newman: Roman Catholic Writings on Development*, ed. J. Gaffney (Kansas City: Sheed and Ward, 1997), 56-7. Perrone speaks in this letter of being "always ready to defend [Newman's] cause." Admittedly, this document referred to a subsequent controversy in which Newman was involved; yet Perrone's mention of being "grateful, first of all, that your kind remembrance of me has lasted," and saying that "[y]ou could scarcely believe how much I have always liked and admired your reverence," indicates its significance in connection to this early period. As for perceptions of their friendship by others: it was certainly known by some of Newman's acquaintances, such as Ambrose St. John, who reported their embracing (Chadwick, *From Bossuet to Newman*, 181); and it also would have been well known to the Roman College Chair of Canon Law, Fr. Mazio, who called on Newman together with Perrone. *LD*, 12:81. By extension, it is likely that this association had,

wrote a Latin exposition of his theory of development with room in the margins for Perrone's comments.[19] This document evidences Newman's attempt to translate his theory into more scholastic language, which was, in general terms, more abstract and ecclesiocentric than the original *Essay*.[20] Although not published until 1935,[21] the document helps to clarify the way in which the theory may have been perceived by Perrone and others of his mindset in Rome.

The *Newman-Perrone Paper* makes evident that the two theologians thought in different ways and differed on important points, such as the precise nature and significance of doctrinal change in history,[22] as well as the role of human subjectivity and the Church in this process.[23] Nonetheless, the document also reveals some affinities between the two men on issues relating to doctrinal change in history and thus deserves attention here.

The document's structure largely precludes systematic analysis of the work as a method to cast light upon the status of Newman's theory of development during this time.[24] Moreover, given the historical contexts of both authors, such an approach to the text would inevitably do it violence for, during this time, Newman was in the early stages of his specifically Roman Catholic education.[25]

---

at the very least, been known among relevant figures in Rome and England during this early period, especially if one takes into account Newman's eagerness to exonerate himself of doctrinal suspicion. Cf. *LD*, 11:289-90.

[19] Chadwick, *From Bossuet to Newman*, 181.

[20] Newman, *Roman Catholic Writings on Development*, Introduction, 5. This generalization is supported by the apparent motivation behind alterations which Newman made to the second edition of the *Essay on Development* at this same time. For a list of these alterations see: Nicholas Lash, *Newman on Development: The Search for an Explanation in History* (Shepherdstown, W. VA.: Patmos Press, 1975), 207-8.

[21] T. Lynch, ed. "The Newman-Perrone Paper on Development." *Gregorianum* 16 (1935): 402-447. Subsequent citations from the text of the *Newman-Perrone Paper* will be from the Lynch edition, not Gaffney's translation.

[22] E.g., Ibid., chapter 4.4, p. 418; Chapter 4, thesis 1, p. 420.

[23] This is especially evident in the section, *De Verbo Dei subjectivo*. Ibid., 407-413.

[24] The published version from 1935 consists of only forty pages of text; and that figure can be reduced by about a third if one accounts for its irregular editing. The first four chapters of the document provide the closest approximation to a systematic presentation of development. However, this section takes up a mere sixteen pages (404-420); and Perrone's responses to Newman here comprise only about fifty complete sentences and fragments. The rest of the document (420-444) consists of twelve theses on various aspects of the issue of development. Perrone's comments here drop to only a fraction of their frequency in the earlier section. In short, the overall form of the document appears to be provisional and each author's contribution uneven.

[25] Such a systematic approach is exemplified in Allen Brent's articles, "Newman and Perrone: Unreconcilable Theses on Development," *Downside Review* 102 (1984): 276-

He was also attempting to develop and make explicit his views on the viability of subjective religious knowledge in a manner acceptable to Catholics.[26] This had been one of the most common objections to the original *Essay*, and Newman would be periodically occupied with this question for his entire life.[27] Perrone, in addition, would have been in the process of forming his own thoughts on the topic of doctrinal change while preparing his book on the definability of the dogma of the Immaculate Conception, which was released only a few months thereafter.[28] In this way, the *Newman-Perrone Paper* should not be read as a text

---

289 and also "The Hermesian Dimension to the Newman Perrone Dialogue," *Ephemerides theologicae Lovanienses* 61 (1985): 73-99. This approach forces Brent to read the document a-historically, by only referencing Perrone's earlier and most systematic work, the *Praelectiones theologicae,* and not taking into account the fact that at the time of the composition of the *Newman-Perrone Paper,* Perrone was himself undergoing a shift in his theological outlook, attempting to grapple with the historical character of Christian doctrine. Consequently, Brent overemphasizes the objectivistic character of Perrone's thinking within the document by failing to take into account the author's deepened appreciation for subjectivity, owed in part to his reading of Möhler in preparation for writing his book on the definability of the Immaculate Conception. That Perrone's exposure to Möhler needs to be taken into account when reading the *Newman-Perrone Paper* is evidenced by the fact that he cites him with strong approval in the document itself (405) and also in his book on the Immaculate Conception. Giovanni Perrone, *De Immaculato B. V. Mariae,* (Rome: Ioannes Baptista Marini and Bernardus Morini, 1847), 136, 142. Such insensitivities lead Brent to conclude that "Rome's failure to censure Newman at this time had a purely diplomatic motivation." Brent, "Unreconcilable Theses on Development," 73. Not only does such an interpretation fail to account for the fact that that Newman and Perrone enjoyed an affectionate friendship, but it ignores significant historical contexts internal to the document in connection to the shifting theological paradigms of the two theologians.

[26] See Newman's prologue in Lynch's edition of "The Newman-Perrone Paper on Development," 404. Oblique language in the document is illuminated by remarks in Newman's letters and diaries. *LD,* 11:289-290.

[27] Chadwick, *From Bossuet to Newman,* 35.

[28] Although I have not been able to determine the precise date of the book's publication, it is clear that Perrone's book was not released until after the composition of the *Newman-Perrone Paper,* in the fall of 1847. Rene Laurentin in, "The Role of the Papal Magisterium in the Development of the Dogma of the Immaculate Conception," in *The Dogma of the Immaculate Conception, History and Significance,* ed. E. O'Connor, (Notre Dame, IN: University of Notre Dame Press, 1958), 309, records that Pius IX congratulated Perrone for this book on 8 October 1847; and the earliest review of the work which I have found was printed on 2 November, and noted that Perrone's work appeared "tout récemment." *L'ami de la religion: Journal ecclésiastique, politique, et littéraire,* vol. 35, 261. In addition, W. G. Ward employed Perrone's works at several points (e.g. 385, 392, 405) in defense of Newman's theory in his *Dublin Review* article of December 1847. In

representing the definitive views of either author, but rather as a friendly and perhaps semi-formal exchange of theological opinion, which helped both thinkers to hone their views. It was, however, never intended for publication.[29]

A literary parallel suggesting that Perrone's book may have been influenced by the *Newman-Perrone Paper* helps to exemplify this point. In thesis two,[30] Newman used a Suárezian distinction between explicit revelation (*in propositionibus*) and what is implied therein to explain that certain elements of the deposit of faith were implicit, until controversy provoked reflection upon a question and a subsequent definition of the Church.[31] Newman then referred to the controversy over the re-baptism of heretics in the third century, arguing that the Church's subsequent decision on the matter ran against the teachings of Cyprian and other bishops and thus constituted a true development of magisterial doctrine. The same historical example appeared again in Perrone's book on the definability of the Immaculate Conception later that year. In the book, one can still observe Perrone's objections in the *Newman-Perrone Paper*; and elements of his own position also come into view.[32] Perrone distinguished here between the deposit of faith *implicite* and *explicite*, yet he is careful to avoid speaking of change within history as development. He instead reasoned that change in the

---

no place, however, did Ward cite Perrone's book on the definability of the Immaculate Conception, which would have been more relevant and helpful than his previous works. This suggests that the book was unavailable, or perhaps only just becoming available, at the time when Ward wrote the article, presumably not long before it was published. William Ward, "Mr. Brownson on Developments" *The Dublin Review* 23 (1847): 373-405. Although he does not provide argumentation for his dates, Franz Michel Willam assumes a chronology parallel to my own in his reading of the document: "John Henry Newman und P. Perrone" *Newman Studien* 2 (1954): 139.

[29] In this respect, my reading of the document aligns with Franz Michel Willam, who describes the two authors as, " ... somit mit zwei Wanderern zu vergleichen, die sich, aus entgegengesetzener Richtung kommend, auf dem gleichen Joch treffen." Ibid., 132.

[30] Lynch, "Newman-Perrone Paper," 424-426.

[31] For more information on Suárez's influence on Perrone, see Kasper, *Die Lehre von der Tradition der Römische Schule*, 45; and on Roman theology in general, see Chadwick, *From Bossuet to Newman*, 21.

[32] Perrone, *De Immaculato B. V. Mariae*, 132-133. It is not the place here to give a full account of Perrone's concept of tradition, but rather to argue that the theological encounter recorded in the *Newman-Perrone Paper* represents a positive step in connection to the theory of development's acceptability, and that this encounter may have been a conditioning factor in the formation of Perrone's own ideas. A full account of Perrone's concept of tradition can be found in, Walter Kasper, *Die Lehre von der Tradition in der Römischen Schule*, 109-181.

historical record is not something which occurs within the deposit of faith itself (*in se*), but is rather a function of our subjective point of view (*quoad nos*).[33]

Perrone was hesitant to speak of the historical character of Christian teaching in Newman's terms. Yet he did not go so far as to deny the appearance of doctrinal change within history—a fact suggesting that Newman's ideas may have pressed Perrone on this issue. It is thus important to admit that differences in outlook can be found in the *Newman-Perrone Paper*.[34] Nevertheless, within this narrative, the theological engagement which the document represents ought to be interpreted as aiding the theory of development's acceptance by the Church at large, at least according to its general contours.

Significant in this regard is the way the theory was subsequently viewed in relation to Perrone's work on the Immaculate Conception. The perspective of one of Perrone's colleagues at the Roman College, Fr. Giacomo Mazio (1800-1851),[35] lends credence to an interpretation which would associate Newman and

---

[33] "Atque haec est illa dogmatum catholicorum explicationis ac veluti progressionis ratio, qua aliqua articulis fidei, non *in se* quidem spectatis, sed *quoad nos* facta est." Perrone, *De Immaculato B. V. Mariae*, 133, original emphasis.

[34] The best systematic study of the *Newman-Perrone Paper* can be found in Walter Kasper, *Die Lehre von der Tradition in der Römischen Schule*, 119-130. Franz Michel Willam, in "John Henry Newman und P. Perrone," 120-145, 350-351, reads the document within its contemporary context and emphasizes discrepancies between the authors on issues of moral certainty. Concise studies can be found in Gaffney, *Roman Catholic Writings on Development*, 1-8. and in Ferdinand Cavalliera, "Le document Newman-Perrone et le développement du dogme" *Bulletin de literature ecclesiastique* 47 (1937): 132-142. Owen Chadwick, in *From Bossuet to Newman*, 181-184, concisely shows that the difference between the two thinkers had much to do with the relationship between an individual's faith and the faith of the Church, with Perrone stressing a 'top down' approach, and Newman the reverse. Although Allen Brent's articles (see above, note 25) may be helpful in drawing connections between Perrone's thinking in the *Newman-Perrone Paper* and his earlier works, they represent a perspective that is otherwise distorting and seemingly hostile to the Roman College.

[35] Although perhaps not as well known as Perrone, Fr. Mazio enjoyed a similarly high stature. He had been the Chair of Canon Law at the Roman College and also one of the censors of the Roman journal, *Annali delle scienze religiose*. Chadwick, *From Bossuet to Newman*, 167-8. Presumably, Mazio and Perrone had been friends or at least close acquaintances, as evidenced by their scholarly interaction (See bibliographical evidence of this in Carlos Sommervogel, *Bibliothèque de la compagnie de Jésus*, Paris: Alphonse Picard, 1894, 5:831) and the fact that the two accompanied one another on visits to Newman. *LD*, 12:76, 12:106. Moreover, it appears that Mazio was the first theological authority in Rome to whom Newman expressed concern about the *Essay on Development*. Wilhelm, "John Henry Newman und P. Perrone," 127. Mazio likely knew English better than his colleagues and seems to have been a keen observer of English affairs, as

Perrone on the issue of development. In his 1849 remarks upon the affair involving Brownson's attacks from America, Mazio claimed that Newman had been correct and that Brownson ought to read Perrone's book on the definability of the Immaculate Conception in order to "clarify his ideas."[36] A review of Perrone's book in the *Rambler* would have perpetuated a similar interpretation, bringing the thinkers together on essential points.[37]

The association of the theory of development with prominent figures like Mazio and Perrone was an important factor in the acceptance of the theory, at least in its basic form. By the end of the 1840s the theory had become a theological position that one could hold without fear of censure. This can be said with confidence, since Newman was granted an honorary doctorate by Pius IX (r.1846-1878) in July 1850 for his *Lectures on Anglican Difficulties*, where one can find elements of the theory of development.[38] This gesture of approbation never would have been made if Newman appeared to hold heterodox views. It is furthermore unlikely that the pope would have actually read Newman's *Essay*, as it went largely unread by even the schoolmen of Rome, despite the fact that its existence was well known and available in French translation.[39] In this way, it appears that the pope's most senior theological consultants, including Perrone, may have had a significant role in commending Newman for official recognition.

Whatever the case may be, there is little doubt that, by 1850, Newman's theory had risen in stature, even if it still aroused the ambivalence of its first appearance and was not accepted by all Catholics in detail. Some of the theologians who were influenced by the theory would include a handful of English apologists,[40] Fr. Mazio, and Salvatore di Bartolo, as well as Perrone himself if not through appropriation, at least by friendly interaction.[41]

---

evidenced by his editorial work. Sommervogel, *Bibliothèque de la compagnie de Jésus*, 5:831). It is thus likely that Mazio played a significant role in bringing Newman and his ideas to Perrone's attention.

[36] Dessain, 183.
[37] Ibid., 185.
[38] Ibid., 185-6.
[39] Chadwick, *From Bossuet to Newman*, 164-184.
[40] Dessain, 181.
[41] Johannes Artz, "Entstehung und Auswerkung von Newmans Theorie der Dogmenentwicklung," *Theologische Quartalschrift* 148 (1968): 173.

The Theory of Development's Role in the Events of 1854-5

The next important stage in the rising status of the theory of development was the definition of the dogma of the Immaculate Conception in 1854. This event had the effect of bringing the problems of history and historical precedent to the forefront of theological reflection in general[42] and it was a main point of dispute in the discussions surrounding the bull that disseminated this teaching, *Ineffabilis*, which was released two months after the decree.

Significantly, the first schema presented to the bull's drafting committee came from Perrone, and it clearly laid forth his ideas from his earlier book on the definability of the Immaculate Conception.[43] In this preliminary document, Perrone speaks of the doctrine as being, in a way, hidden (*veluti latens*), and only dispersed and expressed by degrees.[44] Although this idea differs from Newman's theory of development in its greater stress on the sempiternal character of doctrine, it conceded a lack of unanimity among early Christian sources. When one considers the criticisms which the first schema received and then the definitive document, it is clear that those in control at the time were uncomfortable with allowing much room for theories of doctrinal development.[45] However, the issue was a debated point; phraseology accounting for conflicting witnesses in the tradition shifted back and forth in the drafting stages, as if the theory of development loomed just below the surface of the process.[46] At one important moment in the deliberations, Bishop Michael O'Connor of Pittsburgh (r.1843-1860) even mentioned the theory of development explicitly. However, his remarks were met with the rebuttal of Bishop Thomas Grant of Southwark (r.1851-1870), who said that the Bishop of Pittsburgh's remarks came from

---

[42] Hocedez, *Histoire de la théologie au XIX siècle,* 2:373-374.

[43] Vincenzo Sardi, *La solenne definizione del Dogma dell'Immacolato Concepimento di Maria Santissima: Atti e documenti,* 2 vols (Rome: Tipografia Vaticana, 1905), 2:22-38; esp. 2:24, 2:36 (hereafter, *Atti e documenti*).

[44] "Pia tamen haec doctrina veluti latens quoddam germen neque elata admodum voce, neque a pluribus primum efferebatur; at aetate dilabente explicari paullatim, dein maius capere incrementum, ac demum tantum non in ore omnium esse visa est." Ibid., 25. Later in the document it reads: "Posteriores enim doctioresque christianae Fidei magistri non modo indefinite Mariam Virginem orginaria qualibet culpa illaesam agnoscunt et profitentur, sed paullatim in eam formam unanimes convenient quae modo omnium fere Christifidelium ore usurpatur." Ibid., 27; cited in Kasper, *Die Lehre von der Tradition in der Römischen Schule,* 232.

[45] Sardig, *Atti e documenti,* 2:38-46.

[46] In addition to the language found in Perrone's first schema, schemas III and IV also explicitly mention doctrinal change in the historical record. *Die Lehre von der Tradition in der Römischen Schule,* 232.

Newman, and that talk of "evolution diminish[ed] the power of Tradition." He further reminded everyone that the pope requested the assembly to be silent about the theory in their document.[47] Although these remarks seemingly put an end to the discussion of doctrinal development in the proceedings, it is significant that proposed wording which implied that the doctrine was always explicit (constans doctrina) never made it into the final document.[48] The definitive language of the bull emphasized that the doctrine of the Immaculate Conception always existed in the Church, yet the document was silent about the manner by which the teaching was held. The clearest statement concerning the problem of historical change in the bull described the teaching as ancient, but coming to greater light as the magisterial authority of the Church sought to bring it to greater expression.[49] The significance of this phraseology lies in the fact that the decree does not differ substantially from the understanding of doctrinal change developed by Perrone in his interactions with Newman on the subject. The theory of development thus played a role in the event by conditioning Perrone's writing on the subject, which, in turn, helped to balance the language emphasizing doctrinal constancy in the assembly's deliberations.

A general awareness of the theory among the assembly participants may have also played a role in the affair.[50] In this respect, it is telling that Newman's name was mentioned publicly. Also significant is the fact that Pius IX instructed

---

[47] Sardig, *Atti e documenti*, 2:210-11. I would like to thank Dr. Kenneth Parker for bringing this event to my attention.

[48] Walter Kasper draws attention to this point in his fine treatment of the proceedings. Kasper, *Die Lehre von der Tradition in der Römischen Schule*, 252-254.

[49] "Et re quidem vera hanc de Immaculata beatissimae Virginis Conceptione doctrinam quotidie magis gravissimo Ecclesiae sensu magisterio, studio, scientia, ac sapientia tam spendide explicatam, declaratam, confirmatam, et apud omnes omnis catholici orbis populos, ac nations mirandum propagatam, in ipsa Ecclesia semper extitisse veluti a majoribus acceptam ... Christi enim Ecclesia sedula depositorum apud se dogmatum custos, et vindex nihil in his unquam permutat, nihil minuit, nihil addit, sed omni industria vetera fideliter, sapienterque tractando si qua antiquitus informata sunt, et Patrum fides sevit, ita limare, expolire studet, ut prisca illa caelestis doctrinae dogmata accipiant evidentiam, lucem, distinctionem, sed retineant plentitudinem, integritatem, proprietatem, ac in suo tantum genere crescent, in eodem scilicet dogmate, eodem sensu, eademque sententia." *Official Documents Connected with the Definition of the Dogma of the Immaculate Conception of the Virgin Mary.* (Baltimore, MD: John Murphy & Co., 1855), 35-36.

[50] This is a view also held by Kenneth Parker in his essay on Archbishop Francis Kenrick's actions during the assembly. "Francis Kenrick and Papal Infallibility: How Pastoral Experience in the American Missions Transformed a Roman Ultramontanist," in, eds., K.L. Parker, P. Huff, and M.J.G. Pahls, *Tradition and Pluralism: Essays in Honor of William M. Shea* (Lanham, MD: University Press of America, 2008).

his commission not to speak about development, for it implied that the pope had anticipated the dogmatic definition to be perceived as a manifestation of this principle.

There is little doubt, in fact, that the event was subsequently viewed in this manner. In a pastoral letter, Archbishop Sibour of Paris (r. 1848-1857) taught that the new doctrine ought to be understood in terms of doctrinal development.[51] The idea also appeared in the language of Bishop Dupanloup's (r. 1849-1878) pastoral letter following the decree[52] and perhaps in Bishop Ullathorne's (r.1846-1888) book on the subject.[53] Not surprisingly, Newman and his circle saw the event as undeniable proof of the theory.[54] It was even perceived this way by Newman's former persecutor from America, Orestes Brownson, who apologized to him in a letter shortly before the decree, saying that he had misunderstood what was truly meant by the theory of development. He further promised to make these sentiments public in the next issue of his *Quarterly Review*.[55] Five years after the pronouncement, Brownson even permitted one of his reviewers to state that the theory could "scarcely be denied by anyone conversant with the history of the Church."[56]

The First Vatican Council and Its Roots in the Definition of 1854

Before discussing the evidence relating to the conciliar definition, a few background remarks are needed in order to highlight the significance of the evidence surrounding the definition of the Immaculate Conception. The definition of 1854 was not merely an important reference point for the later ecclesial event. For many churchmen, the definition of the Immaculate Conception and papal infallibility were in fact understood as two manifestations of the same truth.

Soon after the 1854 definition, theologians began developing the notion that papal authority was illustrated in the contrast which the doctrine of the Immaculate Conception stressed between fallen reason and supernatural grace. This idea

---

[51] Bernard Dupuy, O.P., "Newman's Influence in France," in, *The Rediscovery of Newman: An Oxford Symposium*, eds. J. Coulson and A. Allchin (London: Sheed and Ward, 1967), 150.

[52] Sardig, *Atti e documenti*, 2:562.

[53] The Bishop's language is suggestive but not unequivocal. William Ullathorne, *The Immaculate Conception of the Mother of God: An Exposition* (London: Richardson and Son, 1855), 194.

[54] Dessain, 188-189.

[55] Brownson did in fact make good on this promise. See: *Brownson's Quarterly Review* 1.4 (1854): 480. Cited in Dessain, 186-187.

[56] *Brownson's Quarterly Review* 16 (1859): 432.

became more sophisticated and established in the following years.[57] More generally, the Immaculate Conception stood as a symbol of the coherence and integrity of the Church. This was illustrated poignantly by the fact that soldiers around Rome during this era were consecrated to the Immaculate Virgin in defense of the Papal States.[58]

The more scholarly connections between the two doctrines thus ran in tandem with a popular reception in the minds and hearts of the faithful. There is perhaps no clearer manifestation of this convergence than the fact that the relationship between the Immaculate Conception and Infallibility was explicitly added to the Roman Breviary in 1861. In the sixth reading of the Office on the Solemnity of the Immaculate Conception, the text speaks of Pius IX as "assenting to establish, by his supreme and infallible utterance, to solemnly proclaim" the doctrine of the Immaculate Conception as part of the Catholic faith.[59] In addition to bringing this connection into the devotional practices of all priests and religious eight years before the Council would begin, this addition illustrates that the language developed in the 1854 episcopal assembly was becoming an estab-

---

[57] James Hennesey points this out in his article, "A Prelude to Vatican I: American Bishops and the Definition of the Immaculate Conception," *Theological Studies* 25 (1964): 410. During the Vatican Council, Matthias Scheeben would provide the most developed articulation of this idea in his 1870 pamphlet, "Die theologische und praktische Bedeutung des Dogmas von der Unfehlbarkeit des Papsts, besonders in seiner Beziehung auf die heutige Zeit" This work is reprinted in Matthias Scheeben, *Immaculata und Päpstliche Unfehlbarkeit* (Paderborn: Ferdinand Schöningh, 1954), 13-87.

[58] This is recorded in a letter appearing in *l'Univers*. Reprinted by a Member of the House of Commons in, "Article VII: Thoughts on Foreign Relations," *The Church of England Quarterly Review* 33 (January, 1853): 394. For general context concerning threats to the Papal States at this time, see: Owen Chadwick, *A History of the Popes, 1830-1914* (Oxford: Oxford University Press, 1998), 95-160.

[59] "Deiparae autem Vírginis in sua Conceptione de tetérimo humáni generis hoste vietóriam, quam divína elóquia, veneránda traditio, *perpetuus Ecclésiae sensus*, singularis Episcopórum ac fidélium conspirátio, insignia quoque summórum Pontíficum acta atque Constitutiones mirifíce jam illustrabant; *Pius Nonus Póntifex Máximus totíus Ecclésiae votis ánnuens státuit suprémo suo atque infallíbili oráculo solemniter proclamáre* ... ." H. Dessain, P.J. Hanicq, eds., *Breviarium romanum ex decreto sacrosancti Concilii Tridentini restitutum*. (Mechelen, Belgium: Summi Pontificis, S. Congregationis de Propaganda Fide et Archiep. Typographi, 1861), 358-359, emphasis mine. This addition to the prayer book would be used in polemics by the prominent theologian Joseph Hergenröther, who served on the Council's preparatory commission and defended the ultramontanist cause against the attacks of Ignaz von Döllinger. The work was originally published in German in 1870, but appeared in English that same year. Joseph Hergenröther. *Anti-Janus: An Historico-Theological Criticism of the Work Entitled: "The Pope and the Council" By Janus*. J. B. Robertson, trans. (Dublin: W. B. Kelly, 1870), 245.

lished way of speaking about doctrinal change in history. Although the configuration placed more emphasis on the institutional Church, it can be seen that the idea of development would have been easily associated with it. The fact that a figure as informed as Mazio conflated Newman's theory with Perrone's in 1849 certainly suggests this. If this had been the case with Mazio, how much more with so many churchmen at the time who would have been too busy to become bogged down with academic minutiae? To borrow a phrase from Newman, the theory would have been "in the air."[60]

The Conciliar Definition and Its Aftermath

Such was the state of things when the Vatican Council opened on the Solemnity of the Immaculate Conception, 8 December 1869. For purposes here, the link between 1854 and the First Vatican Council needs to be kept in mind, since it illustrates the theory of development's influence on the event in a mediated fashion. There is also evidence that Newman's theory had a direct influence on conciliar deliberations, even if his name never emerged in the council chamber.[61]

If one accepts the maxim that theological ideas often rise or fall in connection to their authors, then Newman's status at the time of the Vatican Council suggests that development was a weighty and established theory. Bishop Dupanloup, an eminent leader opposed to the definition, as well as Pius IX himself, both invited Newman to the proceedings.[62] Newman declined these invitations. Yet the theory of development clearly conditioned conciliar discussions in its author's absence.

The way in which history was employed at the council gives some indication of this. There was, on the one hand, the "scientific" position of Döllinger, who practically identified the facts of history with the normative tradition of the

---

[60] *Apologia,* 77 [195]. Cited in, Walter Ong, "Newman's Essay on Development in Its Intellectual Milieu," *Theological Studies* 7 (1946): 4-5.

[61] It bears noting that one section in the Vatican Council's documents (*Dei filius IV: De fide et ratione*) does make some reference to doctrinal change within history. The passage was not directly related to papal infallibility and its wording followed the precedent initiated at the 1854 assembly. It appears to have been composed without any reference to Newman's theory. Mark McGrath, in "The Vatican Council's Teaching on the Evolution of Dogma: A Study in Nineteenth Century Theology" (PhD. diss. Angelicum, 1960), 116-117, shows that Joseph Kleutgen S.J. (1811-1883), drafted the section in response to the thought of Georg Hermes and Anton Günther.

[62] For a more detailed account of this, see: Fredrick Cwiekowski, *The English Bishops and the First Vatican Council* (Louvain: Publications Universitaires de Louvain, 1971), 73-78.

Church. On the other end of the spectrum was the position of Manning, who viewed history as a purely human endeavor, which held no claims upon tradition manifested in the contemporary magisterium. Despite the great personal influence these figures affected upon the atmosphere of the period, their views on history were extreme. Between Manning and Döllinger stood the majority of churchmen, who, in varying degrees, allowed for some notion of doctrinal change in history.[63] In several respects, the way of thinking about doctrine and history followed the precedent that began in the 1854 episcopal assembly, where the doctrine was viewed as ever the same, yet variable according to deepening human understanding.[64]

The theory of development certainly played a role in this milieu, as Bishop Moriarty's report to Newman made clear. He stated:

> Strange to say, if ever this definition comes you will have contributed much towards it. Your treatise on development has given the key. A Cardinal said the other day '—We must give up the first ten centuries, but the infallibility is an obvious development of the supremacy.' Of course development was ever at work in the Church, but you brought it out and placed it on a pedestal.[65]

In addition to these more general observations regarding the theory of development's influence upon the council, there is more specific evidence deserving consideration. In particular, this has to do with leadership among the largest group opposing the definition, the French Minority bishops. Objections coming from this circle were not so inclined to allow the idea of development into their arguments.[66] However, it appears that even the most reserved among this group had to account for the appearance of doctrinal change within history. Bishop Henri Maret,[67] for example, had been known for his book *Du concile gé-*

---

[63] Klaus Schatz offers this schematization of viewpoints in *Vaticanum*, 3:50. A more detailed account of the way different authorities from the tradition were used during the Council can be found in Schatz, "Päpstliche Unfehlbarkeit und Geschichte in den Diskussionen des Ersten Vatikanums," in, *Dogmengeschichte und katholische Theologie*, eds. W. Löser, et al. (Würzburg: Echter Verlag, 1985), 187-250.

[64] Cf., *Dei filius*, 4.

[65] Letter dated 20 February 1870. *LD*, 25:58.

[66] This would have been in keeping with their aims and also their gallican formation on infallibility. Margaret O'Gara, in *Triumph in Defeat: Infallibility, Vatican I, and the French Minority Bishops* (Washington, D.C.: Catholic University of America Press, 1988), 18, notes that most if not all of these bishops were educated in the gallican tradition and influenced by Bossuet, for whom the unchanging character of tradition was axiomatic. Cf. Chadwick, *Bossuet to Newman*, 5-6.

[67] Henri Maret, Titular Bishop of Sura (r. 1861-1884).

néral et de la paix religieuse, which largely adopted the gallican views of Bossuet.[68] Even in this widely read work,[69] one finds concessions made to doctrinal change within history.[70] Also significant is the fact that two of the French Minority's most important leaders,[71] Bishops Darboy and Dupanloup, were among the few to go on record as viewing the theory of development in a positive light.[72] The theory of development thus may have been a factor in steering the Minority bishops' strategy away from issues of historical precedent and toward issues having to do with the theological constitution of the Church.[73]

The appeals of these bishops proved unsuccessful, and it could be argued that the theory of development had a role to play in breaking down opposition to the new definition. One of the most outspoken opponents to the new definition, Archbishop Peter Kenrick of Saint Louis (r. 1843-1895), gave evidence of this in a letter to John Acton after the Council in March 1871. Explaining himself to Acton, Kenrick stated:

> I have reconciled myself intellectually to submission by applying Father Newman's theory of development to the case in point. The Pontifical authority as at present exercised is so different from what it appears to have been in the early Church, that it can only be supposed identical in substance by allowing a process of doctrinal development. This principle removed Newman's great

---

[68] Charles-Henri Maret, *Du concile génerel et de la paix religiouse: memoir soumis au prochain concile oecumenique du Vatican,* 2 vols (Paris: Henri Plon, 1869-1870), 2:34, 2:82, 2:217.

[69] The two-volume work was translated into German in 1869 and 1870, and provoked polemical responses from Prosper Louis Guéranger.

[70] For example, "Tous les théologiens enseignent qu'une vérité religieuse, pour être definie ou pour devenir un dogme de la foi catholique, doit être expressément, formellement, explicitement révélée de Dieu, en d'autres termes, doit être évidemment cóntinue dans l'Ecriture sainte et dans la tradition. Les conséquences de cette vérité divine ne peuvent devenir objet de foi catholique qu'autant qu'elles sont évidemment et immédiatement liées à leur principe.
Sans dout les conséquences d'une vérité révélée, même celles qui sont évidentes en elles-mêmes, peuvent n'avoir pas toujours été aperçues par tous les esprits, et il existe des vérités de ce genre qui n'ont pas toujours été universellement admises ... ." Ibid., 1:360-361; see also 1:371.

[71] For information on the French minority's leadership dynamics, see: O'Gara, *Triumph in Defeat,* 22-26, 30-33.

[72] Ibid., 4, 14.

[73] The most important action of the French Minority bishops had been their petition objecting to the council's decision to treat the issue of papal primacy before the general constitution of the Church. If the problem of doctrinal change within history had not been a matter largely settled, this strategy may have taken a different course. Cf. Ibid., 4-6.

difficulty and convinced him that, notwithstanding the difference, he should become a Catholic. I thought that it might justify me in remaining one.[74]

It appears that, after many years of uncertainty, Newman's theory of development had come of age.

Conclusion

Taken as a whole, the evidence considered here suggests that the theory of development significantly aided the doctrine of papal infallibility in becoming a defined dogma of the Church. However, Newman's theory did not operate in a vacuum—it functioned amidst a network of intellectual currents converging on the council floor in 1869 and 1870. A monograph-length study would require more attention to be given to some of these currents. In particular, the reception history of Johann Adam Möhler's thinking on the subject of doctrinal change in history, still fragmentary, is one avenue which could shed light upon historical consciousness during this period. The role of Passaglia's thought on the issue is also worthy of attention. In addition, although much evidence exists regarding the reception of the definition of the Immaculate Conception, more work could be done to contextualize theological interpretations of the event in connection to history during the first decades after its occurrence.

These limitations notwithstanding, the role of Newman's theory in the Vatican Council of 1870 is clear. The effect of this theory is evident in the episcopal assembly convened just prior to the bull following the definition of the Immaculate Conception in 1854. This assembly established a precedent for the Vatican Council, both in its defining a new dogma and in the language it used to account for doctrinal change within history. The definition of 1854 also helped to bring the idea of development into Catholic consciousness, influencing the events of 1870. These facts, in addition to the more specific testimonies from the period, lead to the conclusion that Newman's theory was essential in shaping the atmosphere in which in papal infallibility became a dogma of the Catholic Church.

---

[74] Letter from Archbishop Peter Richard Kenrick of Saint Louis to Lord Acton, 29 March 1871. Damian McElrath et al. eds., *Lord Acton, The Decisive Decade 1864-1874: Essays and Documents,* (New York: Humanities Press, 1970), 214.

Henry Manning and Neo-Ultramontanism: The Anglican Context for an Oxford Movement Convert's Faith in Papal Infallibility

Kenneth L. Parker

In 1825, at age eighteen, Henry Manning wrote an essay for his Oxford tutor entitled, "Use and Abuse of Theory." The essay reveals a fine and agile undergraduate mind, keenly aware of the rapidly evolving intellectual life of nineteenth-century Europe. It also reflected a conservative vision of Truth and a conviction about the limits of modern knowledge. After examining the ways natural sciences test and verify theories proposed, he turned to contemporary moral theories. Here he observed, "all is contingent, intangible and abstract." Manning explained that the evidence collected is not subject to experimentation or the rules of observation used by scientists.[1] His concluding analysis raised fascinating issues about the potential evil that may beset theorists in all branches of knowledge:

> According to the constitution of our minds we are apt to admit as truth whatever our will, or affections dictate to us. From this source arise many of the most glaring abuses of theory—The understanding becomes so far tinctured by what it desires to establish, as to find plausible arguments for construction, and specious coincidences for the coherence of its theories. The will taking thus the lead ratiocination becomes the work rather of vivid, and ingenious imagination rather than rigid and uncompromising thought.[2]

The young Manning recognized that in all areas of knowledge, including "religious contemplation," theorists are tempted to "suffer their reason to be outstripped by their desires and to acquiesce in the adoption of crude and fanciful conceits."[3] While all sciences, natural and moral, are temporal, mutable, and subject to change, Manning posed the burning question of his, and perhaps any

---

[1] Oxford, Bodleian Library, MS Eng. Misc.d.1278, "English Essay No. 11," fol. 22.
[2] Ibid., fols. 41-2.
[3] Ibid., fol. 42.

era: Where is eternal, immutable, and changeless Truth to be found? Manning concluded,

> It is to moral truths in their revealed shape we assign these qualities. They are the Eternal and immutable subjects of contemplation. In comparison with these Science is as nothing and the most admirable developments of abstract truth but unprofitable and bootless speculation.[4]

Forty-four years later Manning wrote a letter to his old undergraduate friend, William Gladstone. Their personal friendship, broken by Manning's conversion to Roman Catholicism in 1851, was further complicated in 1869 by their public roles: Manning as the *de facto* Roman Catholic primate of England and Wales, and Gladstone as prime minister of Great Britain. Manning wrote on the eve of the First Vatican Council, where he was a leader of the movement pressing for a sweeping definition of papal infallibility. To Manning's protestations that he was not putting reason and revelation in conflict,[5] Gladstone replied with a lengthy reminiscence of events and times which marked the divergence of their ways of thinking. He called to mind a sermon on the Holy Spirit and the infallibility of the Church written by Manning prior to his conversion to Roman Catholicism.[6] Gladstone observed, "I thought it was too absolute, and argued this, more or less in my reply." He noted that in Manning's explanation of his conversion he had developed "a further exaggeration of that already over-absolute proposition." Gladstone bluntly stated, "you broke altogether away from the teaching of history and experience respecting the methods of God in dealing with his Church."[7]

While Gladstone's critique came from an estranged Anglican friend, many Roman Catholic leaders in 1869 shared Gladstone's assessment of Manning's thought. Lord John Acton and Professor Ignaz von Döllinger were prominent among those outside the council. Many council fathers saw his efforts as overreaching and a departure from traditional Catholic teaching. Archbishop Peter Kenrick of Saint Louis, with direct reference to Manning observed, "We know

---

[4] Ibid., fols. 44-5.

[5] London, British Library, Add. MS 44249, fols. 113-14, Manning to Gladstone, 13 November 1869.

[6] Peter Erb identified this sermon as "The Analogy of Nature," published in: Henry Edward Manning, *Sermons*, 4 vols (London: Pickering, 1850), 4:152-175. The correspondence cited appears to be an exchange in late 1849. See letters in: Peter Erb, ed., *The Correspondence of Henry Edward Manning and William Ewart Gladstone, 1833-1891*, 3 vols (forthcoming), letters 491111mg, 491114mg, 491230gm, 491231mg.

[7] London, British Library, Add. MS 44249, fols. 116-117, Gladstone to Manning, 16 November 1869.

what a happy talent for drawing inferences, even out of figures of speech, is shown by the advocates of Papal authority."[8] Yet the value of Gladstone's observations lies in his experience of Manning from their days as Oxford undergraduates, through their years of enthusiastic support for and involvement in the Oxford Movement, and later the developments that led to Manning's decision to become a Roman Catholic. Manning's leadership of the Roman Catholic Church in England did not alter Gladstone's judgment.

Henry Manning was one of the Oxford Movement converts who found comfort in the dictum, *ubi Petrus, ibi ecclesia*. He stated in 1861, "the one truth which has saved me is the Infallibility of the Vicar of Jesus Christ, as the only true and perfect form of the Infallibility of the Church, and therefore of all divine faith, unity, and obedience."[9] His rapid rise in ecclesiastical authority, seen by some as a cynical grasp for power and by others as the result of humble service in defense of papal prerogatives, resulted in his central role among the Majority bishops of the First Vatican Council.

Two threads in Manning's thought can be found throughout this span of time: the need for a locus of absolute, unchanging, and eternal Truth, and the role of the Holy Spirit in making that Truth manifest in the Church. As Gladstone noted, history was less important to Manning than the principle of absolute Truth received through revealed sources. Indeed, Manning's determined efforts to work out this principle—or theory[10]—to its logical conclusions was a key factor in his conversion to Roman Catholicism and his enthusiastic embrace of what became known as neo-ultramontanism. Relying on a successionist

---

[8] Joannes Dominicus Mansi, ed., *Sacrorum conciliorum nova et amplissima collectio*, 54 vols (Paris: H. Welter, 1901-1927), 52:467. Translation taken from: Raymond Clancy, "American Prelates in the Vatican Council," *Historical Record and Studies* 28 (1937): 111. Kenrick went on to state, "The Most Reverend Archbishop is certainly more Catholic than any Catholic I ever knew before. He has no doubt himself of the infallibility, personal, separate, and absolute, of the Pope, and he is not willing to allow other people to have any." Mansi, 52:469; translation from Clancy, 114.

[9] Edmund Purcell, *Life of Cardinal Manning*, 2 vols (London: Macmillan and Co., 1896), 2:160.

[10] The use of this word is not anachronistic, for nineteenth-century Catholic theologians described gallican and ultramontane claims as competing theories—or opinions—of papal authority. Henry Neville, professor at Maynooth and later rector of Newman's Catholic University, affirmed in 1854 the freedom of Catholics to hold either gallican or ultramontanist theories, "the Gallican is a sound Roman Catholic, in every respect as sound as the Ultramontane." Also see Manning's own articulation of this in 1839: Henry Manning, *The Rule of Faith: Appendix to a Sermon*, 2nd ed. (London: Rivington, 1839), 87.

metanarrative of the Christian past,[11] Manning resolutely refused to acknowledge the value and veracity of historical critiques of neo-ultramontanist claims.

The Early Anglican Years

Manning's early life reflected that of a wealthy middle class Englishman. The youngest of eight children, during Manning's childhood his father enjoyed major successes in the West Indian sugar trade and in Tory politics—though by age twenty-one, the family fortunes had collapsed. A young Balliol student while Newman was an Oriel don and vicar of the University Church, Manning came under Newman's influence and in later life claimed that he never willingly missed Newman's sermons. While Manning's youthful ambition had been to enter politics, the collapse of his family's fortune dashed these hopes, and he found himself reluctantly drawn into holy orders. Though an evangelical by disposition, he fell under the spell of Newman's first "Tract for the Times" in 1833, and a mutual friend reported to Newman, "Manning has revised his opinions and adopts Apostolic Succession."[12] In the summer of 1834, Henry Wilberforce observed "the improvement in him is most remarkable. He is aware of it himself; for he says that a year and a half ago he did not know there was such a thing as the Church."[13] It was a conversion that marked the rest of his life.[14]

By 1834, Manning expressed concern that Newman's doctrine did not take sufficient account of the Holy Spirit's agency, "as a person continually present, helping, teaching, strengthening, guiding and enabling us to use God's appointed means of renewal."[15] This theme perdured and intensified with time.

---

[11] This Eusebian historiography, articulated in the fourth century, used the word διαδοχαί [successions] to emphasize that the authenticity of the original deposit of faith had been handed on through apostolic succession unaltered and undiminished. As Kirsopp Lake stated, Eusebius and Christian historians who followed sought to demonstrate that "the Church had one and only one teaching from the beginning; it had been preserved by the 'Succession' and heresy was the attempt of the Devil to change it." Eusebius of Caesarea, *Eusebius: Ecclesiastical History*, trans. Kirsopp Lake, 2 vols, Loeb Classical Library (London: Heinemanne, 1926), 1:xxxiv-xxxv. Manning's thought reflected this vision of the Christian past. The consistency of his position is striking and it remained an unmovable premise. For Manning, certainty of the Truth he sought required it.

[12] *LD*, 4:92.

[13] Ibid., 4:317.

[14] For an account of his early years, see: Robert Gray, *Cardinal Manning: A Biography* (London: Weidenfeld and Nicolson, 1985), chapters 1-2.

[15] David Newsome, *The Wilberforces and Henry Manning: The Parting of Friends* (Cambridge, MA: The Belknap Press of Harvard University Press, 1966), 202.

Manning's 1835 sermon *The English Church: Its Succession, and Witness for Christ* emphasized the Holy Spirit's enabling work, "whose presence and support was invoked upon us at our ordination, and for the establishment and comfort of our minds in the discharge of our ministerial commission."[16]

In the 1839 *Appendix* to his sermon, *The Rule of Faith*, Manning examined Anglican adherence to the Canon of St. Vincent of Lérins (*quod semper, quod ubique, quod ab omnibus traditum est*). He maintained that the consent of the Christian world was a manifestation of "the voice of God, prolonged from the Apostles to themselves."[17] At that point, he had no problem agreeing with William Palmer that the truth belonging to the universal tradition could be determined by critical historical methods. Using Palmer's words he affirmed that the "'existence of such a tradition from the beginning is a matter of fact, which is to be established on the same sort of evidence as proves any other historical fact.'"[18] Manning maintained that "Christians cannot possibly admit that any doctrine, established by universal tradition, can be otherwise than *divinely, infallibly, true.*"[19] He employed this argument to critique the reliance of both Protestantism and "Romanism" on "living interpreters" of scripture over the consensus of ancient universal tradition. After quoting William Chillingworth's refutation of the Roman theory of papal infallibility, Manning stated, "although this investing of the pope with infallibility is the *Italian* doctrine, the *Gallican* and *British* Romanists placing it in the Church assembled in council ... the *infallibility of the living judge*, whether *pope* or *Church*, is turned against the very ground on which Chillingworth stood ... i.e. *primitive and universal tradition*."[20] In the pages that followed, Manning concluded that Romanists in reality oppose antiquity and universal tradition:

> The infallibility of the *living* Church absorbs all proof into itself. Antiquity, as well as Scripture, is made to follow the interpretation of the present Church. Of antiquity it accepts so much as is in accordance with its existing system; of the rest, some it explains away, some it rejects, some it utterly condemns ... . An-

---

[16] Henry Manning, *The English Church: Its Succession, and Witness for Christ* (London: Rivington, 1835), 5.

[17] Manning, *The Rule of Faith: Appendix*, 62.

[18] Ibid., 112. Original text found in: William Palmer, *A Treatise on the Church of Christ*, 2 vols (Oxford: Rivington, 1838), 2:48.

[19] Ibid., 112. The italics are found in the original text.

[20] Manning, *The Rule of Faith: Appendix*, 87. The italics are found in the original text.

tiquity then is no *rule* of the Church of Rome; it is not even a *proof,* but a pretext.[21]

Manning's doctrine during the 1830s focused on the working of the Holy Spirit in the Church and found its grounding in scripture as interpreted by the consensus of the ancient fathers. Indeed, John Bowden reported to Newman in 1836, "I heard it said the other day of H. Manning, 'It would be very well to bring in the Church every now and then, but *he* never preaches a sermon without it.'"[22] The Holy Spirit's agency at Pentecost as well as the Truth received and preserved through apostolic succession remained fundamental principles for Manning's theological reasoning in the decades that followed.

The Looming Crisis: 1845-1850

In the wake of Newman's conversion in October 1845, Manning declared that "No living man has so powerfully affected me: and there is no mind I have so reverenced."[23] Yet after reading Newman's *Essay on Development*, he declared himself unmoved and considered development the destitute refuge of Protestants and Romanists. The faith had been perfected at Pentecost and the only developments were logical and verbal, "not ideal or *conceptual*."[24] On 6 March 1846 Manning wrote to Gladstone that he had "launched out to try what I can do on the science of proof in Theology." Yet he stated clearly that "I am a long way off from Development." He summed up his observations with doubts about the viability of Newman's theory of development and asserted that whatever its influence, the impact would not be seen soon, "Certainly not for a long time."[25] Just four days later he observed to another correspondent that "the Tridentine Doctors would have severely censured the modern theories of

---

[21] Ibid., 100-101. The italics are found in the original text. John Henry Newman's *Lectures on the Prophetical Office of the Church: Viewed Relatively to Romanism and Popular Protestantism* (London: Rivington, 1837) is quoted at length in the pages that followed to provide concrete examples of this pattern.

[22] *LD*, 5:237, n. 3. Italics in the text.

[23] Emory University, Pitts Library Archives, Manning Collection, Box 1, Folder 22, Manning to Gladstone, 29 October 1845.

[24] Oxford, Bodleian Library, MS Eng. Lett.c.655, fol. 34r, Manning to Robert Wilberforce, 30 December 1845. Italicized text is underlined in the original.

[25] Emory University, Pitts Library, Manning Collection, Box 1, Folder 22, Manning to Gladstone, 6 March 1846.

development, or gradual rise as false, and dangerous—and I hold their principle."[26]

This appeal to the council fathers of Trent signaled a shift for Manning—a transition that had wider implications. Just two months before his conversion in 1851, Manning observed that Newman's essay did convince him of one fact: that while he had found the Rule of Faith (Bible and ancient tradition), he had not determined the Judge.[27] After his conversion, Manning embraced as axiomatic a principle he had vilified in 1839: "A perpetual doctrine tested by a perpetual rule needs a perpetual judge."[28] However, the shift toward this position was already evident in 1846.

By the spring of 1846 Manning raised questions that cast doubt on his critique of the Roman Catholic doctrine of the infallibility of the church. In May 1846, after his sister-in-law Sophie Ryder and her family converted to Roman Catholicism, Manning confided to his journal, "I am conscious to myself of an extensively changed feeling towards the Church of Rome. It seems to me nearer to the truth and the Church of England in greater peril." At the heart of his concern was the apostolic character of the Anglican episcopate. "I have felt that the Episcopate of the English Church is secularised and bound down beyond hope—that there is no [common understanding] to which to appeal for its restoration ... I feel as if a light had fallen on me." He even acknowledged "I am further from the English Church and nearer Rome than I ever was—How do I know where I may be two years hence? Where was Newman five years ago?"[29]

The conversion of a spiritual/theological mentor and cherished relatives had created an emotional and intellectual dissonance that Manning could not shake off. His health declined and a nervous facial tick began.[30] On the day after Christmas 1846, Manning warned Gladstone that in his effort to respond to Newman's essay on development he could not "do things for the nonce, or patch an inconsistent theory."[31]

---

[26] Oxford, Bodleian Library, MS Eng. Lett.c.662, fol. 68r. Manning to unknown correspondent, 10 March 1846.

[27] Oxford, Bodleian Library, MS Eng. Lett.c.656, fol. 107, Manning to Robert Wilberforce, 22 January 1851.

[28] Henry Manning, *The Grounds of Faith* (London: Burns and Lambert, 1852), 51.

[29] Alphonse Chapeau, "Manning the Anglican," in *Manning: Anglican and Catholic*, ed. John Fitzsimons (London: The Catholic Book Club, 1952), 19, 20. Sadly, the contents of Manning's journals are known only through extracts found in the biography written by Edmund Purcell and essays by Alphonse Chapeau. Their current location is unknown.

[30] R.J. Gasquet, *Cardinal Manning* (London: Catholic Truth Society, 1895), 46.

[31] Perry Butler, *Gladstone: Church, State, and Tractarianism* (Oxford: Clarendon Press, 1982), 200-1.

Early in 1847, Manning fell seriously ill and by February he feared that it might be life-threatening. The malady baffled physicians. While Robert Gray hints that the root cause was psychosomatic, what can be said with certainty is that he spent three months confined to his home convalescing.[32] During this period, Manning read works by Pope Leo the Great, Pope Gregory the Great, Augustine, and Optatus.[33] He also studied Melchior Cano's treatment of the infallibility of the Church in his *De Loci Theologici* (1563). As he worked through these theological texts he also drafted volume four of his *Sermons* (published 1850)[34] and came to an overt understanding of a principle he had invoked since 1834. He stated in later autobiographical notes, "I began to find and to express the truth which afterwards brought me into the Church: and has filled my mind with increasing light to this day: I mean the Personal coming, abiding and office of the Holy Ghost ... ." He attributed this insight to Cano.[35]

On 20 April 1847, Manning noted in his diary two questions that vexed him: "1. Is it the will of our Lord Jesus Christ that His flock should be subject to Saint Peter and his successors? 2. Is it part of the mystery of Pentecost that the Church should be infallible?" The notes that followed indicate that Manning leaned toward admitting, "1. The Infallibility of the Church, 2. The Church of Rome that Church."[36]

In a letter to his confessor Charles Laprimaudaye, on 16 June 1847, Manning described an internal turbulence so troubling he had withdrawn from theological discussions with "five men of high excellence and value to us." He expanded on the two questions he had confided to his diary two months earlier:

First.–Is not the infallibility of the Church a necessary consequence of the presence of the third Person of the Blessed Trinity; and of His perpetual office, beginning from the Day of Pentecost? This seems to me revealed in Scripture.

---

[32] Gray, *Cardinal Manning*, 115.

[33] Optatus's singular work, "Against Parmenian the Donatist," provided the starting point for Augustine's work against the Donatists. His argument attacked their "catholicity" and claims to holiness. For an extended study see: José Luis Gutiérrez-Martín, *Iglesia y liturgia en el África romana del siglo IV: bautismo y eucaristía en los libros de Optato, obispo de Milevi* (Roma: CLV, 2001).

[34] Oxford, Bodleian Library, MS Eng. Lett.c.655, fols. 131r-132v.

[35] Chapeau, "Manning the Anglican," 23. See also: Robert Ornsby, *Memoirs of James Hope-Scott*, 2 vols (London: John Murray, 1884), 2:91, for a letter from Manning to J.R. Hope dated 11 December 1850; Oxford, Bodleian Library, MS Eng. Lett.c.656, fol. 108r-v, Manning to Robert Wilberforce, 22 January 1851.

[36] Purcell, *Life of Cardinal Manning*, 1:487.

A perpetual presence, perpetual office, and perpetual *infallibility*—that is, a living voice witnessing for truth and against error under the guidance of the Spirit of Christ—seem inseparable.

Second.—Is it not a part of the revealed will and ordinance of our Lord Jesus Christ, that the Church should be under an episcopate united with a visible head, as the apostles were united with St. Peter? It is not the question of primacy with me so much as *unity of the episcopate. "Episcopatus unus est."*[37] I take St. Peter to have been the first of the apostles, as the Primate of Christendom is the first of bishops; in spiritual order or power all being equal.[38]

One month later Manning embarked on a Roman holiday. While physical recuperation provided the pretext, he remained focused on his interior turmoil. On 5 July 1847 Manning recorded in his diary, "To-morrow by the will of God I go forth, it may be for a year, it may be for ever. I feel to be in His hands. I know not what is good for myself."[39] While his progress to Rome is recounted in detail elsewhere, diary entries provide an inventory of religious practice on the continent—Catholics always cast in a positive light and Protestant deficiencies recorded in detail.[40] He finally arrived in Rome on 28 November 1847, and seemed enthralled by the five months there. Unlike Newman, who felt ill at ease among the Italians, Manning embraced the Roman ethos.[41] Though Manning and Newman met on three consecutive days, neither recorded the substance of their discussions, and Newman left for England in early December.[42]

It is not surprising that, in January 1848, Manning reported to Robert Wilberforce, "Things seem to me clearer, plainer, shapelier and more harmonious; things which were only in the head have got down into the heart."[43] A month later he wrote:

> There are truths so primary and despotic that I cannot elude them ... Such is the Infallibility of the Mystical Body of Christ on Earth, through the Indwelling of

---

[37] It was this very point that brought Manning into conflict with Archbishop Kenrick at Vatican I, for Kenrick argued that Manning's theory of papal infallibility absorbed all episcopal authority into the papal office, and effectively nullified the apostolic character of bishops dispersed throughout the world.

[38] Ibid., 1:471.

[39] Ibid., 1:342.

[40] Ibid., 1:343-61.

[41] Ibid., 1:362-417. Manning's enthusiasm for Pius IX's Rome is reminiscent of Wiseman's description of the ethos cultivated by Pius VII in the years after 1815. See: Nicholas Wiseman, *The Last Four Popes* (Boston: Patrick Donahoe, 1858), 30.

[42] Gray, *Cardinal Manning*, 121; *LD*, 12:154.

[43] Oxford, Bodleian Library, MS Eng. Lett.c.655, fol. 62r-v.

the Holy Spirit. I could as soon disbelieve the Canon of Scripture, or the perpetuity of the Church. Infallibility is not an accident; it is a property as inseparable by the Divine Will as perpetuity. This is evident to me from Holy Scripture, from Catholic Tradition, from internal and necessary relations of Divine Truth and Divine acts, as well as from reasons which alone would prove nothing.[44]

While Manning sojourned in Rome, Prime Minister John Russell nominated Oxford's Regius Professor of Divinity, Renn Dickson Hampden, to the bishopric of Hereford in December 1847. Despite the protest of bishops Hampden was consecrated in March 1848.[45] This struck Manning as a direct blow to the apostolic character of the Church of England and an unmistakable example of the worst form of Erastian abuse—the appointment of a heretic to episcopal office by a Whig prime minister.

Despairing, Manning confided to Robert Wilberforce in February 1848 the personal angst Hampden's case generated in him. Shedding forever the appeal to universal ancient tradition, he stated:

It is useless to offer me antiquity for my foundation. What do I know of antiquity? At my next birthday, if I live, I shall be forty. I must rest on something which itself rests continuously on antiquity, whose consciousness is therefore continuous, running down from the Day of Pentecost to this hour.

He concluded, "God knows that I would rather stand in the lowest place within the Truth, than in the highest without it. Nay outside the Truth the higher the worst. ... If I could but know *one* great truth, all would be clear."[46]

Although Manning had a lengthy private audience with Pius IX on 8 May 1848, three days before his return to England, he made no record in his diary beyond, "Audience to-day at the Vatican." Decades later he explained, "I remember the pain I felt at seeing how unknown we were to the Vicar of Jesus Christ. It made me feel our isolation."[47]

On his journey back to England, Manning passed through Milan and visited the tomb of Charles Borromeo, his future patron saint. He later reported that at the tomb he prayerfully yearned to know if Borromeo, who represented for him

---

[44] Ibid., fol. 63v.

[45] Hampden's appointment as Regius Professor of Divinity in 1836 was a *casus belli* for members of the Oxford Movement, primarily because he argued for a relaxation of dogmatic principles in Christianity.

[46] Ibid., fols. 63v-64r, 64v. Printed text found in: Edmund Purcell, *Life of Cardinal Manning*, 1:512-13. The italicized text is underlined in the original.

[47] Ibid., 1:416.

the Council of Trent, was right and Anglicans were wrong. In the midst of this supplication, he realized that the deacon was singing the gospel for that day, and the last words of John 10:16 came as an answer to his question: "'*et erit unum ovile et unus pastor*'" [and there shall be one flock and one shepherd].[48]

If Manning was Romeward bound, this determination at least appeared to dissipate on his return to England. Gladstone remembered vividly a walk in St. James's Park in July 1848 when Manning professed his conviction that the previous year, with the insight of a man near to death in 1847, "'I had an absolute assurance in heart and soul, solemn beyond expression, that the English Church—I am not speaking of the Establishment—is a living portion of the Church of Christ.'"[49] Indeed, Keble reported to Pusey that same month that Manning had returned from Rome a stalwart Anglican.[50] Even more striking was his published July 1848 "Charge," as archdeacon of Chichester. In this sixty-two page document, Manning defended the Church of England in the wake of Hampden's consecration as bishop of Hereford. Because Hampden had not been convicted of heresy by a church tribunal and had subscribed to the *Thirty-nine Articles*, Manning argued, the Church of England stood vindicated.[51] Yet when he sent a copy of the "Charge" to his former tutor, friend and confidant, George Moberly, he explained that, "My opinions are what they were when I wrote to you from Rome. My Charge is the case for the Church of England."[52] This statement appears to give a lie to his anguished comment to Robert Wilberforce from Rome that "I would rather stand in the lowest place within the Truth, than

---

[48] The Vulgate actually reads: "*et fiet unum ovile et unus pastor.*" Quote found in: Chapeau, "Manning the Anglican," 26. It is worth pondering why this biblical text was transmuted in Manning's memory from the more developmental verb—"*fiet*" [will become]—into the more static—"*erit*" [shall be]. There is also a problem of historical fact that is hard to reconcile. Manning in his last years dated his private audience with Pius IX on 8 May 1848 Purcell, *Life of Cardinal Manning*, 416. However, the gospel text he claimed to have heard in Milan was the reading for the second Sunday after Easter, which was 7 May 1848.

[49] Purcell, *Life of Cardinal Manning*, 1:570. While this account was based on Gladstone's recollections in 1894, Gladstone pointed to a letter he wrote to Manning in November 1850, in which that conversation was summarized and used to admonish Manning. Ibid., 1:581.

[50] Georgina Battiscombe, *John Keble: A Study in Limitations* (London: Constable, 1963), 304.

[51] Henry Manning, *A Charge Delivered at the Ordinary Visitation of the Archdeaconry of Chichester, July 1848* (London: John Murray, 1848).

[52] John Bodley, *Cardinal Manning. The Decay of Idealism in France. The Institute of France: Three Essays* (London: Longmans, Green, and Co., 1912), 27.

in the highest without it."[53] Some argue that not having relinquished his position as archdeacon, Manning had an obligation to present the official position. Others point to a desire not to scandalize friends while his mind remained unsettled. Those disposed to believe the worst accuse Manning of duplicity. His most recent biographer concluded that "Manning was ready to err on the side of hope." No conclusive judgment is possible.[54]

Yet Newman, for one, expressed exasperation as early as March 1848, when Henry Wilberforce shared with Newman a letter Manning had written, in which he stated that a "deep gulf" divided Newman and Manning. Newman responded, "What does Manning *mean* by telling *you* that there is a 'deep gulf between him and me' … while he tells all Catholics that he is already quite *one* with us. You are a clever fellow, but you will not reconcile these sayings." Using Manning's own words of advice to Henry, Newman concluded that Manning's public posture was "'necessary for your position'" in the Church of England.[55]

Through the later half of 1848 and throughout 1849, Manning's vacillation continued. His private anguish seemed counterbalanced by a sense of the good he could accomplish in the public sphere. Indeed he was a powerful force, as F.D. Maurice noted concerning his role in negotiating a compromise over state involvement in church-run schools in June 1849:

> There was one man in that room who can save the Church from its confusion if he has a mind to do so. This is Manning. … His power with the clergy is very great, greater certainly than that of any man living. I do hope he has a sense of responsibility which belongs to the exercise of it.[56]

Manning's resolve and sense of duty seemed intact during Holy Week 1849, when he wrote to Mary Wilberforce, "My deep belief is that He wills me to stay as I am; and all those whom He has submitted to me."[57] Yet by Advent of

---

[53] Oxford, Bodleian Library, MS Eng. Lett.c.655, fol. 64v. Printed text available in: Purcell, *Life of Cardinal Manning,* 1:513.

[54] Butler, *Gladstone,* 200-1; Purcell, *Life of Cardinal Manning,* 1:569-70; Bodley, 27-8. James Pereiro, *Cardinal Manning: An Intellectual Biography* (Oxford: Clarendon Press, 1998), 108.

[55] *LD,* 12:183.

[56] Frederick Maurice, ed., *The Life of Frederick Denison Maurice, Chiefly Told in His Own Letters,* 2 vols (London: Macmillan and Co., 1884), 1:545.

[57] Oxford, Bodleian Library, MS Eng. Lett.c.655, fol. 110r. Printed text available in: Newsome, *The Parting of Friends,* 326.

the same year, he admitted to her, "I have felt and do feel an overwhelming fear lest I should be under an illusion."[58]

Manning had spent much of 1849 consumed by the Gorham Case. George Gorham, an evangelical cleric whom the Bishop of Exeter had refused to install in a living because of his rejection of baptismal regeneration, had taken the bishop to court. Despite a series of lost court cases, Gorham continued to appeal until he reached the ultimate British court, the Judicial Committee of the Privy Council.[59] While Britain had been untouched by the wave of revolutions that swept Europe in 1848, one Frenchman noted that revolution in England's religious order had come in the form of "*le père Gorham.*"[60] Manning poured over Anglican canon law, and applied it "'like arguments from pure mathematics.'"[61] His anxiety focused on a specific question: "'whether the Church of England be a Divine or a human society.'"[62] By January 1850 Manning had the answer to his question. In a letter to Samuel Wilberforce, dated 24 January 1850, Manning explained:

> [I]t is indifferent which way the judgement may go. Indeed a decision in favour of the true doctrine of Baptism would mislead many. A judgement right in matter cannot heal a wrong in the principle of the Appeal. And the wrong is this: 'The Appeal removed the final decision of a question involving both doctrine and discipline out of the Church to another centre and that a Civil Court.'[63]

As he struggled with the current events of 1849, Manning revised the fourth volume of his sermons, drafted during his 1847 illness,[64] and saw them through to their final proofs in the latter months of that year. In this collection Manning articulated the dramatic alteration in his ideas about the nature of Truth, the Church, and the working of the Holy Spirit.[65] In "The Analogy of Nature,"

---

[58] Oxford, Bodleian Library, MS Eng. Lett.c.655, fol. 138r. Printed text available in: Shane Leslie, *Cardinal Manning: His Life and Labours* (New York: P.J. Kenedy and Sons, 1954), 36.

[59] Gray, *Cardinal Manning*, 131-2.

[60] Arthur P. Stanley, *Essays Chiefly on Questions of Church and State: From 1850 to 1870* (London: John Murray, 1884), 16.

[61] *Guardian*, 17 July 1850, as quoted in: Arthur W. Hutton, *Cardinal Manning* (London: Methuen and Co., 1892), 66.

[62] Purcell, *Life of Cardinal Manning*, 1:548.

[63] Newsome, 350. Manning worked out elements of this argument in his 12 and 18 January 1850 letters to Robert Wilberforce. See: Oxford, Bodleian Library, MS Eng. Lett.c.655, fols. 150r-158v.

[64] Ibid., fols. 131r-132v.

[65] For a close analysis of this volume see: Pereiro, *Cardinal Manning*, 80-104.

which Gladstone described in 1869 as a troubling shift in Manning's thought, Manning posed a question which echoed the problem explored in his undergraduate essay: "What is the proper faculty or instrument by which the truth is to be apprehended?" The answer to this rhetorical homiletic question was simple in its directness: "By faith." In a starkly bifurcated analysis, Manning stated unambiguously that we either know Truth "by discovery or reception ... by reasoning or by faith." To underline this conclusion he stated emphatically, "there is no third way."[66] Truth had been given "to the prophets, by the inspiration of God; to the Apostles, by the descent of the Holy Ghost, by the presence and guidance of Christ."[67] That gift had been received by faith and was perpetuated by faith. "It was not first *given*, then left to be *discovered*; first consigned to faith, then to be proved by reason."[68] For Manning, the ultimate proof rested in his understanding of apostolic succession, the human agency through which the Holy Spirit preserved and perpetuated revealed Truth. If the Holy Spirit remained and communicated sanctifying grace, the same must be said of doctrines originally given at Pentecost. "Surely the traditions of grace and the traditions of truth are both sustained by the same perpetual and infallible presence."[69] After attacking Butlerian appeals to the analogy of nature and to discerning truth through reasoning, Manning stated, "faith means trust in divine authority. ... But faith is an infused grace of God."[70] In "The Intuition of Faith," Manning clarified that "Faith is a spiritual consciousness of the world unseen, infused into us, in our regeneration, by the supernatural gift of God."[71] Tying the infallibility of God to the infallibility of the Church, he presented his reader with a striking dilemma:

> The infallibility of the Church is made up of these two elements; perfect certainty in the object revealed, and spiritual illumination in the subject which perceives it, that is, the Church itself. Shake this foundation, and faith becomes uncertainty; and what is uncertainty, as a rule of life or as a principle of action? ... What gives to faith its confidence of trust, its enduring strength in action, its intense insight in contemplation? Certainty founded on revelation. And what is the very first idea of revelation but a clear and infallible knowledge of the truth given direct from God?[72]

---

[66] Henry Manning, "The Analogy of Nature," published in: Henry Edward Manning, *Sermons*, 4 vols (London: William Pickering, 1850), 4:168.
[67] Ibid., 168-9.
[68] Ibid., 169.
[69] Ibid., 169-70.
[70] Ibid., 171.
[71] Ibid., 377.
[72] Ibid., 171.

Manning assured his reader that preservation and perpetuation of Truth was an office of the Holy Spirit, always present in the mystical body of Christ. "[T]he presence of an infallible Teacher is as necessary to the infirmities of the human reason, as the presence of an omnipotent Comforter is necessary to the infirmities of the human will; that both the will and reason, without such a presence, omnipotent and infallible, would be in bondage to evil and to falsehood."[73] While not explicitly stated in his sermons, Manning's line of reasoning pointed toward conclusions that he had communicated only to his journal: that the bishop of Rome was the infallible judge of doctrine, by virtue of his role as Peter's apostolic successor and the ultimate expression of the unity of the episcopate.

Despite refining the theological case for leaving the Church of England and becoming a Roman Catholic, Manning continued to hold onto his Anglican affiliation through 1850 and into 1851. On 11 March 1850, two days after the positive outcome of Gorham's appeal, Manning led a group of clergy in drafting a repudiation of the Gorham decision, which appeared in *The Times* of London on 20 March.

On 5 August 1850, Manning admitted to a female disciple that the Gorham case had taken its toll. He explained,

> I always felt that the Low Church had no objective Truths, and the High Church little subjective religion. Now I see that in the Catholic System the objective and the subjective are the concave and the convex ... God and man are one by Incarnation. A Theology of 300 years is in conflict with a Faith of 1,800 years. I was born in the 300. My mature thoughts transplant me into the 1,800.[74]

Though his reception into the Roman Catholic Church did not occur until months later, the final trajectory was evident to all but the most willfully obtuse—Gladstone foremost among these. While in letters to Robert Wilberforce he continued to go over and over the case for Rome and against the Church of England, this "ratiocination" had more to do with convincing himself that his decision was justifiable, rather than simply following the desires of his heart. The voluminous correspondence with Robert Wilberforce demonstrates this point. By September 1850, the decision had been made.[75]

---

[73] Ibid., 172.
[74] Leslie, *Cardinal Manning*, 91.
[75] Oxford, Bodleian Library, MS Eng. Lett.c.656, fols. 33r-179v. Gray, *Cardinal Manning*, 135.

Five years before Manning's conversion, the turn in his thinking was evident in private papers and correspondence. Focused on questions of the agency of the Holy Spirit and revealed truths, Manning turned away from the concept of ancient consensus in doctrine as a guiding principle, and toward a "living judge" of scripture and tradition, whose authority and insight derived from the perpetual and infallible presence of the Holy Spirit working through the supreme episcopal office—the Bishop of Rome. Manning's five year struggle, so reminiscent of Newman's Littlemore years, drew him toward the same destination, but via a very different route. Here one finds the tension between inductive and deductive reasoning which characterized their age. Newman struggled with historical inconsistencies and human failures. Doctrinal development proved a theory that resolved his difficulties. Manning's line of reasoning eschewed arguments from historical evidence. He demonstrated a decided preference for abstract principles from which he drew conclusions that had an unassailable internal logic. If eternal, immutable, and changeless truths are found only "in their revealed shape,"[76] and the Holy Spirit is the agency of that revelation, human sciences had nothing to offer compared with the authoritative living voice of the divinely appointed successor of St. Peter.

From Catholic Convert to Primate of England

This quest found its goal in the ultramontane doctrine of the Roman scholastics. While Newman remained ever under a cloud of suspicion in Rome,[77] Manning developed a bond with the Roman College professor, Giovanni Perrone, which evolved into a powerful alliance during the 1860s. Fifteen years after his conversion, through the intercession of another Oxford Movement convert, George Talbot (chamberlain to Pope Pius IX), Manning became the most influential episcopal figure in the English-speaking Catholic world.

He exerted the weight of his influence in promoting the permanent and unchanging character of the Truth proclaimed by the Catholic Church. Manning's

---

[76] Oxford, Bodleian Library, MS Eng. Misc.d.1278, "English Essay No. 11," fols. 44-5.

[77] In February 1847, Newman wrote to Nicholas Wiseman, reporting that the influential professor Carlo Passaglia and Dr. Alexander Grant, rector of the "Scotch" College openly opposed his book on development. *LD*, 12:42. Giovanni Perrone proved more open to engaging Newman on this subject. See: C. Michael Shea's essay in this volume. Mgr. George Talbot viewed Newman with suspicion and as late as April 1867, wrote to Manning that "Dr. Newman is the most dangerous man in England." Purcell, *Life of Cardinal Manning*, 2:318. For more on George Talbot, see Donna Reinhard's essay in this volume.

conviction rested on an ancient vision of the Christian past articulated by Eusebius of Caesarea, who argued that the Truth given by Christ to the apostles had been preserved unaltered by their successors. Using a clear and unambiguous application of successionist historiography, Manning stated in 1865, "the divine action of the day of Pentecost is permanent, and pervades the world so far as the Church is diffused, and pervades all ages, the present as fully as the past, to-day as fully as in the beginning."[78] For Manning, the faith was revealed and taught before history, fact, and antiquity existed. One did not look to the past for knowledge of faith, for "the enunciation of the faith by the living Church of this hour, is the maximum evidence, both natural and supernatural, as to the *facts* and the *contents* of the original revelation."[79] According to Manning, the papacy maintained this unbroken continuity. "By that one long chain of Pontiffs, two hundred and fifty and more, linked in perfect continuity, connected as indissolubly as the generations of men and the successions of time, we are in direct contact now, through the person of Pius IX., with St. Peter, Prince of the Apostles and Vicar of Jesus Christ."[80]

Manning and others proved powerful influences on Pius IX in the 1860s, and encouraged his conviction that their age of uncertainty and change required a definition of papal infallibility. For Manning the infallibility of the Church depended on the infallibility of the pope, not the bishops. "The Vicar of Christ would bear no proportion to the body if, while it is infallible, he were not."[81] In 1867 the pope announced that the first general council since Trent would gather in Rome. While the intention to define papal infallibility was not stated, it was widely assumed to be a principal reason for this extraordinary event. At the council, Manning was the ultimate insider. Leader of the Majority bishops, confidante of the pope, and member of influential council commissions that controlled the agenda, Manning sought a sweeping definition of papal infallibility.

Manning considered the liberal Catholic intellectuals of Germany, France, and England among the chief opponents of his campaign, and gave special attention to their primary weapon: history. Manning's understanding of papal

---

[78] Henry Manning, *The Temporal Mission of the Holy Ghost* (New York: D. and J. Sadlier, 1887; 1st ed., 1865), 83.

[79] Ibid., 205. This argument is also found in the pre-papal publications of Gregory XVI (Mauro Cappellari). See: Mauro Cappellari, *Il Trionfo della Santa Sede e della Chiesa contro gli assalti dei novatori combattuti e respinti colle stesse loro armi* (Rome, 1799), 19.

[80] Henry Manning, *Sermons on Ecclesiastical Subjects*, 2 vols (London: Burns, Oates, and Co., 1872), 2:17.

[81] Manning, *Temporal Mission*, 95.

infallibility defied their appeal to the Church's past, taking the successionist understanding of history to its ultimate extreme. In a later work, responding to a quote attributed to him, Manning stated:

> The triumph of dogma over history ... means this: the Church defines its doctrines in spite of you, because it knows its history better than you. Its dogmas include its history, and its history is part of its consciousness, sustained by divine assistance ... which perpetuates faith."[82]

Henry Manning certainly had Lord Acton in mind, among others, when making this statement. Acton sought to organize and encourage the Minority bishops during the First Vatican Council and proved tireless in his efforts to oppose Manning's goal. The young historian and dedicated Catholic found Manning's understanding of the Church and Truth disturbing as he sought to reconcile his Catholic faith with his formation in historical research. He rejected Manning's conviction that "faith cannot be proved, that it is a sort of inspiration and illuminism." He quoted Manning saying, "I don't say that it is the truth [papal infallibility]; I only say that it is the Catholic doctrine." Acton doubted Manning's belief "that Conclaves are decided by the Holy Ghost" and rejected the concept that popes are "exempt from the ordinary laws of historical reasoning and judgment."[83] For Acton, neo-ultramontanism was a theory, pushed to its ultimate extreme. Manning, among others like him, damaged the viability of Acton's own vision of the "objectiveness" of Catholic Truth. Acton concluded, "already infallibility [has] undermined this theory, inasmuch as it preferred the theological to the historical argument. They refuse to be bound by the evidence of history."[84]

The pleasure of reading Manning's works lies in the absence of ambiguity in his thought, and the deep conviction and certainty of what he believed. The consistency of his epistemological foundation (divine revelation mediated by the Holy Spirit), which he articulated as a young Anglican undergraduate, developed and amplified as a youthful theologian, and took to its logical conclusion in his life as a Catholic, gives greater clarity to his activities at the First Vatican Council. Yet the weakness of his conclusions can also be found in his undergraduate analysis, as well as the observations of his (former) friend William Gladstone and his young ideological foe John Acton. To what extent was his enthusiastic embrace of papal infallibility a theorist's desire "to admit as truth

---

[82] Henry Manning, *Religio Viatoris* (London: Burns and Oates, 4th ed., nd), 79.
[83] Cambridge University Library, Add. MS 5542, fol. 27.
[84] Ibid., fol. 32.

whatever our will, or affections dictate to us"?[85] Is there a sense in which he, like other religious theorists, "suffer their reason to be out-stripped by their desires and to acquiesce in the adoption of crude and fanciful conceits"?[86] Gladstone and Acton would certainly have agreed with such a critique. Yet if dogma did triumph over history at the council, it was a Pyrrhic victory; for the theory of another Oxford Movement convert, John Henry Newman, came into its own during the twentieth century.

---

[85] Oxford, Bodleian Library, MS Eng. Misc.d.1278, "English Essay No. 11," fols. 41-2.

[86] Ibid., fol. 42.

Canterbury's Rejoinder
Pusey, Gladstone, and The Neo-Ultramontanism of Manning

Michael J. G. Pahls

On 25 March 1851, Henry Edward Manning (1808-1892) made his formal break with the Church of England, legally resigning his archdeaconry. From there he returned over the Blackfriars Bridge to Southwark to enter the Roman Catholic cathedral. He then knelt before a monstrance containing the blessed sacrament and uttered his first Hail Mary. He did this as a man who had lost confidence in the power of the Church of England to maintain the integrity of Christian faith in the face of what he believed to be an intrusive intervention of the *saeculum* in sacred affairs.

Although occurring well over a century and a half ago, the event has proven to be enduringly significant—for within fourteen years, Pope Pius IX would name Manning the Archbishop of Westminster and Catholic Metropolitan of England. From this exalted seat of ecclesiastical power, Manning played a profoundly instrumental role in the process leading to the definition of papal infallibility.

In this essay I will retrace Manning's journey from Anglicanism into Roman Catholicism and his rapid emergence as "ultra of the ultras" among Catholic ultramontanes. I will then trace out the contrasting yet complimentary objections of his primary Anglican respondents—Oxford's Regius Professor of Hebrew, Edward Bouverie Pusey (1800-1882) and British Prime Minister, William Ewart Gladstone (1809-1888). By drawing attention to this nineteenth-century conversation among former friends of diverging concerns, I hope to illuminate the enduring political, ecumenical, and theological consequence of papal infallibility.

Manning, Pusey, and the Judicial Committee of the Privy Council

Just over a year prior to that first Hail Mary, on 9 March 1850, the Judicial Committee of the Privy Council successfully ordered Bishop Henry Phillpots of St. Just Church to reinstate an Evangelical Anglican clergyman to his priestly office. George Cornelius Gorham (1787-1857) had been deposed for his denial that the sacrament of baptism carried with it the objective effect of baptismal regeneration. Gorham's theological commitments represented a grave error to Phillpots, Manning, and other members of the high church party in the Church of England. Far more problematic, however, was the fact that the Privy Council was dominated by laymen—six lawyers with Lord Lansdowne alongside the Archbishops of Canterbury and York, and the Bishop of London—and it was also a secular court sitting in judgment over a doctrinal controversy. Indeed, even prior to the Judicial Committee's decision, Manning objected to the jurisdictional forum itself.

> [I]t is indifferent which way the judgment may go. Indeed, a decision in favour of the true doctrine of Baptism would confuse many ... the Appeal removes the final decision of a question involving both doctrine and discipline out of the Church to another centre and that a Civil Court.[1]

For Manning the fact that a secular court should wield the power to impose a theological judgment on the church proved that the Church of England was merely a man-made creation of the English parliament. Conversion to Roman Catholicism, a move made five years earlier by John Henry Newman (1801-1890), became the only remaining means by which he could reclaim a lost center of Christian authority. From this moment on Manning would become Anglicanism's greatest Victorian opponent.

Manning's wife had died of consumption long before his withdrawal into the Roman Communion, so there was no domestic obstacle to his passing within a week from the Catholic laity into the priesthood. In less than fourteen years, he was named Archbishop of Westminster and entered into the intimate confidences of Pius IX (1792-1878). Just prior to his episcopal appointment, a second action of the Judicial Committee of the Privy Council renewed the agitation that had provoked his conversion. This time the committee acted to intervene in the joint cases of Dr. Rowland Williams (1817-1870) and Mr. Henry Bristow Wilson (1803-1888) resulting from their contributions to the 1860 collection, *Essays and Reviews*. Williams, was Vice Principal and Professor of Hebrew at St. Peter's College, Lampeter. He had written to commend the liberal German biblical criticism of Christian C.J. Bunsen. In the essay he famously compared Bunsen's conservative critics to "degenerate senators before Tiberius."[2] Wilson was pri-

---

[1] Manning to Samuel Wilberforce 24 January,1850. Quoted in David Newsome, *The Wilberforces and Henry Manning: The Parting of Friends* (Cambridge, MA: Belknap/HUP, 1966), 350.

[2] Rowland Williams, "Bunsen's Biblical Researches," in *Essays and Reviews* (London: Longman, Green, Longman, Roberts, & Green, 1860), 62. Williams continued with

mary editor of the collection and argued in his own essay for the provisional nature of theological truth and a broader liberty to dissent from the historic formularies of Anglicanism.[3] The two were prosecuted for heterodoxy in the Court of Arches and eventually found guilty of three articles brought against them. When the decision was reversed on appeal to the Judiciary Committee, the earlier ignominy of the Gorham decision was underscored. Whereas the Gorham decision merely served to adjudicate between broadly held High and Low church opinions of the sacrament of baptism, the Williams-Wilson judgment seemed to mark a decision against Anglicanism and in favor of unbelief. So disturbing was this to Manning's former Oxford Movement colleague, Edward Bouverie Pusey, that Pusey undertook a campaign to discern the precise implication of the decision. Writing to Sir Roundell Palmer and Sir Hugh Cairns, asking fifteen questions regarding the force of the judgment, he secured assurances that the decision pertained exclusively to the case under consideration and that the most to be inferred was that the two Anglican clergyman were not bound to explicitly affirm "every part of every book of Holy Scripture was written by the Holy Spirit, and is the Word of God."[4] Neither were they required to explicitly disclaim as heretical "the ultimate pardon of [even] the wicked" as being possibly "consistent with the will of Almighty God."[5] This delimited opinion of the case certainly mitigated possible damage following upon more liberal readings, but as with Manning in the wake of the Gorham decision, Pusey remained anxious about a theological case being decided in a civil forum. In September 1864, he issued a pamphlet promulgating the opinions he had secured from Palmer and Cairns and arguing for a minimalist rather than a maximalist interpretation of the decision.[6] As part of this pamphlet, he celebrated non-Anglican friends of the Church of England while decrying those who would rejoice at her destruction:

> While I know that a very earnest body of Roman Catholics rejoice in all the workings of God the Holy Ghost in the Church of England (whatever they

---

a sharp condemnation: "They stand balancing terror against shame. Even with those in our universities who no longer repeat fully the required Shibboleths the explicitness of truth is rare. He who assents most, committing himself least to baseness is reckoned wisest", Ibid.

[3] See Henry Bristow Wilson, "Séances Historiques De Geneve—The National Church," Ibid., 173-248.

[4] Liddon, *Life of Pusey*, 4:86.

[5] Ibid.

[6] Edward Pusey, *Case as to the Legal force of the Judgment of the Privy Council, in re Fendall v. Wilson; with the Opinion of the Attorney-General and Sir Hugh Cairns, and a Preface to those who love God and his Truth* (Oxford: Parker; London: Rivington, 1864).

think of her), and are saddened in what weakens her who is, in God's hands, the great bulwark against infidelity in this land, others seemed to be in an ecstasy of triumph at this victory of Satan.[7]

One reviewer of Pusey's pamphlet in *The Weekly Register*—Fr. Lockhart—reflected a popular belief that the term "bulwark" originated with John Henry Newman. Newman himself later disclaimed the sentiment, however, responding on 19 November 1865 that he only intended the term—as used in his *Apologia*—to indicate that "the National Church has hitherto been a serviceable breakwater against doctrinal errors more fundamental than its own."[8] There could be no dispute regarding the subject of Pusey's rebuke, however, and having recognized his own countenance in the description, Manning published in 1864 an open letter entitled *The Workings of the Holy Spirit in England*.

Even as an Anglican, Manning had developed clear convictions about the infallibility of the Church and about true doctrinal knowledge as its peculiar manifestation.[9] Reflecting on his late-Anglican period in 1870, Manning wrote,

> I had by that time a profuse and immutable conviction that the Holy Ghost perpetually and infallibly guides the Church and speaks by its voice. I lingered still in hope that the Church of England was a part of that Church in which He dwells and through which He perpetually speaks.[10]

The issue, at least according to the Catholic Manning, came down to whether the Church of England was truly part of the Church universal and thus graced with infallibility—a gift of the Holy Spirit:

---

[7] Ibid., 34.

[8] Henry Liddon observed that Pusey had never read the portion of the *Apologia* in which the statement appears. Newman expressed a belief that the expression had originated with Joseph de Maistre. Liddon, *Life of Pusey*, 4:95, n. 1.

[9] Of this James Pereiro has written, "The problem was presented in clear terms in Manning's mind: the end of man is eternal life, and one of the indispensable means to reach it is the knowledge of God. Man attains eternal life by growing into the image and likeness of God which he received from his Creator, and, as he wrote in 1842—the knowledge of God's revelation is 'a means to the restoration of man to his image', 'a necessary condition to man's restoration to the divine image.'" See: James Pereiro, "'Truth Before Peace': Manning and Infallibility," *Recusant History* 21 (October 1992): 218. Pereiro quotes here from Manning's *The Unity of the Church* (London: John Murray, 1842), 177, 236-7. Cf. also the essay by Kenneth Parker in this volume.

[10] Henry Manning, *Sermons on Ecclesiastical Subjects*, 2 vols (London: Burns, Oats, and Co., 1870), 1:7.

'*Me lusit amabilis insania*,' [A fond illusion led me astray,] which the facts before my eyes rudely dispelled. As a disciple of the Church of God, infallible in all ages by virtue of the perpetual presence and assistance of the Spirit of Truth I had no decision to make. The Church of England forsook me, not I it.[11]

In his 1864 pamphlet, Manning replied to Pusey's not-so-veiled rebuke as a man who had found again the role of the Spirit and with it a confident epistemological footing in Catholic neo-ultramontanism.[12] Identifying specific players in William Ward's "internecine conflict ... between the army of [infallible] dogma and the united hosts of heresy, indifferentism, and atheism," he believed that adherence to Anglican heresy would drag a Christian soul, almost of necessity, into the latter two errors.[13] The Williams-Wilson judgment only buttressed this conviction.

Manning did acknowledge the bare validity of Protestant baptisms and thus a minimal work of the Holy Spirit outside the Roman Catholic communion. He did this only begrudgingly, however, arguing that this was in spite of, rather than because of, the Church of England.[14] Whatever truth may have remained in Anglicanism merely represented borrowed capital from Rome. His elegant summation denied that the Church of England was part of the visible Church of Christ and thus was no bulwark against infidelity.

If the Catholic faith be the perfect revelation of Christianity, the Anglican Reformation is a cloud of heresies. If the Catholic Church be the organ of the Holy Ghost, the Anglican Church is not only no part of the Church, but no Church of Divine foundation. It is a human institution, sustained, as it was founded, by

---

[11] Ibid., The Latin quote is an adaptation of: Horace, *Odes,* Book 3, Ode 4, lines 5-6. In the Modern Library translation of Horace's *Odes*, it is subtitled, "Power of the Muses." Horace, *The Complete Works of Horace*, ed. Casper Kraemer, Jr. (New York: Modern Library, 1936), 223.

[12] Cuthbert Butler defines neo-ultramontanism as a belief that the "infallible element of bulls, encyclicals, etc., should not be restricted to their formal definitions but ran through the entire doctrinal instructions; the decrees of the Roman Congregation, if adopted by the Pope and published with his authority, thereby were stamped with the mark of infallibility, in short 'his every doctrinal pronouncement is infallibly rendered by the Holy Ghost.'" See: Cuthbert Butler, *The Vatican Council 1869-1870* (Westminster, MD: Newman, 1962), 57-8. While Butler's description focused on the beliefs of fellow Anglican convert, William Ward, Butler suggested that "[Manning] was more than disposed to accept them." Ibid., 61.

[13] William Ward, "Preliminary Essay," in: *Essays on the Church's Doctrinal Authority* (London: Burns & Oates, 1880), 24.

[14] Ibid., 10. Of the latter, Manning distinguished between "the working of grace *in* the Church of England" from "the grace *of* the Church of England." Ibid., 25.

human authority; without priesthood, without sacraments, without absolution, without the Real Presence of Jesus upon its altars.[15]

In Manning's estimation, to the extent that the Church of England continued to exist, infidelity would invariably find refuge. The individual soul would thus be left with a choice, not between Catholic or non-Catholic Christianity, but fundamentally between Catholicism and atheism. Manning summoned his powers to convert his fellow Englishmen as from darkness to light and employed extraordinary means to prevent the lapse of Catholics into Anglicanism. Indeed, the potential for mass conversions in England was among his strongest selling points when advocating for papal infallibility among the Roman Curia.

Pusey's Eirenicon

The public row between Manning and his former Oxford compatriot led Pusey to undertake a project that he titled *The Church of England a Portion of Christ's One Holy Catholic Church and a Means of Restoring Visible Unity*.[16] The work originally began as an apology for the Church of England, retracing the broad steps of Newman's *Tract 90*, arguing for a catholic sense of the Anglican *Thirty-nine Articles* and their general compatibility with the canons and decrees of the Council of Trent. Midway through the project, however, he reconceived the work as a plea for reunion between the Church of England and the Church of Rome. Calling the work an "Eirenicon," he addressed it as a letter to the recognized *agent provocateur* of the Oxford Movement, John Keble (1792-1866).

In a letter dated 6 November 1865, Pusey wrote to Newman describing his hopes for the project as an attempt to secure from Rome an explicit clarification with regard to which parts of its system of theological praxis were a matter of faith (*de fide*) and which were not. The distinction between the official doctrine of Rome and its popular, tacitly approved practices had been a feature of Newman's thinking since the publication of *Tract 90* during his Anglican period, and Pusey was already on record as approving of the *letter* of the Council of Trent. The council, however, did not treat in great detail the vast practical system of pious opinion and devotion surrounding, in particular, the cult of the Virgin Mary. Of this Pusey wrote,

---

[15] *The Workings of the Holy Spirit in the Church of England, A Letter to the Reverend E.B. Pusey, D.D.* (London: Burns & Oates, 1864), 49.

[16] *The Church of England a Portion of Christ's One Holy Catholic Church and a Means of Restoring Visible Unity: An Eirenicon in a Letter to the Author of "The Christian Year"* (London: Rivingtons, 1864). Henceforth, *Eirenicon I*.

> Now if, as I believe, the system in regard to the Blessed Virgin is the chief hindrance to reunion, and if a declaration by authority that something which does not necessarily involve this (as the Council of Trent with [Bishop John] Milner's explanation) is alone of faith, would remove that chief hindrance to reunion, then an intelligible ground is given for the request.[17]

Pusey completed a first draft of the *Eirenicon* in the spring of 1865 and shortly thereafter presented a copy to Henry Liddon. At Liddon's suggestion, he added an appendix to the work treating specifically the 1854 dogmatic definition of the Immaculate Conception. In composing the appendix he made careful examination of the 1851 *"Pareri dell": Episcopato Cattolico sulla definizione dogmatica dell' immacolato concepimento della B.V. Maria,* which collected the various opinions of Catholic bishops in response Pius IX's 1849 encyclical, *Ubi Primum*.[18] He also studied the 1854 Apostolic Constitution, *Ineffabilus Deus*, itself. A letter to Rev. W.J. Copeland indicates Pusey's perception of the deep connection between the Immaculate Conception and the doctrine of papal infallibility which lay barely concealed beneath:

> What a strange way they are driving on? The last result of [Ward's] *Dublin Review* is that the Pope is personally infallible as to facts too, not connected with faith or morals, and that, however he utters his pronouncements. Bellarmine is left far behind. So his Italian government is to be a matter of faith too, and that the Pope never did anything wrong to the Greeks.[19]

Written from concerns that were historical, theological, and preeminently ecumenical, Pusey hoped to vindicate the claim of the Church of England to be a portion of the Church Universal, defending the validity of its doctrine, its orders, and its sacraments. He also explored in detail instances of popular and quasi-

---

[17] Quoted in Liddon, *Life of Pusey*, 4:98. This letter is mentioned in Newman's reply to Pusey dated 10 November 1865. *LD*, 22:99-101. The limitations of space preclude, here, a full account of Bishop John Milner's 1818 work, *The End of Religious Controversy*. Throughout his correspondence in the period leading to the first *Eirenicon*, Pusey regularly alluded to Milner as an influential guide in his own reading of the Council of Trent. The chief weakness of the work for Pusey lay in his being a non-authoritative source. Indeed, the planned publication of the *The End of Religious Controversy* proved so controversial in the 1780s that its release was delayed almost twenty years at the request of Milner's then bishop.

[18] *"Pareri dell": Episcopato Cattolico sulla definizione dogmatica dell' immacolato concepimento della B.V. Maria,* 10 vols (Rome, 1851-1854).

[19] Quoted in Liddon, *Life of Pusey*, 4:105-6.

authoritative Roman praxis that had historically perpetuated the separation between England and Rome. Pointing to what he called the "vast system as to the Blessed Virgin which to all of us has been the special 'crux' of the Roman system," Pusey argued that the Council of Trent failed to define details of doctrine and practice despite their condemnation by Reformation era Protestants. Of course, there was no word of condemnation or suppression in the decrees and canons either and this created ambiguity as to their explicit theological weight. Pusey observed,

> The Church of England and the Council of Trent have long seemed to me at cross purposes. In some cases at least, the Council of Trent proposed the minimum of [sic] which it would accept, but left a maximum, far beyond the letter of the Council to be thereafter, as it was before, the practical system of the Church. The Church of England in her Articles protested against that maximum, the practical system which she saw around her; but, in many cases, she laid down no doctrine at all on the subject upon which she protested. She made negative statements to show against what she protested, but set down no positive statement to explain what, on the same subject, she accepted.[20]

Turning to the question of papal infallibility in particular, Pusey cited numerous historical instances where Christians of late antiquity seemed ignorant of and even hostile towards, Rome as a final court of theological appeal.[21] Rather than being rooted in revelation and observed in "the times nearest the apostles," Pusey's record detailed Roman usurpation of ecclesial authority. Buttressing his perspective as something more than mere Protestant ideology, he emphasized the dissent of the Eastern Churches and the continued status of impaired communion between Roman Catholicism and Eastern Orthodoxy. Just under the surface of numerous presenting doctrinal differences between Orient and Occident, Pusey perceived more fundamental disagreements concerning papal supremacy and its proper exercise beyond the Roman jurisdictional boundaries.[22] Pusey could also appeal to the disputed nature of the question within the Roman Communion itself. Writing five years prior to the promulgation of *Pastor Aeternus*, he argued,

> 'papal infallibility' [is not] an article of faith anywhere. The Eastern Church, in its whole length and breadth, agrees, of course, with us. But in the West too, the Gallican Church, also, which holds the consent of the Universal Church to be

---

[20] Pusey, *Eirenicon I*: 266-7.
[21] Ibid., 68-9.
[22] Ibid., 96-7.

essential to infallibility, could not hold the infallibility of the Pope, by himself, without such an Œcumenical Council.[23]

Pusey's works were premised on the fundamental conviction that the impaired communion between the Churches of England and Rome were fundamentally reconcilable without sacrificing the claim of either to antiquity. Above all, he was convinced that a unified Christendom was preferable to communions continuing apart from the other. He concluded with a musing question,

> [I]s there then no issue to the present division of Christendom? Is disunion to be the normal state of the Church, for which we all pray that God would give her unity, peace, and concord? God forbid! I have never expected to see that external unity of intercommunion restored in my own day; but I have felt it to be an end to be wished for, and prayed for.[24]

Pusey traveled through France in the following year, collecting a number of bishops who responded favorably to his *Eirenicon*. Indeed, this reply to Manning would eventually receive high praise from learned Anglican and Roman Catholics readers alike. Based on this success, he added a second (1869) and third volume (1870) to his *Eirenicon* project, addressing both to Newman after Keble's death. These treat Mariology and the prospects of reconciliation respectively. Sadly, Pusey's efforts were effectively undermined by the definition of papal infallibility and its seeming closure of the very dialog he hoped to advance. Writing to Newman shortly after the definition on 26 August 1870, Pusey pronounced a fitting eulogy upon his project:

> Before the Council, I wondered whether I might live to see the union of the Churches: you will have seen and mourned how that has already repelled minds. The last Eirenicon has sunk unnoticed to its grave the first as you know was popular both against my expectations.[25]

Near the end of his life in 1882 he lamented that "the Vatican Council was the greatest sorrow I ever had in a long life."[26]

---

[23] Ibid, 34.
[24] Ibid., 98.
[25] Quoted in Liddon, *Life of Pusey*, 4:193. Cf. *LD*, 25:197-198.
[26] Edward Pusey, *The Spiritual Letters of Edward Bouverie Pusey*, eds. J.O. Johnston and W.E. Newbolt (London: Longmans, Green & Co., 1898), 220.

William Ewart Gladstone and the Pragmatics of the Papacy

William Ewart Gladstone was the prime minister of Great Britain in the late 1860s and enjoying a period of prominence on the international stage. An old schoolmate of Manning, he too possessed a remarkable theological acumen and remained a faithful Anglican churchman of the old high church party. Bypassing Pusey's concern over matters historical and theological, however, Gladstone's contemplation of Roman Catholicism and his correspondence with Manning on the subject of papal supremacy remained strikingly pragmatic—even to the point of appearing insufficiently Protestant and "krypto-Catholic" in the eyes of third-party readers. In the last years of his life, Gladstone defended this general strategy of engagement with Rome in a letter to Willard Maynell:

> I may describe myself in few words: strongly anti-Roman in certain respects, but profoundly reluctant to raise theological controversy in these perilous days, to the hazard of the common interests, which are far before the special. I was therefore most reluctant to write, and the motive was not theological, nor, I think, was the language.[27]

Relying on the narrative supplied in William Palmer's *Compendious Ecclesiastical History from the Earliest Period to the Present Time* (1840), Gladstone was committed to the principal of the local identity of the Church and strongly believed that each nation should declare its own indigenous character when it came to matters of religion.[28] This commitment was so pronounced in Gladstone's thinking that standard Protestant apologies for Anglicanism were often underemployed. Corresponding with Maud Stanley, a wavering Anglican who was considering conversion to Roman Catholicism following the Gorham decision, Gladstone evinced no particular duty to defend the theological superiority of the Church of England. Rather, he generally equated the claim of both churches to antiquity and argued that Mrs. Stanley should remain an Anglican in fidelity to the nation and the integrity of the national church: "My position is this: you are bound by duty and allegiance to the Church of England."[29]

---

[27] This section of a letter from Gladstone to Willard Meynell, dated 15 October 1892, appears in Peter Erb, ed., *The Correspondence of Henry Edward Manning and William Ewart Gladstone, 1833-1891*, 3 vols (forthcoming) §12, n. 2. I have been given access to pre-publication sections of this work and offer my special thanks to Dr. Erb for his kindness.

[28] D.C. Lathbury, ed. *The Ecclesiastical and Religious Correspondence of William Ewart Gladstone*, 2 vols (New York: Macmillan, 1910), 2:24-5.

[29] Ibid., 31.

This general principle also animated Gladstone's most important treatment of papal infallibility: his 1874 *The Vatican Decrees in their Bearing on Civil Allegiance*. Appearing almost five years after the promulgation of *Pastor Aeternus*, *The Vatican Decrees* was actually intended to refute Manning's *Caesarism and Ultramontanism* of 1874. There Manning had asserted the right of the Roman Catholic Church not to submit to the state in the face of the Bismarck's policies of *Kulturkampf* in Germany.[30] Speaking of the "hopeless and visionary effort to Romanise the Church and People of England," Gladstone summarized the ultramontane policies of the Vatican as a violent and subversive affront to national integrity.

> Rome has substituted for the proud boast of *semper eadem* a policy of violence and change in faith; when she has refurbished, and paraded anew, every rusty tool she was fondly thought to have disused; when no one can become her convert without renouncing his moral and mental freedom, and placing his civil loyalty and duty at the mercy of another; and when she has equally repudiated modern thought and ancient history.[31]

Newman moved swiftly to answer Gladstone's charges with a persuasive defense of English Catholics as good subjects of the crown in his own 1875 *Letter to the Duke of Norfolk*, but Gladstone remained unrepentant. In February of the same year he re-asserted his position unaltered with the publication of *Vaticanism: An Answer to Reproofs and Replies*. The following year he concluded his case against Manning's ultramontanism, condemning its "hostility to mental freedom at large" and "incompatibility with the thought and movement of modern civilization."[32]

While this commitment to the local identity of the church led him to reject the ultramontanism of Manning, it also led him to strongly support the integrity of Roman Catholicism in Italy. Turning to Catholicism in Rome, therefore, Gladstone did not mirror Manning's posture toward the Church of England. While Gladstone did hope to challenge what he believed to be errors in historical fact and to chasten extravagant claims for the papacy—"To save the Pope and the Catholic Church from itself," as he termed it—his strong desire was to see the flourishing of Roman Catholicism's spiritual and moral authority in

---

[30] For a brief overview of Manning's work see: Jeffrey P. von Arx, "Archbishop Manning and the *Kulturkampf*," *Recusant History* 21 (1992): 254-266.

[31] William Gladstone, "The Vatican Decrees in their Bearing on Civil Allegiance," in *Rome and the Newest Fashions in Religion* (Leipzig: Bernhard Tauchnitz, 1875), 22.

[32] William Gladstone, "Courses of Religious Thought," in *Gleanings of Past Years 1860-1879, Volume 3: Historical and Speculative* (London: John Murray, 1879), 105.

Europe generally if not in England particularly.[33] In a letter to Ignaz von Döllinger, dated 22 June 1862, Gladstone cast himself in direct opposition to those he called "enemies of the Roman Church—who wish to see her, not improved—but destroyed, and the Papal Supremacy, not reformed, but rejected." Regarding the notorious mismanagement of the Papal States as scandalous, Gladstone depicted his advice that the pope relinquish temporal power as that of a friendly critic. Continuing in that same letter to Döllinger, Gladstone wrote,

> I deeply lament the scandal and real damage to religion which must result from these proceedings, I wish heartily that all its best tendencies may be fully developed, and all its worse ones neutralized; most of all must I cherish this desire in regard to the greatest of them all, and one which must clearly have in the counsels of Providence its own special work to perform.[34]

On the occasion of a private audience with Pius IX four years later, Gladstone reaffirmed this advice, explicitly arguing that it would further the spiritual vocation of the Roman Communion.

The tendency toward pragmatism and his bent to promote the general good of Christian faith in Europe seems to have likewise informed Gladstone's contemplation of Manning and the proceedings of the Vatican Council. In a letter to Odo Russell, dated 20 December 1869, Gladstone wrote,

> It is curious that Manning has so greatly changed his character. When he was Archdeacon with us, all his strength was thought [to] lie in a governing faculty & in its wise moderation. Now he is ever quoted as the Ultra of the Ultras, & he seems greatly to have overshot his mark. The odds seem to be that the child yet unborn will rue the calling of this Council. For if the best result arrive in the triumph of the Fallibitarians, will not even this be a considerable shock to the credit and working efficiency of the Papal system[?][35]

In the end, Gladstone concluded that the more the pope tried to establish his extraordinary *de jure divino* authority and powers, the less *de facto* authority and power he really had. To the extent that Rome continued to cast off necessary restraint, Christianity as a whole would suffer loss.

---

[33] Letter from Gladstone to Clarendon, 21 May 1869, in D.C. Lathbury, *Ecclesiastical and Religious Correspondence*, 45. Cf. Letters to Clarendon dated 24 August and 14 September 1869. Cited in: Jonathan Philip Parry, *Democracy and Religion: Gladstone and the Liberal Party, 1867-1875* (Cambridge: Cambridge University Press, 1986), 293.

[34] Lathbury, *The Ecclesiastical and Religious Correspondence*, 34.

[35] H.C.G. Matthew, ed., *The Gladstone Diaries: With Cabinet Minutes and Prime-Ministerial Correspondence* (Oxford: Oxford University Press, 1982), 7:202.

Conclusion

Robert Gray wrote that "[Manning] had become a Catholic because he had discovered in the one infallible Church the authority which he needed as a sure grounding for his faith, and he was not inclined to imagine that a prescription that had worked so well for himself would fail for the world at large."[36] From 1865 onward, Manning located this confidence in the authority of Roman Catholicism in the office of the papacy. He was central to the maneuvering to bring the subject of papal infallibility before the Vatican Council, and then in guiding the council through its discussion and debate process. Manning proved central in the broader public debates of the doctrine, advocating the definition, reproving Catholic and non-Catholic dissenters alike, and generally serving as lightening rod. When the council concluded with a more qualified definition than he himself had advocated, Manning's joy was undiminished. The infallible authority of the church could finally be exercised efficiently to protect the faithful from the dangers of modernity and to check what Manning once described as "the exaggerated spirit of national independence."[37]

For Pusey and Gladstone the neo-ultramontane seizure of ecclesial power and the assertion of papal infallibility as its divine guarantor would be disastrous to the integrity of Christendom and to the influence of the faith on Europe. In Pusey we see an ecumenical sensibility, utilizing historical and theological argument to provoke a situation where Rome—or, rather, the Bishop of Rome—would not be acting alone and in isolation from the entirety of the baptized faithful. In Gladstone, we see a pragmatic impulse, seeking to bring about a situation where the pope could wield spiritual and moral authority in a way that Europe could receive as service and pastoral care. Both of these contrast with Man-

---

[36] Robert Gray, *Cardinal Manning: A Biography* (New York: St. Martin's, 1985), 226.

[37] *The Oecumenical Council and the Infallibility of the Roman Pontiff* (London: Longmans, Green, and Co., 1869), 52.

ning's insistence on a configuration of church authority that would proceed on the projection of power and assertion of divine right. One might argue that Pusey and Gladstone proved more insightful than their alienated convert friend. Another Vatican Council, and a different pope, took steps in their direction, and away from Manning's chosen path.

WILLIAM GEORGE WARD, THE DUBLIN REVIEW AND NEO-ULTRAMONTANISM

HUDSON RUSSELL DAVIS

The reputation of William George Ward (1812-1882) has been shaped by one statement he made concerning papal infallibility during the middle portion of his life. The pugnacious and forthright Ward, goaded by a friend, reportedly said, "I should like a new papal Bull every morning with my Times at breakfast."[1] His desire for logical completeness led him to make such bold statements that even he later admitted were "pressed ... much too far."[2] Yet Ward's forceful nature and vigilant pursuit of authority played a significant role in the definition of papal infallibility during the First Vatican Council in 1870. R. W. Church (1815-1890) wrote, "I suppose it really would not have happened but for Manning and Ward."[3] Henry Manning (1808-1892) and his contribution to the debates of the First Vatican Council are well recognized but the contentious Ward remains an obscure and unappreciated figure.[4] Even natural allies were ambivalent about his work. In a letter dated 10 September 1852, Monsignor

---

[1] Wilfrid Philip Ward, *William George Ward and the Catholic Revival* (New York: Longmans, Green, and Co., 1912), 14. Wilfrid Ward's book is the source for this comment. Ward spoke these words after being challenged by a friend but no date is given. According to Gilley, the conversation took place during the First Vatican Council but no corroborating evidence has been found. Sheridan Gilley, "Ward, William George (1812-1882)," in *ODNB*.

[2] William George Ward, *Essays on the Church's Doctrinal Authority*, (London: Burns and Oats, 1880), 432. See also: Ward, *William George Ward and the Catholic Revival*, 264.

[3] Richard William Church, *Life and Letters of Dean Church* (London: Macmillan and Co., 1895), 185.

[4] K. T. Hoppen has produced the most recent treatments of Ward's ideas. K. Theodore Hoppen, "William George Ward and Nineteenth-Century Catholicism," (Unpublished PhD dissertation, University of Cambridge, 1966). Also see: K. Theodore Hoppen, "W. G. Ward and Liberal Catholicism," *Journal of Ecclesiastical History* 23 (1972): 323-44; K. Theodore Hoppen, "Church, State, and Ultramontanism in Mid-Victorian England: The Case of William George Ward," *Journal of Church and State* 18 (1976): 289-309.

John Talbot (1816-1886) actually accused Ward of having "no respect whatever for Episcopal Authority, and very little even for that of the Holy See."[5] While the irony in this accusation, given Ward's neo-ultramontane views, is striking, it demonstrates the passion he elicited from both friend and foe alike.

This study will bring to light the role of William Ward within the Oxford Movement and his continued influence as a Catholic convert. While Ward is not ordinarily treated as a central figure in the Oxford Movement, the first part of this essay will show that his influence upon the Movement's major figure, John Henry Newman, was significant. The second portion of this essay will elucidate Ward's unique version of neo-ultramontanism and the influence he exerted to promote an expansive definition of papal infallibility at Vatican I through his editorship of the *Dublin Review*.

Background

William George Ward was born in London to William Ward of Northwood Park, a famous cricketer and Tory member for the city, on 21 March 1812.[6] His childhood was marked by a deep love of the theater and mathematics and he nurtured both passions at every turn.[7] He so loved mathematics that at age nine he honed his skills using the principle of logarithms. Some described him as a clumsy and reclusive youth.[8] In 1830, at the age of eighteen, Ward began his studies at Oxford where the awkward boy became a skilled orator.[9] Thomas Mozley (1806-1893) described the Ward of those years as perplexingly brilliant. Mozley wrote in *Reminiscences*: "[Ward] was a vast deal too sharp for me. I had a good answer ready for him in time—that is, half an hour too late."[10]

Ward was good-natured but forceful with his opinions. He was unrelenting in arguments, sometimes driving his opponents and friends to exhaustion. He

---

[5] Brian Fothergill, *Nicholas Wiseman* (London: Faber; Garden City, NY: Doubleday, 1963), 204.

[6] Wilfrid Philip Ward, *William George Ward and the Oxford Movement* (New York: Macmillan, 1889), 1.

[7] Ibid., 3.

[8] J. Lewis May, *The Oxford Movement: It's History and its Future, A Layman's Estimate* (London: John Lane, The Bodley Head, 1933), 102. W.P. Ward, *Oxford Movement*, 3.

[9] Ibid., 19-20.

[10] Thomas Mozley, *Reminiscences: Chiefly of Oriel College and the Oxford Movement*, 2 vols (Boston: Houghton, Miftlin and Co., 1882), 1:227.

was a young man who was often equally ready to shock or to please.[11] Fairweather described him as "one of the most uproarious bulls ever to invade a theological china-shop."[12] This very pugnacious nature was, however, tempered by his own humility, which Newman recognized as a great asset. Newman wrote of Ward, "I know of no one who has so anxiously wished to correct the faults imputed to him, who is so thankful to be told of them, so encouraged by being told of improvement in him, so vexed at charges brought against him."[13]

Possessing a sharp philosophical mind, Ward was drawn to the ideas of John Stuart Mill and Jeremy Bentham. His son Wilfrid wrote, "The strongest directly intellectual influence exercised on him was that of Mill and Bentham."[14] He never accepted in full their Utilitarianism but his intellectual formation was profoundly shaped by their thought—particularly that of Mill.[15] Gladstone observed that Ward owed more of his mental culture to the writings of John Mill than to all the Anglican divines put together, "Mr. Newman excepted."[16] Mill and Bentham appealed to the highly philosophical and logical nature within Ward. He had a desire for completeness of thought and Mill provided this concise and rigorously logical philosophy. His son explained that Mill satisfied an "appetite for drastic reform, and the moral qualities of candour and love for truth."[17] Without fully embracing Mill's utilitarian teachings Ward warmed to Mill's practical usefulness, his moral attitude, and his emphasis on distribution rather than accumulation of wealth.[18] Later, Ward would use these ideas to judge the church by its practical usefulness to human life.

In the Michaelmas of 1830, when he went up to Oxford as a Commoner of Christ Church, it was Thomas Arnold's Broad Church theories and not Newman that first drew the young William Ward.[19] This influence continued to hold sway

---

[11] Raymond Chapman, *Faith and Revolt: Studies in the Literary Influence of the Oxford Movement* (London: Weidenfeld and Nicolson, 1970), 51.

[12] Eugene R. Fairweather, *The Oxford Movement* (New York: Oxford University Press, 1964), 159.

[13] Newman to Mozley, 29 January 1842, *LD*, 8:444.

[14] W. P. Ward, *Oxford Movement*, 60.

[15] The respect with which Mill regarded Ward can be seen in his letter to Ward. He wrote, "You are the clearest thinker I have met for a long time who has written on your side of these great questions." John Stuart Mill, *The Later Letters of John Stuart Mill, 1849-1873*, eds. Francis E. Mineka and Dwight N. Lindley, 17 vols (Toronto, Canada: University of Toronto Press, 1972), 16:1240.

[16] W. E. Gladstone, "The Ideal of a Christian Church," *Quarterly Review*, 75 (December 1844), 183.

[17] W. P. Ward, *Oxford Movement*, 61.

[18] K. Theodore Hoppen, "Church, State, and Ultramontanism," 292-293.

[19] Ibid., 290; W. P. Ward, *Oxford Movement*, 20.

through much of the 1830s. In strong contrast to Newman and the Oxford Movement, Arnold was distinctly liberal and deeply hostile to the Tractarians, calling them "mischievous" and comparing them to the "Judaizers" of the New Testament who suffer not from "intellectual error" but "moral wickedness."[20] In contrast to the Tractarians, Arnold suggested that the church take a broader approach to the issues confronting it by admitting dissenters and showing a greater sympathy to the state.[21] It was these more liberal views that drove the Tractarians to pursue a more "catholic" church both in ritual and doctrine. This more liberal portion of Arnold's teaching was less attractive to Ward, who subscribed to Arnold's "religious philosophy" while giving little heed to the proposed "political manifestations."[22] Ward and others who followed Arnold found the Tractarian position a far more logical complement to their own doctrinal and social understandings.[23] Eventually, Ward came to disdain Arnold's concept of individualism—that "private individuals" should "depend more on the word of those *more holy* than themselves."[24] He concluded that Arnold offered insufficient grounding for authority. He wrote,

---

[20] Thomas Arnold, "The Oxford Malignants and Dr. Hampden," *Edinburgh Review* 63 (1863): 233, 235, 238. He also wrote, "Now with regard to the Newmanites. I do not call them bad men, nor would I deny their many good qualities. ... but fanaticism is idolatry ... it is clear to me that Newman and his party are idolaters." Arthur Penrhyn Stanley, *The Life and Correspondence of Thomas Arnold*, 3rd ed., 2 vols (Boston: Ticknor and Fields, 1860), 2:46-47.

[21] Arnold, after a long discussion on dissenters, concluded that the church received both harm and help from dissenters. He wrote, "Yet we have seen, on the other hand, that differences of religious opinion ... are absolutely unavoidable; and that since there exists on earth no infallible authority to decide controversies between Christians, it is vain for any one sect to condemn another ..." Thomas Arnold, *Principles of Church Reform* (London: Society for Promoting Christian Knowledge, 1962), 107. See also: Hoppen, "Church, State, and Ultramontanism," 290.

[22] Ibid., 290. Ward also began his criticism of Arnold's sermons with a commendation of Arnold's ideas. He wrote, "The great idea which Dr. Arnold seems to us to have grasped and to put forth in every variety of shape in his sermons, is the duty of doing all to the glory of God ..." William George Ward, "Arnold's Sermons," *British Critic*, 30 (1841): 300.

[23] Arnold offered little grounding for those seeking safety from the multiplicity of religious sects and opinions. He wrote concerning the church's history, "... infallibility being nowhere to be found, it was merely opinion against opinion; and however convinced either party might be of the truth of its own views, they had no right to judge their opponents." This was, of course, unacceptable to the Tractarians and the rigorism of Ward. Arnold, *Church Reform*, 101.

[24] W. G. Ward, "Arnold's Sermons," 344 (emphasis original).

But what does Dr. Arnold and those who think with *him* in this matter substitute? he [sic] attacks the prophetical office of the Church as founded by the Apostles, and gives us as our prophets grammarians and philologists. Humble believers are to look for Christian truth from the lips, not of those who are better Christians, but better critics; not of those who have more experience in holy living, but in manuscripts and Greek constructions; not of those who succeed the Apostles, but of those who succeed 'Porson and Hermann.'"[25]

Arnold's thought directly contradicted Ward's desire for completeness and unity of thought. He supposed that there was no way to achieve unity of faith since there was no "infallible authority to decide controversies," a concept which irked Ward.[26] Rather than seeking such an "infallible authority," Arnold advocated a "different system" in which there was greater unity through "varieties of opinion."[27] This could not have been more contrary to Ward's own thinking. His refusal to have intellect alone "placed aloft as our one guide in exploring the depths of Scripture" caused him to press towards an external infallible guide for conscience.[28] Arthur Stanley coaxed a reluctant Ward to sit in on one of Newman's public lectures and Ward was impressed. In 1838 Newman published *Tract 85* in which he argued for the authority of the Church and its tradition against exclusive reliance on scriptural authority.[29] This offered Ward a

---

[25] Ibid., 344-45 (emphasis original).

[26] Arnold, *Church Reform,* 107.

[27] "Is it not, then, worth while to try a different system? And since disunion is something so contrary to the spirit of Christianity, and difference of opinion a thing so inevitable to human nature, might it not be possible to escape the former without the folly of attempting to get rid of the latter; to constitute a Church thoroughly national, thoroughly united, thoroughly Christian, which should allow great varieties of opinion, and of ceremonies, and forms of worship, according to the various knowledge, and habits, and tempers of its members ..." Ibid., 107-08.

[28] W. G. Ward, "Arnold's Sermons," 345. In contrast to Ward, Arnold wrote concerning infallibility, "It is false that there exists in the Church any power or office endowed with the gift of infallible wisdom; and therefore it is impossible to prevent differences of opinion. But the claim of infallibility was not only false, but mischievous; because it encouraged the notion that these differences were to be condemned and prevented, and thus hindered men from learning the truer and better lesson ..." Arnold, *Church Reform*, 100.

[29] Nockles wrote, "In *Tract 85* Newman ... appealed to [Edward] Hawkins's sermon in his use of the *argumentum ad hominem* to justify doctrines such as the Trinity on the authority of Tradition alone because they were not explicitly enshrined in the letter of Holy Scripture. He directly echoed Hawkins's argument that 'the more fundamental the doctrine ... the more likely would it be rather implied than directly taught in the writings

trustworthy locus of authority—the Church—and the intellectual justification he needed to transfer his allegiance from the individualism of Arnold to the Oxford Movement.[30]

The Oxford Movement

By the latter part of 1838 Ward soon became a devoted follower of Newman and quickly made his sharp intellect felt within the Oxford Movement.[31] The quiet, awkward youth had become a confident and combative thinker; and, though not intentionally pugnacious, had a penchant for finding controversy. His analytic mind required struggle for intellectual growth.[32] Ward's childhood obsession with mathematics drove him to seek the same precision in doctrinal matters. He later wrote that his combativeness was due to "a certain hankering after premature logical completeness which" he came to "recognize as prominent among my intellectual faults."[33] Thus his contributions to the Oxford Movement were due, in many ways, to his desire for mathematical precision in theology and strong personality.[34]

Newman's influence on Ward was profound. As his Romeward views became more evident, many wondered why he remained Anglican at all. In 1844, Ward's response to inquisitive Catholics showed the boldness with which he often spoke. He answered, "You Catholics know what it is to have a Pope. Well—Newman is my Pope. Without his sanction I cannot move."[35] Ward went so far

---

of the Apostles.'" Peter Benedict Nockles, *The Oxford Movement in Context* (Cambridge: Cambridge University Press, 1994), 110. See also: W. P. Ward, *Oxford Movement,* 81-82.

[30] W. P. Ward, *Oxford Movement,* 136. Leo Joseph Walsh, "William G. Ward and the Dublin Review" (PhD dissertation, Columbia University, 1962), 18-19.

[31] W. P. Ward, *Oxford Movement,* 36.

[32] Owen Chadwick, *The Mind of the Oxford Movement* (London: Adam & Charles Black, 1960), 62. Wilfrid Ward wrote, "Mr. Ward himself in later years, while retaining in the main his own views, considered that he had been in some respects too exacting." W. P. Ward, *Catholic Revival,* 264.

[33] W. G. Ward, *Essays on the Church's Doctrinal Authority,* 432.

[34] Unlike other high churchmen, he was not drawn to a study of history. He wrote that he was "wholly unversed in history," and confessed that, "even with ecclesial history, my acquaintance was merely second hand." W. G. Ward, *Essays on the Church's Doctrinal Authority,* 32. His son Wilfrid sought to temper this point. He wrote, "This statement must be somewhat qualified if it is to be reconciled with some of his Oxford writings. But he certainly disliked the dry details of history, where they threw no light whatever on the philosophy of life." W. P. Ward, *Oxford Movement,* 32, n. 1. See also: Fairweather, *Oxford Movement,* 159.

[35] W. P. Ward, *Oxford Movement,* 240.

as to say, "to him ... I owe the inestimable blessing of having become a Catholic at all."[36] He confessed that, though they did not always agree, his views were in a large part shaped by Newman. He wrote,

> What I have to state, then, is this, I was enmeshed in the toils of a false philosophy, which could have had no other legitimate issue, except a further and further descent towards the gulf of utter infidelity. From this thraldom, the one human agency which effected my deliverance was F. Newman's teaching. ... Take any one of F. Newman's utterances in his Protestant works on the one hand; and take any one of my own convictions on moral and religious matters on the other hand; it is often impossible for me even to guess, how far the former may have been simply the one exciting cause of the latter.[37]

Newman's influence was especially profound in the area of conscience, which Ward appropriated and personalized.[38] He came to consider conscience more important than reason and saw conscience as synonymous with faith. For him the two were inextricably linked.[39] Conscience was not analytic reason, nor was it logic or proof; but reason alone was an insufficient guide. While reason was not incapable of attaining knowledge of God, it must ultimately be subject to conscience.[40] He wrote, "Conscience alone can guide us aright; and by following our intellect instead of our conscience, we shall be led even more fearfully and widely astray ... ."[41] He did, however, consider individual con-

---

[36] William George Ward, *On Nature and Grace: A Theological Treatise* (London: Burns and Lambert, 1860), xlii.

[37] Ibid., xli-xlii.

[38] For a detailed treatment of Newman's view of conscience see: S. A. Grave, *Conscience in Newman's Thought* (Oxford: Clarendon Press, 1989), and James Kaiser, "The Concept of Conscience According to John Henry Newman," (Unpublished PhD dissertation: The Catholic University of America, 1958).

[39] Ward wrote: "Viewed then in the concrete, as found in the devout believer, we may regard *conscience* and *faith* to be one and the same faculty: considered as submissively bending before external authority and ever deriving more of doctrinal truth, we call it faith; considered as carefully obeying the precepts of which it has knowledge, and as laboriously realizing and assimilating the truths of which it has possession, we call it conscience." William G. Ward, *The Ideal of a Christian Church* (London: James Toovey, 1844), 512.

[40] Ibid., 276-277.

[41] Ibid., 280. At times Ward seemed to suggest a nearly anti-intellectual basis for faith. He wrote, "When the spirit of heresy is perplexed, it leans upon human authority; plunges for relief into books or manuscripts. ... Heresy seeks enlightenment in the library." His own life of scholarship, however, suggests that he is not anti-intellectual. At issue for Ward was the use of "books and manuscripts" or libraries as sources of ultimate

science to be inadequate, unreliable, and in need of an external authoritative guide. Ward stated:

> I deny altogether, that the intellect's appointed way of arriving at Truth, is that of unbiased and uncontrolled inquiry. I assert the very contrary. I maintain, that so soon as the intellect quits the region of pure mathematics, it absolutely requires, for its healthy action, the being compelled constantly to compare its conclusions with some external standard.[42]

Rather than an intuitive understanding of morality Ward pointed towards the spiritual authority of the Church as guide.

In 1839, due to severe spiritual turmoil in which he found himself less critical of Rome and unsure of his own position, Newman took a less prominent role in the Oxford Movement.[43] This withdrawal of the spokesman left room for the assertive Ward who emerged as the leader of a younger generation of Tractarians. From that point on the tone of the Oxford Movement changed. While Newman had fostered loyalty to the Anglican Church, Ward "had no clinging love for the Church of his birth."[44] He and his younger crop of Tractarians brought a new urgency to the Movement.[45] They lacked the same moderation of the founders and sought to press for change. In his *Apologia* Newman wrote "these men cut into the original Movement at an angle, fell across its line of thought, and then set about turning that line in its own direction."[46] And in the fall, September of 1839, Newman wrote to Frederick Rogers, "At this moment

---

authority. William George Ward, "Pius IX and the '*Civiltà Cattolica*,'" *Dublin Review*, 7. 59, n.s. (1866): 423.

[42] W. G. Ward, *On Nature and Grace*, xxii.

[43] During the summer of 1839, Newman had been engaged in a historical study that shook his foundation. At the same time he was given Wiseman's article, "Anglican Claim," which compared the Anglican Communion to the Donatists of old. While it was not new information, Newman found himself challenged by an altered perception of the analogical implications of the historical data and his contemporary situation. He concluded that the Anglican claim to catholicity was not valid and the claim of Rome more secure. In his mind "… the theory of the *Via Media* was absolutely pulverized." *Apologia*, 111 [229]. See Jay Hammond's essay in this collection for a close examination of this period.

[44] W. P. Ward, *Oxford Movement*, 138, 206.

[45] Sydney Leslie Ollard, *The Anglo-Catholic Revival* (London: A. R. Mowbray & Co. Ltd., 1963), 39. Frederick Oakley, "Historical Notes of the Tractarian Movement (Part II)," *Dublin Review*, 1.53, n.s. (1863): 505.

[46] *Apologia*, 151 [266].

we have sprung a leak, and the worst of it is that those sharp fellows, Ward, Stanley & Co., will not let us go to sleep upon it."[47]

While Newman internally suffered great indecision, externally the younger Tractarians made noise that further unsettled his mind. Thomas Mozley described the volatile personalities of Ward and his colleague Oakley:

> Prominent, if not foremost of the group that contended round Newman, but fighting battles of their own, were two men, Oakley and Ward. Both of them, having received their new impulses, went ahead, disregarded warnings, and defied control. As it had entirely been their own choice to come [into the Oxford Movement], so they consulted their own choice in going.[48]

While Newman himself respected Ward, he showed some apprehension concerning Ward's recasting of Newman's words and conclusions. He wrote to Pusey (1800-1882), "You must not take him as a fair reporter about me. Everyone colours what he hears by his own mind—from one instance Ward has told me, I see he has done so too."[49] In October of 1841 Newman wrote to Nicholas Wiseman (1802-1865) to correct a misrepresentation by Ward. He wrote, "He tells me he understood me then to contemplate, and to convey to Mr. Spencer my anticipation of a time when I and others should join the Church of Rome. I must in honesty say that I did not intend any such intimation, and am sorry to have conveyed it."[50] Whatever Newman wrote in his original letter, Ward had pressed it until it led to Rome.

Newman struggled, as did the rest of the early Tractarians, to walk the *via media*, to secure for themselves the melding of both the catholicity they saw in Rome and the loyalty they felt to the Anglican Church. Upon joining the Oxford Movement Ward became intimate with Newman, seeing him nearly daily, and continually pressed "the Roman argument and disparaging the purely Anglican view of the Movement."[51] The moderates of the Oxford Movement, those who subscribed to the Newman's *via media*, were content to push for change within the Anglican Church. Their desire was to transform the Church of England in her full truth and beauty. In his October 1841 letter to Wiseman, Newman wrote that his desire was "not to conciliate" the Anglican Church to Rome but to

---

[47] Newman to Frederick Rogers, 22 Sept. 1839, *LD*, 7:154.
[48] Mozley, *Reminiscences*, 1:4.
[49] Newman to Pusey, 3 Aug. 1851, *LD*, 8:237.
[50] Newman to Wiseman, 14 Oct. 1841, Ibid., 297.
[51] Wilfred Phillip Ward, *The Life of John Henry Cardinal Newman*, 2 vols (London: Longmans, Green, and Co., 1912), 1:68.

"strengthen it in itself."[52] He added, "I feel no call of duty to change my communion, being thankful for the grace ... dispensed in it."[53] This strengthening was essentially the proposed purpose of the Movement.

But for Ward, things were different. In the same year, 1841, years before his departure to Rome, Ward wrote a letter to John Rouse Bloxam, "The restoration of active communion with that Church is the most enchanting earthly prospect on which my imagination can dwell."[54]

Newman understood that Ward and many of the new members of the Movement felt a pressing need to choose between a more elastic view of the *Thirty-nine Articles* or secession to Rome.[55] They found it intellectually difficult to subscribe to the *Thirty-nine Articles* and to call their Anglican Church "Catholic." Many suggested that it was these young zealots, and particularly Ward, who pressed Newman to publish *Tract 90* in 1841.[56] According to Archbishop Tait, "Ward worried him into writing Tract 90."[57] Indeed, the impetuous and relentless Ward gave Newman no peace before the publication of *Tract 90* and no rest after.[58] Such was the force of Ward's personality and the strength of his convictions. Though designed to pacify them, Ward and the younger Tractarians were dissatisfied with *Tract 90*. For Ward the document, meant by Newman as a means of securing the catholicity of the Anglican Church and thereby avoiding secession to Rome, was stripped of its power.[59] Nothing but Rome would do.

Having a strong philosophical mind and being willing to push inferences to logical conclusions, Ward acted as a thorn in the side of Newman. Wilfred Ward wrote, "Ward was continually forcing on Mr. Newman so-called irresistible in-

---

[52] Newman to Wiseman, *LD*, 8:297.

[53] Ibid.

[54] W. P. Ward, *Oxford Movement*, 194.

[55] Ibid., 152.

[56] "The logicians, with the hilarious hoplite Ward at their head, pestered and bewildered [Newman], and he answered them according to their...logic!" Yngve Brilioth, *The Anglican Revival: Studies in the Oxford Movement* (New York: Longmans, Green and Co., 1933), 118.

[57] W. P. Ward, *Oxford Movement*, 152.

[58] In *Tract 90* Newman argued for the catholicity of the *Thirty-nine Articles*. He concluded that the *Articles* must be read with the Catholic Church as a standard and that they could not be in conflict with that church. *Tract 90* caused a stir within the Oxford Movement and hastened the Romeward journey of many members. Brilioth, *Anglican Revival*, 117-126. Chadwick, *Mind of the Oxford Movement*, 24-25. Nockles, *Oxford Movement in Context*, 136-142. W. P. Ward, *Oxford Movement*, 156-184. See also Benjamin O'Conner's essay in this collection.

[59] W. P. Ward, *Oxford Movement*, 208.

ferences: 'If you say so and so, surely you must also say something more?'"[60] Ward's mathematical mind craved logical consistency; something that, while important to Newman, was not everything. Newman thought it a nuisance to be "forced beyond" what he could "fairly accept."[61] He endured the pressure of Ward's "keen perception," confessing:

> I do not know the limits of my own opinions. If Ward says that this or that is a development from what I have said, I cannot say yes or no. It is plausible, it *may* be true. I cannot assert that it is not true, but I cannot, with that keen perception which some people have, appropriate it.[62]

Newman was continually forced to face and accept conclusions he would have preferred to ignore. He was pressed, particularly by Ward, to admit and approve "extreme" ideas he would have avoided if left to himself. So, while Ward may not have moved Newman against his will, he applied severe and unrelenting pressure in the Romeward direction until Newman could find no avenue of escape. His desperate words to Frederick Rodgers in September 1839, showed the stress Ward and others exerted on Newman's conscience. He wrote, "How are we to keep hot heads from going over? Let alone ourselves."[63]

As for Ward, he had taken a solid stand on the issue by 1844. He wrote,

> ... two principles especially, closely and indissolubly connected with each other, seem to me so vitally important at the present time, that I could wish their very names were familiar to us all 'as household words': the one, the absolute supremacy of conscience in moral and religious questions, the other, the high sacredness of hereditary religion.[64]

For Ward, conscience was a guide; but it was weak, feeble, and unable to make proper judgments "unless supported by some strong external motive."[65] The "external motive," for Ward, was supplied by the Church's infallible authority, and in particular, the papacy. While Ward would not "move" without Newman, he became increasingly bold in his disdain for the Anglican Church and his adoration of the Catholic Church. His views were finally made obvious when he published *The Ideal of a Christian Church* (1844).

---

[60] Newman to Frederick Rogers, 22 September 1839, *LD*, 7:154.
[61] *Apologia*, 157 [271].
[62] Ibid., (emphasis original).
[63] Newman to Frederic Rogers, 22 September 1839, *LD*, 7:154.
[64] W. G. Ward, *The Ideal of a Christian Church*, 43-44. Ward had picked up the nickname "Ideal Ward" during his time at Oxford. W. P. Ward, *Catholic Revival*, 375.
[65] W. G. Ward, *Ideal of a Christian Church*, 219.

Ideals of a Christian Church

While Newman's *Tract 90* (February 1841) marked a turning point in the Oxford Movement, Ward's publications proved catastrophic for its future. Ward first set about defending *Tract 90* against attacks, but his own pamphlets, *A Few Words,* and *A Few Words More in Defense of Tract 90,* caused further trouble.[66] In *Tract 90,* Newman had left the discussion open as to whether the Reformers were Catholic, but Ward declared that they were not Catholic. Newman suggested that the formularies might be construed as ambiguous but Ward declared them unambiguously Protestant.[67] Ward admitted that he wrote these pamphlets hoping that "putting these charges against the Reformers more fully out [sic] might be serviceable."[68] He saw it as his duty to "hint or openly state [Newman's] extremely unfavorable views of the English Reformers."[69] Ward sought to take the inferences made by Newman to their logical conclusion.

In 1841, responding to intense criticism, Ward produced several articles for the *British Critic* that pressed his Romeward point. Intense criticism from Mr. Palmer of Worcester, however, led to the termination of the *British Critic* in October 1843, temporarily muting Ward's impact. He therefore set out to write a tract in answer to the criticism from Palmer and during the Long Vacation 1844 that tract grew to be a book—*The Ideal of a Christian Church*.[70] He reportedly told Robert J. Whitty, "I am writing a pamphlet which is fast becoming a fat book ... ."[71] In *The Ideal,* Ward declared his Romeward focus in plain language. He wrote: "The times are dark, and a curtain of gloom hangs over the future; but on its dark face we may discern brightening in prismatic hue a vision of past beauty,—the Holy Catholic Church."[72] While Newman had strained to reconcile the *Thirty-nine Articles* of the Anglican Church with the desired catholicity of the Oxford Movement, Ward refused to compromise any longer. The tract was intended to clarify Ward's views; and it did, but it also marked the final chapter in Ward's Anglican life.

Ward lauded the Catholic Church and defamed the Church of England, boasting that he preaching doctrine consonant with Rome and gloating that he

---

[66] Oakley, "Historical Notes-Part II," 505.

[67] W. P. Ward, *Oxford Movement,* 161-62.

[68] William George Ward to Robert Scott, Oxford, 27 April 1841. Quoted in W. P. Ward, *Oxford Movement,* 168.

[69] Ibid.

[70] W. P. Ward, *Oxford Movement,* 249. Ollard, *Anglo-Catholic,* 78.

[71] William George Ward to Father Whitty, Quoted in W. P. Ward, *Oxford Movement,* 240.

[72] W. G. Ward, *Ideal of a Christian Church,* 52.

had received no sanction. He wrote: "We find, oh most joyful, most wonderful, most unexpected sight! We find the whole of Roman doctrine gradually possessing numbers of English Churchmen."[73] He went on to confess that he had been teaching against the Articles and that he had long held all of the Roman doctrines and yet "no argument had appeared of any force against my positions."[74] The insult was not just that he held those doctrines, or that he taught those doctrines, but his bold declaration that no one had officially corrected or sanctioned him and his teachings. He accused the hierarchy of approving his views by their silence and inaction. The reprisal came swiftly.

On 13 February 1845, Ward's book received an unequivocal condemnation. Oxford's Hebdominal Board stripped him of his degrees and made him an undergraduate.[75] The spring and summer of 1845 found Ward with his characteristic optimism and cheerful good nature. He continued to teach as an "undergraduate" and enjoyed the joke. As the summer came to a close, Ward ended his career as an Anglican priest and Oxford fellow. In September 1845, he was received into the Roman Catholic Church. Newman, whom the convocation had not expressly sanctioned, felt the mounting pressure. His disciple had followed Newman's own ideas to their logical conclusion—Rome. In October 1845, John Henry Newman brought his own spiritual struggle of many years to a close by entering the Roman Catholic Church. Newman himself was convinced that Ward had played a critical role in the unfolding drama that led so many to Rome. On 15 February 1845, he wrote to Ward,

> That your part has been an important one in the course of events which are happening, though we are as yet too near to understand it, is beyond all doubt and there is every reason to think it will not be less important in time to come. No decree of Council or Convocation, unless a special divine power goes with it, can destroy opinion, or those who are organs of it. *It is* impossible to anticipate things—but one may say, I trust, without presumption, that your course is only just begun.[76]

---

[73] Ibid., 565.

[74] "No argument has appeared of any force against these positions; and, what is more to the purpose, no condemnation of them by any authoritative tribunal. Three years have passed, since I said plainly, that in subscribing the Articles I renounce no one Roman doctrine: yet I retain my Fellowship which I hold on the tenure of subscription, and have received no Ecclesiastical censure in any shape." Ibid., 567.

[75] Wilfrid Ward, *Oxford Movement*, 343; For several documents relevant to the proceedings against Ward and his "degradation," see: *LD*, 10:534-557.

[76] Newman to William George Ward, Feb. 15, 1844, *LD*, 10:556-557 (emphasis original).

The Dublin Review *and the Neo-ultramontanism of William Ward*

In 1846, after his reception into the Catholic Church, Ward retired to his house near St. Edmonds College, Hertfordshire, England, and lived in quiet seclusion. He assisted in the church offices, socialized with the students and lecturers, and became generally familiar with the Catholic Church he had only admired from afar. In 1849, after the death of his uncle, Ward inherited some property on the Isle of Wight, but did not take up residence there. Instead, in 1851, he accepted an appointment by Cardinal Wiseman to teach moral philosophy at St. Edmonds College. A year later, though a layman, he was appointed Professor of Dogmatic Theology and dutifully instructed the young seminarians.[77] In 1858 he left the college and retired to his property on the Isle of Wight; but the quietness of country life did not hold him. He returned to St. Edmonds College in 1861 after publishing his philosophical work *On Nature and Grace,* a work flowing from his lectures at St. Edmonds.[78]

Ward's return to the public sphere in 1861 saw him once again embroiled in controversy. At that time the debate on papal infallibility was brewing between 'liberal' Catholics and neo-ultramontanes. Ward entered the debate through his contributions to the *Dublin Review*. He began to advocate not only concepts of primacy and supremacy—but also personal infallibility of the pope. This neo-ultramontanist vision of the papacy was for Ward "the symbol of that principle of unity and effective authority, which had enabled the Church to stand immovable amid a society whose structure had been shaken to its foundations."[79] The papacy was perceived as a safeguard against the decay taking place in the society of the nineteenth century. The pope, with his infallible authority, was a rock "amidst the ocean of modern European politics."[80]

Ward was not alone in advocating papal infallibility, but by the extremity of his view he stood apart. All Ward needed was a platform to promote his views, and increasingly, the *Dublin Review* obliged. In the early 1860s the more liberal

---

[77] W. P. Ward, *Catholic Revival,* 3. Gilley, "Ward, William George," ODNB.

[78] W. P. Ward, *Catholic Revival,* 216-17.

[79] Ibid., 84. Ward's observation of the decaying society was evident in his treatment of *Mirari Vos* (1865). He commented that the pontiff "has been involved through his whole reign in so unrelenting a succession of political distresses." And Pius, in issuing the Syllabus, was combating "corruption of morals and the propagation of a pestilential indifferentism." Pius combated "a vast and heterogeneous mass of hideous error." William G. Ward, "The Encyclical and Syllabus," *Dublin Review,* 4.56, n.s. (1865): 442.

[80] He wrote that his strong language and persistence in the *Dublin Review* was for the purpose of instructing the faithful in this profound truth of the faith, "... in recognizing the infallibility of that See in its widest and fullest extent ..." William George Ward, "Two Criticisms on the Dublin Review," *The Dublin Review,* 8.60, n.s. (1867): 165.

Acton sought to gain control of the *Dublin Review*; but in 1863, Manning, after receiving control of the *Dublin Review* from Cardinal Wiseman, named Ward its editor.[81] Ward accepted the position with humility.[82] He wrote to Newman before assuming control, "I have had the impudence to accept the editorship of the *Dublin Review.*"[83] Yet, in his typically forceful fashion, Ward set out to "make the *Dublin Review* a means of pushing forward the *conspiratio bonorum.*"[84] He took control in July 1863 and made it a voice for promoting his own version of papal infallibility.

Threads of Ward's Oxford Movement experience were woven into the fabric of his neo-ultramontane stand. Ward's youthful flirtation with the Arnoldian liberalism was long past. What Ward admired about Arnold was his biblical interpretation, his humanitarian ideals, and his disdain for worldly gain and his "real and open-hearted way of looking at Holy Scripture."[85] Yet his eventual disenchantment with Arnold had come because of Arnold's commitment to individual rather than ecclesial authority. In the same way, Montalambert's call for "complete separation of church and state, and religious toleration for all" raised the specter of liberal political reforms of the early 1830s. Döllinger's advocacy for the "abandonment of scholastic theology" for a theology grounded in historical research contributed to Ward's view that restraint of conscience was needed as a safeguard for the intellect and orthodoxy.[86] He saw the spiritual power of the church, and particularly the supreme authority of the papacy, as the only safeguard against the anarchy he saw all around him. Ward's very desire to become Catholic was marked by his desire to find this one sure and infallible guide for his conscience. In contrast to the liberal Catholic call for separation of church and state Ward wrote,

> The temporal ruler would regard it as his highest privilege to co-operate with the Church, in a due attitude of subordination, towards the fulfillment of her Divine commission. Meanwhile, he would hold it as among the most sacred

---

[81] Walsh, "William G. Ward and the *Dublin Review*," 2-3. W. P. Ward, *Catholic Revival*, 155. See also: Hugh A. MacDougall, *The Acton-Newman Relations: The Dilemma of Christian Liberalism* (New York: Fordham University Press, 1962), 25.

[82] Later, remembering his sense of inadequacy Ward wrote, "One reason, which alone would have made me profoundly distrustful of my power to edit a *Review*, is my incompetence on all matters of literature and secular politics." W. P. Ward, *Catholic Revival*, 155, 409. The *Dublin Review*, under Wiseman and later under Wilfrid Ward, was primarily a review of literature. Walsh, 57.

[83] W. P. Ward, *Catholic Revival*, 155.

[84] Ibid.

[85] W. G. Ward, "Arnold's Sermons," 303.

[86] Walsh, 82.

and elementary of his duties, to use the force of his command for the purpose of repressing any attempts to introduce into the country heresy or schism. ... He would cooperate with the Church in exercising a strict censorship over the press, as regards any matters that even indirectly connected with moral and spiritual truth. The various nations of Europe would thus be united in bonds of sympathy, animated by the same spirit, directed towards the same end, while the common father of Christendom would be their international arbiter where contentions might arise.[87]

Ward's ideal world was thus a world in which conscience had a strict guide and the temporal power was ultimately submissive to the church. His views invited great opposition from liberal Catholics, led by Acton, and made Ward's brand of neo-ultramontanism the flashpoint of controversy in the years preceding Vatican I.[88] Some detractors accused him of holding views that were "injurious to souls."[89] Ward was deeply hurt. Convinced that his efforts were beneficial to the Church and its head, the pope, Ward felt compelled to speak boldly.[90] He wrote, "I am myself hardly aware of any motive which ever prompted me to write a single line, except my desire of forwarding God's cause in the world."[91] This sense of high motive did not temper the intensity and rigidness of his views nor did it deter his critics. Ward adapted an already existing

---

[87] W. G. Ward, "Encyclical and Syllabus", 497. The degree to which this was a residual influence of Bentham and Mill's political philosophy deserves further consideration.

[88] In Acton, Ward found an obvious target as they represented distinct poles of Catholic thought during the Victorian era. Hoppen, "Church and State," 289. Acton was the incarnation of Catholic liberalism, advocating a freedom so extensive that one must tolerate heresy to preserve unity—so precious was liberty. The collision with Ward was inevitable. Acton did not dismiss the ultramontane theory but sought to define it in such a way that it was more inclusive and liberal. He wrote, "When a man has really performed this double task—when he has worked out the problem of science or politics, on purely scientific and political principles, and then controlled this process by the doctrine of the Church, and found its results to coincide with that doctrine, then he is an Ultramontane in the *real* meaning of the term ..." (emphasis mine). Lord Acton, "Ultramontanism," in *Essays on Church and State* (New York: Thomas Y. Crowell Company, 1968), 84. See also: Josef Lewis Altholz, *The Conscience of Lord Acton* (Houston, TX: Univ. of St. Thomas, 1970).

[89] W. G. Ward, *Essays on the Church's Doctrinal Authority*, 33.

[90] Ibid.

[91] Ibid. Ward took comfort in the fact that his views "were cordially approved by my two ecclesiastical superiors, Cardinal Wiseman and his Successor." He wrote, "I have found Cardinal Manning's counsel and exhortations simply invaluable; both as assisting me to steer the right course, and as giving me spirit to pursue that course." Ibid.

ultramontanism and brought to it his desire for mathematical completeness of thought. He carried the ideals of the ultramontane theory to conclusions that had an internal logic that seemed inescapable—to those who accepted foundational assumptions. Those who stood outside the ultramontane tradition found his claims dangerously extreme.

Key Points in Ward's Neo-ultramontanism

To understand Ward's view of papal infallibility, two key points stand out. First, Ward asserted that since the church—with the pope as her head—is responsible for instructing the faithful it is important to seek out and obey in full the church's—and thus the pope's—explicit declarations and subtle "intimations." These "intimations," he suggested, are to be considered infallible in essence, because they are directed by the Holy Ghost. He stated that God demands,

> ... unlimited obedience to the Roman, as distinguished from all other churches; unalterable attachment to Roman traditions and observances; and acceptance of the infallible authority, in dogma and discipline, over every other power on earth, of the Vicar of Jesus Christ—the recognition that his every doctrinal pronouncement is infallibly directed by the Holy Ghost—[these] are corner-stone conditions of his proclaiming approbation of any individual before mankind.[92]

Second, Ward considered it vital that the church's declarations and presumed infallible "intimations" should receive not just external *consent* but also inner *assent*.[93] Where Acton and Newman called for academic and intellectual freedom Ward urged that, "independence of the intellect, just like independence of the will, is not man's healthy state, but his disease and calamity."[94] His rem-

---

[92] W. G. Ward, "Pius IX and the Civiltà Cattolica" in *The Dublin Review: Volume 7 New Series, July-October 1866* (London: Burns, Lambert, & Oates, 1866), 418. He also wrote, "The only bound to their authority which the Popes of Rome have ever recognized, is that appointed directly and immediately by God Himself; and which the Holy Ghost inspires themselves infallibly to declare." Ibid., 419.

[93] W. G. Ward, *Essays on the Church's Doctrinal Authority*, 470. Ward taught, "If the Church is infallible in her whole magisterium, she is infallible inclusively in that large body of explicit instruction, which she issues for the guidance of her children." This view of the Church's infallibility was naturally extended and applied to the pope. William George Ward, *The Authority of Doctrinal Decisions Which Are Not Definitions of Faith* (London: Burns, Lambert, and Burns, 1866), xv.

[94] W. G. Ward, *Essays on the Church's Doctrinal Authority*, 320.

edy was complete submission to God and his "discoverable intimations."[95] While most of his opponents would concede that the church was infallible in its doctrinal decisions and that the pope was infallible when he spoke *ex cathedra*, Ward pressed for an even broader understanding of infallible pronouncements. He reasoned that if infallibility could flow from God's intimations and thus the church's intimations, then surely they can flow from the pope's teachings and even his intimations.[96] He located his view within a tightly constructed flow of logic that perplexed his opponents.

When treating the scope of papal infallibility, Ward argued that the pope need not declare his teaching *ex cathedra* for them to bear the mark of infallibility. He wrote, "The Pope can be said with sufficient correctness to speak *ex cathedra*—although he may put forth no Dogma to be believed *de fide*—whenever he teaches Catholic Doctrine infallibly as Universal Doctor."[97] He concluded, therefore, that Pius IX spoke infallibly in many "Apostolical Letters and Allocutions" in the same way that his predecessors acted to secure the orthodox faith in their own "Letters and Constitutions."[98] Ward viewed these papal declarations given on doctrine as actions of the church's pastor or universal teacher and thus—*ex cathedra*.[99] The former popes were "condemning the 'chief errors'" of their times just as Pius IX condemned the errors of his time. This was especially troubling to his opponents who lauded the intellectual freedom condemned by Pius IX's *Syllabus of Errors* (1864).

In his discussion of the *Syllabus,* Ward concluded that Pius IX dealt with the "vast and heterogeneous mass of error" of the time by issuing a "large apostolic denunciation."[100] In Ward's view, Pius had issued a corrective to "a large number of tenets both philosophical and strictly theological [condemned] in company with politico-religious errors, which altogether savor of the same

---

[95] Ibid., 321.

[96] Concerning the minor rulings of the church Ward wrote, "The Church is infallible, not only when she anathematizes certain propositions as heretical, but also when she stigmatizes them with some minor censure: when e.g. she proscribes them as erroneous, approaching to heresy, false, scandalous, temerarious, &c., &c." Ibid., 436.

[97] Ibid., 460.

[98] Ibid., 461.

[99] Ibid. "When the pope solemnly condemns certain prodigies of opinion predominant in a certain age, he speaks beyond all doubt ex cathedra." Ibid. 462.

[100] Ibid., 443. "The *Syllabus Errorum* was a list of the propositions condemned as erroneous in earlier Encyclicals and Allocutions. The fresh emphasis given to the Papal protests by their collection and republication and the vehement tone of the Encyclical created a great sensation." W. P. Ward, *Life of John Henry Cardinal Newman,* 2:79. W. P. Ward, *Catholic Revival,* 145.

school."[101] At issue were the ideas of "liberty of worship and of the press" which Ward considered a breeding ground for "corruption of morals and the propagation of pestilential indifferences."[102] For this very reason Ward saw Pius's *Syllabus* as a great confirmation of his own views. He reasoned that if the *Syllabus* was infallible then all the previous declarations it restated were infallible. So the Letters and Allocutions from which the Syllabus drew could be seen as *ex cathedra* and thus infallible. Ward later retracted this extreme view of infallibility that characterized his *Dublin Review* editorship but not before it became a deep point of contention between him and other Catholic thinkers. This expansive understanding of what could be considered infallible was one of the chief reasons his opinions generated such opposition.[103]

This extreme view made it not only difficult to judge when the pope spoke *ex cathedra* but also difficult to discern when he did not. Ward himself did not suffer such confusion. For him it was simple—the pope spoke and the faithful obeyed. He wrote, "All that was required is that the Pope should, either in the Papal Act itself, or else in *any other way whatever*, sufficiently manifest his intention of teaching the whole Church ..."[104] It becomes clear why Ward, when pressed, declared that he would like a "papal Bull every morning." Since the pope could offer constant infallible guidance—why should he not? Ward wrote, "Is not an increase of Infallible Truth greatly to be desired?"[105] He was not seeking in a cavalier fashion to find everywhere something infallible but to find a safeguard for the church through a constant flow of divine and infallible truth. Thus Pius IX did not have to pronounce "definitions of faith" in order to speak *ex cathedra*, he simply needed to offer instruction to the Church or rebuke to its adversaries. Ward wrote concerning Pius IX, "Yet his reign has been no less remarkable for those other doctrinal determinations, which, though not definitions of faith, yet peremptorily claim the interior assent of his spiritual children."[106]

---

[101] W. G. Ward, *Essays on the Church's Doctrinal Authority*, 443.

[102] Ibid.

[103] He wrote, "I freely confess that when I set forth this thesis in some of my writings, I extended it too far. [Published during the earlier controversy.] For I thought all those acts of Pius IX were ex cathedrâ in which those propositions are censured which were afterwards condemned in the syllabus. This view I now retract. For grave theologians have instructed me, that from the mere fact of these acts being quoted in the syllabus no general proof ensures that they were issued ex cathedrâ; but that each must be separately examined." Ibid., 462.

[104] Ibid., 463 (emphasis mine).

[105] Ibid., 321.

[106] Ibid., 441.

This extreme view of infallibility drew the indignation of his adversaries and friends alike.[107]

The second controversial point in Ward's view of papal infallibility flowed naturally from his acceptance of the first. If the pope spoke infallibly, and that infallibility was the church's infallibility drawn from Christ himself, then the faithful are required to submit not only their actions but also their will and intellect to these decrees. What was required, according to Ward, was an *inner assent*. As the quote above reveals, even the pope's lesser declarations demanded the "interior assent of his spiritual children."[108] This attitude was ever present in his considerations of papal infallibility and caused trouble with the liberal factions of the Catholic Church who saw intellectual freedom threatened.[109]

Rather than intellectual freedom, Ward spoke of "intellectual captivity."[110] Catholics, according to Ward, "owe [the decrees of the pope] interior assent; such as that with which a docile son accepts the paternal instructions: the same in kind, but far firmer in degree."[111] His line of reasoning did not allow for intellectual dissent on doctrinal decisions. Rather, for the Catholic believer the

---

[107] This extreme understanding of papal authority was what Acton feared. In 1863 he wrote: "It is necessary to notice briefly an opinion held by some who are either ignorant of the Catholic system or especially hostile to it, that an arbitrary authority exists in the Church which may deny what has been hitherto believed, and may suddenly impose upon the faithful, against their will, doctrines which, while there is not warrant for them in the past, may be in contradiction with the existing and received conclusions of ecclesiastical, or even profane, science." Acton, "Ultramontanism," 79-80. Ward, by his own assessment, was ignorant of history and felt that the pope's infallible teachings should hold sway over the will of the faithful without regard to historical precedent.

[108] W. G. Ward, *Essays on the Church's Doctrinal Authority*, 441. Ward had already declared during his Anglican days that "whatever proportion of our clergy there may be, who feel the direction and assistance of the individual conscience to be their own primary duty, they have certainly not learnt that opinion from our Church." W. G. Ward, *Ideal of a Christian Church*, 322.

[109] Acton had little sympathy for those who held such views, He wrote: "Intellectual indolence conspired with the ignorance of the age to promote these theories. Men were glad to find a formula which saved them the trouble of thinking, and a view which enabled them to shut their eyes. For the defense of a thesis is far easier than the discovery of truth. The followers of a system dreaded lest the knowledge of facts should interfere with the certainty of their opinions, and lest the resistless stream of history should be let in upon their settled and compact conclusions." Acton, "Ultramontanism," 42. See also: Walsh, 82.

[110] W. G. Ward, *Essays of the Church's Doctrinal Authority*, ix-x, 321.

[111] W. G. Ward, *Authority of Doctrinal Decisions*, xvi.

infallible teaching of the pope was "obligatory on his absolute interior assent."[112] He wrote, "Catholic faith involves unqualified belief in and submission to the intrinsic as well as extrinsic inspirations of Rome."[113] This conclusion put him in direct conflict with the more liberal Catholic thinkers such as Acton and Ignaz von Döllinger, who saw intellectual freedom as a necessity.[114] Ward considered such dissenters to be "minimizing Catholics" and "pseudo-Catholics" who refuse "to accept these decrees as *infallible* [and] disavows any obligation of accepting them with interior assent."[115] His demand that his opponents not only accept his views but also yield interior assent caused resentment.

For Ward, conscience was an inner assent based on surety from "external motive."[116] He wrote that a person "preserves his feelings and affections in a real, however latent, subordination to his conscience, and thus preserves his conscience itself in subordination to God."[117] It was this subordination of the conscience that led Ward to press his conclusions beyond that of other ultramon-

---

[112] Ibid., xi-xii. Ward argued that all *ex cathedra* decrees obligated the faithful to interior assent. He ran into difficulty in extending the number of *ex cathedra* decrees beyond the comfort level of most. See also: W. G. Ward, *Essays of the Church's Doctrinal Authority*, 497.

[113] W. G. Ward, "Pius IX and the Civiltà Cattolica," 418.

[114] Acton viewed conscience as a critical possession of man that should not be surrendered. His understanding of "conscience" differed radically from Ward's conflation of "conscience" with "faith." He wrote: "The conscience of man is his most divine possession. Jesuits give up conscience to authority, therefore they forfeit the rights of men, which are the rights of conscience, and have no claim to toleration." John Acton, *Letters of Lord Acton to Mary, Daughter of the Right Hon. W. E. Gladstone* (London: George Allen, 1904), 39. Rather than Ward's idea of conscience submitted to authority, Acton spoke of liberty of conscience. He wrote in 1858, "The Christian notion of conscience imperatively demands a corresponding measure of personal liberty. The feeling of duty and responsibility to God is the only arbiter of a Christian's actions. With this no human authority can be permitted to interfere. We are bound to extend to the utmost, and to guard from every encroachment, the sphere in which we can act in obedience to the sole voice of conscience, regardless of any other consideration." John Acton, *History of Freedom and Other Essays* (London: Macmillan and Co., Ltd., 1907), 203.

[115] William G. Ward, "Dr. Pusey on Ecclesiastical Unity," *Dublin Review*, 8.60, n.s. (1867): 91 (emphasis original). See also: W. G. Ward, *Essays of the Church's Doctrinal Authority*, 319; He wrote, "the fallible acumen which criticizes, patronizes, or explains away infallibility, is applauded, even by many educated men among pseudo-Catholics." W. G. Ward, "Pius IX and the Civiltà Cattolica," 423.

[116] W. G. Ward, *Ideal of a Christian Church*, 219.

[117] Ibid., 205.

tanes.[118] "Consent" to papal authority was not enough, one must offer "inner assent." Obedience was required; but one's inner assent must follow.[119]

Ward understood himself, as editor of the *Dublin Review,* to be performing a great service to the church. He wrote, "I have been confident in maintaining my main theses, because it seems to me so absolutely unquestionable, by any one who takes pains to examine, that the church teaches them."[120] In the year preceding Vatican I Ward used the *Dublin Review* to push his particular vision of papal infallibility—a vision Newman and others found irresponsible because Ward's concept of "inner assent" left no room for private dissent.[121] Newman accused Ward of using his voice in the *Dublin Review* to present his views as though they were the views of the church without making apparent that others of "equal authority thought otherwise."[122] In 1867, he wrote to Ward:

> Pardon me if I say that you are making a Church within a Church, as the Novatians of old did within the Catholic pale, and as, outside the Catholic pale, the Evangelicals of the Establishment. As they talk of "vital religion" and "vital doctrines," and will not allow that their brethren "know the Gospel," or are Gospel preachers, unless they profess the small shibboleths of their own sect, so you are doing your best to make a party in the Catholic Church, and in St. Paul's words are dividing Christ by exalting your opinions into dogmas. ... I protest then again, not against your tenets, but against what I must call your

---

[118] The distinctions between "ultramontanes" and "neo-ultramontanes" were the differing "extremeness" of their conclusions. Ward reflected an extreme vision that was shared by neo-ultras, but would have been difficult to swallow for Francis Kenrick, an ultramontane apologist for papal authority. See: Kenneth L. Parker, "Francis Kenrick and Papal Infallibility: How Pastoral Experience in the American Missions Transformed a Roman Ultramontanist," in *Tradition and Pluralism: Essays in Honor of William Shea,* eds. K.L. Parker, P. Huff, and M.J.G. Pahls (Lanham, MD: University Press of America, 2008).

[119] W. G. Ward, *The Authority of Doctrinal Decisions,* xvi.

[120] Ibid., xxvii-xxviii.

[121] In 1875 Newman wrote Ward a harsh letter, accusing him of making his "own belief the measure of the belief of others." Newman judged his article "tyrannical." See W. P. Ward, *Catholic Revival,* 273. Wilfrid Ward, the sole witness to the letter, attests that he saw his father burn it. Newman also lamented having to defend papal infallibility against Protestant detractors—Gladstone in particular—and wrote, "men like W. G. Ward have in part to answer for it." Newman to R. W. Church, 10 Dec. 1874, *LD,* 27:170.

[122] W. P. Ward, *Catholic Revival,* 255. As far as Newman was concerned it does not follow that "because there is a gift of infallibility in the Catholic Church, that therefore the parties who are in possession of it are in all their proceedings infallible." *Apologia,* 231 [334].

schismatical spirit. I pray God that I may never denounce, as you do, what the Church has not denounced.[123]

Newman labeled Ward's view of papal infallibility "incomplete and unpractical."[124] Ward struggled with Newman's rebuke and wrote soberly to Ryder, "Remember how enormously J. H. N. has always influenced my mind."[125] In response to criticism from Newman and others, Ward wrote, "Far be it from me to deny, that arrogance and a hundred other faults enter largely into my moral composition; and I shall be unfeignedly grateful to those, who see in my writing manifold traces of those faults, if they will pray for my improvement."[126] Ultimately, Newman found Ward's stubbornness a hindrance to any meaningful communication on the subject of infallibility.[127]

In 1869, Ward's strong assertions were denounced by Bishop Dupanloup, who wrote that it was up to the "learning and knowledge of the great teaching Church as a whole," to decide the church's doctrine.[128] Ward was forced to submit and withdraw his overreaching statements. Once again Ward found himself

---

[123] John Henry Newman to William George Ward, 9 May 1867, *LD*, 23:217.

[124] W. P. Ward, *Catholic Revival*, 251. Gaius Atkins observed, "[Newman] was opposed to the dogma because he thought in theory that one dogma a century was enough and because his habit of mind predisposed him to a belief in the infallibility of the Church rather than the temporal head of it." Gaius Glenn Atkins, *Life of Cardinal Newman* (New York: Harper & Brothers Publishers, 1931), 235. Newman did not support the definition of papal infallibility in the late 1860s but in his *Apologia* confessed his loyalty and submission to the church and its Pontiff. He wrote, "I believe the whole revealed dogma as taught by the Apostles, as committed by the Apostles to the Church, and as declared by the Church to me. I receive it, as it is infallibly interpreted by the authority to whom it is thus committed, and (implicitly) as it shall be, in like manner, further interpreted by that same authority till the end of time. And I submit myself to those other decisions of the Holy See, theological or not, through the organs which it has itself appointed, which, waiving the question of their infallibility, on the lowest ground come to me with a claim to be accepted and obeyed." *Apologia*, 224-225 [330].

[125] W. P. Ward, *Catholic Revival*, 233. Newman's earlier words concerning Ward's humility were proven true. Ward "wished to correct the faults imputed to him." Newman to Mozley, 29 January 1842, *LD*, 8:444.

[126] W. G. Ward, *Authority of Doctrinal Decisions*, xxvii.

[127] In 1875, Newman observed to Emily Bowles, "I wrote to Ward, saying how I wished he would live in peace with me and others—he answered that he desired it of all things, but that faith was a greater thing than peace, and it was a great grief to him that I would not take his views. Every thing would go right, if I did." Newman to Emily Bowles, 24 January 1875, *LD*, 27:204.

[128] W. P. Ward, *Catholic Revival*, 257-8.

at the center of controversy and his ideas condemned. He submitted to the censure without contention.

However, Ward did not waver from his conviction that he had found his infallible *external guide* and desired to be guided by the church's great head—the pope.[129] He was by no means convinced that he was wrong and wrote to Frederick Ryder, "We consider that we have rendered important service both to the Church and to yourselves, by enlarging on the vast extent of her infallible determinations."[130]

Vatican I completed its deliberations in 1870 with a definition of papal infallibility. Ward's most extreme neo-ultramontane views were not incorporated into the definition. Yet while *Pastor Aeternus* did not include his extreme views on infallibility, he was able to point out, "nothing had been ruled inconsistent with his teaching."[131] He had, as far as he was concerned, been vindicated and the liberals had lost. The power of the church, and the infallible authority of the papacy, had been secured. He hoped the seduction of an immoral society had been averted.

Conclusions: Ward's Conscience Finds Rest

Ward's role in the 1860's infallibility debates cannot be understood outside the context of his earlier Oxford Movement background. The force of his personality ensured that he would voice his opinion despite the consequences. His understanding of conscience and utility, developed during his Anglican days, remained the intellectual ground on which he sought to defend and expand the scope of papal infallibility. Ward's earlier passion for mathematically precise logic, understanding of conscience became essential tools in his forceful promotion of papal infallibility.

While Ward could be viewed as a contentious soul, he sought submission rather than liberty. Yet having no doubts about the personal infallibility of the pope, he demanded the same certainty in others—a certainty others found unten-

---

[129] Earlier, in 1841, Ward had written, "... advance of spiritual life cannot proceed equally and healthily without some guide external to the individual; he cannot otherwise be preserved from narrow-mindedness and idiosyncrasy ... Nor can this external guide be adequately supplied, otherwise than by some living source, to which he may come to draw as it were inspiration from its pure fountain, and derive the contagion of it living breathing example." W. G. Ward, "Arnold's Sermons," 333.

[130] William G. Ward, "Doctrinal Apostolic Letters," *Dublin review*, 10.62, n.s. (1868): 87.

[131] W. P. Ward, *Catholic Revival*, 263-64.

able. His contentious and unbending opinions refused to allow for a diversity of thought and thus permitted his protagonists no rest.

In the office of the papacy he found an immovable external guide. The papacy was protection against individual judgment gone awry and utter submission to the pope (both external consent and internal assent) was an aide to his feeble conscience. He wrote, "the cultivation of conscience is indissolubly bound up with self-denial."[132] Ward understood "self-denial" to be a morally pure life, but a morally pure life; for him demanded a well-guided conscience that in turn required a proper external guide—an infallible interpreter of God's Word and Catholic tradition.

If there is one clear conclusion from the life of William George Ward it is that he lived a life consistent with beliefs pressed to their logical conclusions. He lived a life of mathematical precision that refused to accept anything less than principles pressed to their ultimate limits. He unwaveringly applied and defended what he believed and he did so with little equivocation or regard for the conscience of others. It was his unyielding tone that left little room for negotiation or compromise with those who opposed him.

Ward showed a remarkable willingness to live out the principles he espoused. He concluded *The Authority of Doctrinal Decisions* with a profound statement of his complete readiness to obey any and all declarations from an infallible pope. He wrote: "Take any statement which may have been made by me with the greatest confidence: if the Holy Father shall see reason to censure it, my conviction of its unsoundness will be (not merely far greater in degree, but) indefinitely higher in kind, than my present persuasion of its truth."[133] His comments to Newman summarized the journey of a restless soul whose rebellion was more a cry for order and discipline than anything else. In 1875 he wrote to Newman,

> Now I am daily more and more convinced that my aim has been the true one; but I am more convinced that I have fallen into grievous mistakes of judgment from time to time, whether as regards what I have said, or (much more) my way of saying it. Never was a man more unfit than I to play any kind of first fiddle. You supplied exactly what I needed; corrected extravagances, corrected crudities, suggested opposite considerations, pointed out exaggerations of language, etc. etc. I have never been able even approximately to replace you. If you will not laugh at the expression, I will say that I have felt myself a kind of intellectual orphan. I may say in my own praise that my censors have compli-

---

[132] Ibid., 261.
[133] W. G. Ward, *Authority of Doctrinal Decisions*, xxviii.

mented me on my submissiveness; but I have always wished to submit myself much more could I have found a guide whom I trusted."[134]

While Ward had replaced the "pope" of his Anglican years—Newman—with the pope in Rome, he never severed the emotional attachment that had always sought Newman's approval and approbation. Despite their differences, Newman exhibited a generous spirit in return. In 1875, Newman wrote to Ullathorne concerning Ward,

> I know perfectly well how affectionate his feelings are towards me, and I may truly say I never have borne him ill will and felt towards him any resentment for a moment, but have always expressed my admiration, to himself as to others, of his perfect frankness and sincerity. He has never whispered against me—he has spoken out as a man … .[135]

Ward showed his willingness to receive rebuke and quite often confessed his own shortcomings. Rather than a man who reveled in conflict the evidence presents a man troubled by strife and misunderstandings. He wrote to his critics, "No part of my work in carrying on the *Dublin Review* is so trying and distasteful to me, as my personal conflict with individuals; nor have I ever entered on such a conflict otherwise than with extreme reluctance, and in obedience to what I thought a plain duty."[136] Whether from age, wisdom, or both, this was not the famed pugnacious youth whose pugilistic spirit helped cripple the Oxford Movement.

Ward's forceful personality may have had a profound influence on Newman in the last days of his life as an Anglican, but Newman was not lost on Ward. Their Catholic years, marked by interpersonal tension and misunderstanding, nevertheless manifested a bond forged during their life as Anglicans. Ward's comments to Newman seem almost too intimate for a public forum. Yet his adolescent quest for certainty, and his latter day words of self-doubt and sorrow over trusted relationships broken, resonates as a universal human experience. Ward's relationship with Newman, his humility in conflict, the consistency of his thought, and the stated intentions of his efforts, should soften the caricature of Ward so often found in the literature. Though his passion was for mathematical precision and certainty in matters ultimately grounded in mystery, he need not be dismissed as "extravagantly a one-sided individual," since his quest for

---

[134] William George Ward to John Henry Newman, 20 January 1875, quoted in W. P. Ward, *Catholic Revival*, 274.
[135] Newman to Ullathorne, 9 February 1875, *LD*, 27:216.
[136] W. G. Ward, *Authority of Doctrinal Decisions,* xxvii.

truth and trustworthy authority reflect a common human pursuit.[137] Indeed his passion revealed the complex dimensions of his life and thought.

In February of 1882 William George Ward became sick; and though optimistic for a quick recovery, continued to deteriorate. Soon his memory began to fail and his physical health worsened. In a note to his son Wilfrid, he wrote, "If ever I recover I shall take one lesson to heart which I have learned in thinking over my past life during my illness, and that is to make more allowance than I ever did for the inevitable differences between one mind and another."[138] Sadly it was this very failure to "make allowance" that produced so many enemies for Ward. It was his stubbornness that reduced his legacy to a narrow caricature.

Some who had known him at the height of his vigor remarked that seeing him in this state was like watching "a great ship breaking up to pieces and going down in the storm."[139] Yet whatever he had left in his wake, it seems that the man, judging the youth, had caught sight of a broader horizon.

---

[137] George Henry Frederick Nye, *The Story of the Oxford Movement: A Book for the Times* (London: Bemrose and Son, Ltd., 1899), 98-99.

[138] W. P. Ward, *Catholic Revival*, 415.

[139] Ibid., 416.

ENGAGING THE DEBATES FROM THE PERIPHERY: THE CONTRIBUTION OF NEGLECTED OXFORD MOVEMENT CONVERTS IN THE INFALLIBILITY DEBATES

DONNA R. REINHARD

While our society typically assigns fame or infamy to individuals, rarely does a person act in isolation. Keeping this assumption in mind, an exploration of the roles of obscure Oxford Movement converts is important in order to develop a richer appreciation of the variety of voices and influences involved in the infallibility debates leading up to the First Vatican Council. This essay will uncover some of the contributions and potential influence of converts who are rarely in the standard narratives.

In 1847, Jules Gondon published a series of three lists that comprised of total of 165 men and women who converted to Roman Catholicism due to the work of the Tractarians. In 1926, Bertram Windle listed 180 men and women whom he considered to be significant people associated with the Oxford Movement. This list included over sixty-five men who converted to Roman Catholicism due to their involvement in the Movement.[1] Of this group of converts, friendships forged during this time of struggle, study, service, and fellowship continued to support and offer stability for the major figures as they wrestled with the issues of the day. Differences in opinion over political, educational, and doctrinal differences added to the tension of the times. Marriages and common goals after conversion forged alliances. Differences in temperament and spirituality strained relationships.

---

[1] Windle's work lists members of the Oxford Movement in alphabetical order with some bibliographic information. Jules Gondon's work specifically addressed the converts of the Oxford Movement, and lists the converts according to date of reception into the Catholic Church. Gondon's work covered the years between 1841 and 1846, and listed fifty-five Anglican clergy, fourteen Oxford laymen, fifteen Cambridge laymen, and over eighty distinguished others. The only notable omissions in Gondon's work are Frederick Capes and Maria Rosina Giberne. Bertram C. A. Windle, *Who's Who of the Oxford Movement* (New York: The Century Co., 1926). Jules Gondon, *Conversion de cent cinquante ministres anglicans, membres des universités anglaises, et personnes de distinction: avec une notice sur MM. Newman, Ward et Oakeley* (Paris: s.n., 1847).

This essay explores the contributions of sixteen people who converted due to the Oxford Movement: twelve from Oxford, two Cambridgemen, and two women who converted due to their association with the Tractarians. I have divided these converts under two primary categories, each with two sections, to delineate the means by which the converts engaged in the debates. Appendix A at the end of this essay summarizes the contributions of these converts.

Under the first major category, engaging the debates through publications, the headings subdivide the contributions into indirect—those who provided opportunities for others to publish—and direct—those who published sermons, treatises, or essays related to papal infallibility. The indirect contributions section focuses on how Robert Ornsby, Henry William Wilberforce, brothers John Moore Capes and Frederick Capes, and James Spencer Northcote created opportunities in publishing for those who publicly engaged in the infallibility debates.[2] This leads to the second category, "influence through writing." Included in this section are published sermons by Robert Isaac Wilberforce and Frederick William Faber, a metaphysical paper by John Dobrée Dalgairns, a treatise by Thomas Francis Knox, and several works by St. George Jackson Mivart.

The second major category of entering the debates from the periphery examines the more indirect influence through personal contacts and connections. These contributions are divided under two headings: those who used personal contacts and positions of influence to provide fellow Oxford convert Henry Edward Manning access to the council and those who served major figures of the debates through long and short term relationships that encouraged or agitated those major figures. The first of these sub-sections is a brief discussion of the opportunities seized by Robert Aston Coffin and George Talbot which ultimately provided Manning a position of power at the council. The second subsection considers how, through friendship and pastoral care, neglected Oxford converts were indirectly involved in the infallibility debates. While each major Oxford Movement figure had confidants and disciples,[3] this section will be limited to four people: Frederick Oakeley and Ambrose St. John, as well as two

---

[2] While these men also wrote essays and entered the debates through editorial work, this section of the essay will focus on their work of opening up room in the debates for those on the periphery.

[3] For information on Manning's work as a spiritual director and especially his relationship with Priscilla Maurice and Virginia Crawford, see Peter Erb's and Robin Gard's articles in *Victorian Churches and Churchmen: Essays Presented to Vincent Alan McClelland*, ed. Sheridan Gilley (Sullfolk: Boydell Press, 2005).

women who received pastoral care from John Henry Newman: Maria Rosina Giberne and Emily Bowles.[4]

Providing Opportunities to Enter the Debate: Ornsby, Wilberforce, the Capes Brothers, and Northcote

While some Oxford Movement converts entered the debates directly through their writings, other converts set the stage for lay involvement in the infallibility debates by establishing or controlling periodicals early in the debate. The technology of the time allowed for rapid dissemination of inexpensive publications. It is no surprise that those who were involved in the Tractarian Movement, with its focus on the printed word to carry their message, continued this strategy. Joseph Altholz noted that as early as 1846, some of the Oxford Movement converts were interested in journalistic ventures.[5] Therefore, it is important to look at the involvement of the Oxford Movement converts in the birth and formation of three major religious periodicals of the time: *The Tablet, Weekly Register*, and *The Rambler*. A fourth important periodical, the Dublin Review, has been dealt with elsewhere in this volume.

The first periodical, Frederick Lucas's *The Tablet*, provided an outlet for Robert Ornsby (1820-1889), close associate of Newman,[6] to work as an assistant editor. Ornsby worked in this capacity between his conversion in 1847 and his acceptance of a professorship of Greek and Latin literature at Newman's Catholic University in Ireland in 1854.[7] This periodical was, from the outset, ultramontane.[8]

---

[4] Both of these women were friends of Newman from his Tractarian days in Oxford. Joyce Sugg, *Ever Yours Affly: John Henry Newman and His Female Circle* (Leominster, Herfordshire: Gracewing Publishing, 1996), 1.

[5] Josef L. Altholz, *The Liberal Catholic Movement in England: The "Rambler" and its Contributors, 1848-1864* (London: Burns and Oates, 1962), 9.

[6] Ornsby was also married to the sister of John Dobrée Dalgairns, another Oxford Movement convert who will be discussed in the next section. Dalgairns was one of the ultramontane London Oratorians. His influence upon Ornsby provides interesting insights.

[7] Thompson Cooper and Richard Smail, "Ornsby, Robert (1820–1889)," in *ODNB*.

[8] Lucas founded *The Tablet* in 1840. The influence of *The Tablet* increased dramatically during this time, but success is typically credited to the owner and editor, Frederick Lucas, who moved the headquarters from London to Dublin in 1849 and took up the cause against the 1801 Act of Union. After Lucas' death in 1855, the paper was purchased by John Wallis and used as a means of attacking liberal Catholics in parliament and supporting the ultramontanist cause, going so far as to enforce a policy forbidding debate on papal infallibility. The far-reaching effects of *The Tablet* under the direction of

The second notable periodical became the liberal rival to the ultramontane *Tablet*.[9] In 1854, Henry William Wilberforce (1807-1873), brother of Robert Wilberforce and close friend of Newman, took on the *Catholic Standard*, becoming both proprietor and editor of this London weekly. He renamed the periodical the *Weekly Register* the following year.[10] Wilberforce was credited with reviving this periodical, which had declined from its previous important status.[11] He supported liberal Catholic Sir John Acton as well as Newman in their critique of the Catholic hierarchy.[12] However, the pace of his publishing endeavor was too taxing. In 1863 the Weekly Register was put up for sale and was sold the following year.[13] While Wilberforce retired from publishing, he remained active in journalism but confined his work to writing articles and reviews for the *Dublin Review*.[14]

The third publication of interest, *The Rambler*, was founded by the Capes brothers, Frederick (1816-1888) and John Moore (1813-1889), in 1848.[15] Windle described the journal as "brilliant, but tactless, inconsiderate, and offensive, especially to the old Catholics, and is a frequent subject of correspondence among the more prominent members of the Movement after their conversions."[16]

Wallis was in part due to the periodical's rise in readership prior to Wallis' purchase. Ornsby's direct effect upon this increase in popularity would be difficult to determine, given the changes made in the publication at this time. Sylvanus Urban, *The Gentleman's Magazine*, vol. 44 new series (London: John Bowyer Nichols and Sons, 1855), 652. Michael Walsh, "History of *The Tablet*," (The Tablet Publishing Company, 1990 [http://www.thetablet.co.uk/history.shtml accessed 3 December 2005]).

[9] For the use of the term "liberal" in this essay, see the essay by Benjamin O'Connor in this volume.

[10] H.W. Wilberforce converted in 1850. Windle, *Who's Who*, 239. David Newsome reports that Wilberforce had an almost "idolatrous veneration" of Newman. Newman trusted Wilberforce with close confidence. David Newsome, *The Parting of Friends: A Study of the Wilberforces and Henry Manning* (London: John Murray, 1966), 112-13, 405.

[11] Windle, *Who's Who*, 239.

[12] Newsome notes that Wilberforce's tone was more reserved in print than it had been in his Anglican days. Newsome, *The Parting of Friends*, 405.

[13] Ibid.

[14] Ibid. Considering that the *Weekly Register* leaned to the liberal side of the debates and that the *Dublin Review*, with Cardinal Wiseman's influence, leaned to the neo-ultramontane, it might be of interest to explore whether Wilberforce's views changed prior to the First Vatican Council.

[15] Altholz lists John Moore Capes as the founder while Windle lists Frederick. Altholz, *The Liberal Catholic Movement*, 11. Windle, *Who's Who*, 95. John converted in 1845. Gondon, *Conversion de cent cinquante ministres anglicans*, 87.

[16] Windle, *Who's Who*, 95.

The periodical leaned toward liberal Catholicism from its inception.[17] The publication began as a monthly, but within two months shifted to a weekly. While this was a means of dealing with current events in a timely manner, this change made *The Rambler* a direct competitor of *The Tablet* at a time when *The Tablet* had fallen from the bishops' favor for supporting the Irish cause, attacking one of Wiseman's friends, opposing attempts at diplomacy with Rome as well as "publishing some letters which were deemed disrespectful to the Holy See."[18] However, this direct competition did not last long due to the need to expand in size and scope. *The Rambler* once again became a monthly magazine in September of 1848.[19] As episcopal support of *The Tablet* waned in the 1850s, even as the publication's advocacy of ultramontane ideals increased, it waxed for the *The Rambler*, which was an embarrassment for Frederick Capes and caused him to fear that "Wiseman was forming a 'convert party,'" with the goal of *The Rambler* to eclipse completely *The Tablet*.[20]

According to Altholz, between 1850 and 1852, *The Rambler* was more cautious, which corresponds with the time Newman served as theological censor for the periodical.[21] However, even at this time, the periodical continued to come under scrutiny of Rome.[22] Frederick Capes was the editor of the magazine from its inception in 1848 until 1854, with the exception of the period between 1853

---

[17] Altholz, *The Liberal Catholic Movement*, 12-3.
[18] Ibid., 12.
[19] Ibid.
[20] Ibid., 13.
[21] Windle reports that Newman refused, but Altholz notes that Newman quietly worked in this capacity from 1850-52, and received considerable criticism from the Continental Orators for "conducting a secular magazine." When Frederick Capes denied this allegation, he took the opportunity to also refute the rumors that the magazine was under Cardinal Wiseman's control or that it was a Jesuit publication. Windle, *Who's Who*, 95; Altholz, *The Liberal Catholic Movement*, 20.
[22] In a letter to Fr. Coleridge on 30 August 1867, Newman wrote: "There was the Rambler matter—The Cardinal and our Bishop urged me to interfere with the conductors—and thanked me when I consented. It involved me in endless trouble and work. The correspondence is a huge heap. I have been obliged to arrange and complete it with notes and collateral papers, that I may ultimately be shown to have acted a good part, at that future time when people will speak out the slanders which they only whisper now. This was the work of four or five years, and what came of it?" *LD*, 23:325-6.

and 1854, when fellow Oxford convert James Spencer Northcote[23] (1821-1907) filled in for him.[24]

The influence of the Capes brothers was not limited to providing a venue for others to enter the debate, but also providing their own commentary on the debate. One of the two Capes brothers wrote what Windle described as a bitter and untrue depiction of "Newman's attitude to the papal infallibility," which resulted in "two scathing letters on the topic, one to the 'Guardian,' the other to the 'Pall Mall Gazette.'"[25]

While these five men do not appear to have written works that were significant in the infallibility debates leading up to the council,[26] these periodicals were used as an intellectual outlet and means for debate. These men offered venues for both liberal and neo-ultramontane voices to be heard.

Influence through Writing: Wilberforce, Faber, Knox, Dalgairns, and Mivart

The work of these converts will be presented in chronological order based upon the publication date of the convert's primary work discussed in this essay. Thus, the order of presentation will be Robert Wilberforce (1851), Frederick Faber (1860), Thomas Knox (1867), John Dalgairns (1871), and St. George Mivart (1899). Wilberforce's work sets the stage and provides insight into an ongoing concern for the converts. The next three works are from members of the

---

[23] Northcote was received into the Roman Catholic Church in 1845, a year after his wife was received. Windle, *Who's Who*, 187.

[24] Ibid. According to John Capes, Northcote was more successful as a contributor to *The Rambler* than as an editor. In a letter to Mrs. Richard Simpson, John Capes wrote that "his cautiousness, and dry antiquarianism, made the sale fall off so much, that I felt obliged to resume the work as soon as I could." Letter of John Capes to Mrs. Richard Simpson (date uncertain), Altholz, *The Liberal Catholic Movement*, 23.

[25] Windle, *Who's Who*, 96. Windle noted that it is "very difficult to disentangle these two in the letters of the period."

[26] A possible exception is the work of John Capes. Prior to selling the publication to Simpson and Lord Acton, John Capes published the article "Four Years' Experience with the Catholic Religion," which chronicled his conversion. In this essay he stated that he followed "the more probable of the two alternatives," implying "that the Catholic claims could not be *proved* and that religion should be decided as a matter of personal experience and preference." This stirred private criticism that he had "substituted theological 'probabilism' for the traditional Catholic teaching of the *certainty* of faith." He continued developing this concept in two subsequent books: *Reasons for Returning to the Church of England* (1871) and *To Rome and Back* (1873). Patrick Allitt, *Catholic Converts: British and American Intellectuals Turn to Rome* (Ithaca, NY: Cornell University Press, 1997), 93. Italics are his.

London English Oratory and express ultramontanist views. Mivart represents the liberal view, and the voice of a layperson and scientist.

Robert Isaac Wilberforce (1802-1857), a close friend of John Henry Newman prior to Newman's conversion. He became closer to his brother-in-law Henry Manning after Newman's conversion in 1845, when Wilberforce helped Manning lead the Tractarians.[27] In 1851, three years before his conversion to Catholicism,[28] Wilberforce published *A Sketch of the History of Erastianism* which contained two sermons preached at St. Mary's Church for the University of Oxford: the first, "The Reality of Church Ordinances" during Advent of 1850 and the second, "The Principle of Church Authority," on 18 May 1851. In *A Sketch of the History of Erastianism*, Wilberforce explored how five issues of church authority—"orders, mission, communion, patronage, and interpretation of doctrine"—were assigned after the Reformation.[29] In the first essay of the volume, the underlying issue is with whom or what does church authority lie.[30] In the final essay, the sermon "The Principle of Church Authority," Wilberforce advanced his argument to the conclusion that by allowing spiritual matters to be tried in the civil system, the Anglican Church was no longer exercising her rightful spiritual authority.[31] According to Windle, both the Catholic and the

---

[27] Windle, *Who's Who*, 240-1. During this time, Manning and Wilberforce worked closely together in their theological research. Edmund Sheridan Purcell, *The Life of Cardinal Manning*, 2 vols (New York: Macmillian and Company, 1896), 2:25-48. Manning's letters to Wilberforce demonstrate the depth of their friendship and Wilberforce's role as a sounding board for Manning as he anguished over concepts of infallibility. See Kenneth Parker's essay in this volume. Their expansive correspondence is preserved and merits further study. See: Oxford, Bodleian Library, MS Eng. Lett.c.655, 656, and 662. Newsome noted that as early as 1843, Manning sought to enter into Robert's confidence. He also reported the "furious argument" between Henry and Robert Wilberforce regarding whether they should continue relationships with Newman after his conversion. Newsome, *The Parting of Friends*, 302, 310, 381.

[28] Ibid., 416.

[29] Erastianism, as defined by Wilberforce is "that system of opinions and that course of action, which deprive the Church of Christ of independent existence, and resolve it into a function of the civil government." He proposed that "pure Erastiansim" was fully displayed within the Anglican Church in 1850. Robert Isaac Wilberforce, *A Sketch of the History of Erastianism; Together with Two Sermons on The Reality of Church Ordinances, and on the Principle of Church Authority*, 2nd ed. (Derby: John and Charles Mosley, 1851), 2, 4, 77, 79, 86.

[30] The pastoral issue of the essay was the laity's confidence in the proper dispensing of the sacraments and an authoritative response to faith controversies. Ibid., 78-95.

[31] This work is, according to Windle, the equivalent of *Essay on Development* for Newman. Windle, *Who's Who*, 240-1. In this sermon, Wilberforce argued that the disputes of the early church were "concluded by the authority of those, who by office were

Anglican Churches had hoped for important contributions coming from Wilberforce.[32] Gladstone considered Wilberforce to be "one of the most learned men of the Movement," and bemoaned his conversion.[33] Manning was reported to have stated that Wilberforce was "the most powerful theologian of his generation."[34] However, on 3 February 1857 Wilberforce died of a fever during his journey to Rome to study for the priesthood, ending his contributions to the debates thirteen years before the Council.[35] His primary contribution to the debates was an articulation of the Tractarian concern regarding the relationship between church and state in the context of issues of authority that would continue to plague some of the converts.

While the impact of Wilberforce's writings, at the least, reflect ideas that influenced Manning, a sermon published in 1860 by Frederick William Faber (1814-1861) had a more direct impact on the infallibility debates. Faber had desired to be received by the Roman Catholic Church as early as 1845, but Newman influenced his delayed departure from the Anglican Church.[36] After

---

successors of the Apostles." The successors of the apostles, "the Bishops of the Church Catholic," are the means by which the entire church is connected together, and it is through them that the Lord's presence is represented. However, while the Church of England claimed "to be the depository of a Divine truth, which she has a superhuman commission to deliver; but the worldly power has in reality taken possession of her frame, and gives expression to its will through her organs of utterance. She claims to be the salt of the earth, and she is in reality trodden under foot of men." While this decline occurred over a long period of time, "its consummation was the transference of the right of deciding respecting doctrine from spiritual to civil rulers, from those who possess authority in Christ's spiritual kingdom, to those whom God's providence has invested with natural power." Wilberforce, *A Sketch of the History of Erastianism*, 134, 145-6.

[32] Wilberforce was an able systematic theologian, was competent in Hebrew, was "a very competent German scholar," had "an immense knowledge of patristic sources," and had "a fair grasp of Catholic theological writings" as early as 1847. His three great dogmatic works were written between 1848 and 1853: *The Doctrine of the Incarnation*, *The Doctrine of Holy Baptism*, and *The Doctrine of the Holy Eucharist*. Newsome, *The Parting of Friends*, 373-4. Note that his reception into the Catholic Church was in the midst of these writings in 1850. For studies of Wilberforce's sacramental works, see: E. R. Fairweather, *The Oxford Movement* (New York: Oxford University Press, 1964) and Alf Härdelin, *The Tractarian Understanding of the Eucharist*, Acta Universitatis Upsaliensis. Studia historico-ecclesiastica Upsaliensia, 8 (Uppsala, 1965).

[33] Windle, *Who's Who*, 240-1.

[34] Newsome, *The Parting of Friends*, 381.

[35] Windle, *Who's Who*, 240-1; *LD,* 17:516, 519.

[36] Chapman noted that Faber realized that he could not trust his volatile nature, and not only was his hero-worship of Newman obvious, but "[h]e needed Newman as a guide,

Newman converted, there was no reason for Faber to wait. He was ordained and joined the Oratory at Birmingham with Newman in 1847;[37] but differences in temperament and preferences were best resolved through community division, leading to the formation of the Oratory in London. This placed both men as leaders among the English Oratorians, Newman at Birmingham and Faber at London. However, disagreements between the two men over the operation and rule of the houses led to Newman needing to defend himself against charges sent against him from the London Oratory.[38] This attracted the attention of the Curia.

Faber, who had been the Oxford Movement's hope for a poet, wrote hymns as well as spiritual works.[39] In 1860, he published *Devotion to the Pope*, an ex-

---

to protect him from himself." Ronald Chapman, *Father Faber* (Westminster, Maryland: The Newman Press, 1961), 112, 17-8.

[37] Faber had been ordained as an Anglican priest on the Feast of St. Philip Neri, the founder of the Oratory, on 26 May 1839. He was received into the Catholic Church on 16 November 1845. His ordination into the Catholic priesthood was 3 April 1847. In the summer of 1848, his two-month novitiate was under Newman; after which, on 28 July, he became the novice master. The London Oratory was started in January of 1849, Faber was sent to London in April, and the London Oratory opened in May of the same year. Faber was made the rector of the London Oratory. When the London Oratory became independent in the fall of the same year, Faber was elected as the superior. Raleigh Addington, ed., *Faber Poet and Priest: Selected Letters by Frederick William Faber, 1833-1863* (Cowbridge and Bridgend, Glamorgan: D. Brown and Sons, 1974), 28-29.

[38] At issue was hearing the confession of nuns. Sheridan Gilley, *Newman and His Age* (Westminster, MD: Christian Classics, 1991), 285-8. Addington, *Faber Poet and Priest*, 29. Chapman, *Father Faber*, 261-90. However, differences in temperament between the two men were also an underlying issue. Placid Murray noted that while Cardinal Wiseman's desire for Newman and his friends to be in "some such body as the Oratorians," it was ultimately Newman who chose the religious organization. However, Wiseman can be credited with encouraging Faber to join Newman in the Oratory. When Faber, with his companions, joined the newly formed Oratory, Wiseman considered this as a "most choice Christmas gift" for Newman. However, this gift was a difficult one to live with. John Henry Newman, *Newman the Oratorian: His Unpublished Oratory Papers*, ed. Placid Murray (Leominster, England: Gracewing, 2006), 88, 96.

[39] Ronald Chapman noted that Faber influenced the poet William Wordsworth, who considered Faber to have "considerable poetic talent." Some feared that, because of Faber's influence, Wordsworth "might become a full-blooded Tractarian—or worse." Faber was considered to be "a startling phenomenon in mid-nineteenth century London." While Charles Dickens displayed "the emotional reaction of the natural man" to Utilitarianism, "Faber's was the emotional reaction of the spiritual man." Chapman, *Father Faber*, 68, 71, 299-300. Mary Heimann noted that Faber wrote a hymn titled "God bless our Pope," which influenced popular piety and the course of the infallibility debates in England. Mary Heimann, *Catholic Devotion in Victorian England* (Oxford: Claredon Press, 1995), 139. Faber is also well-known for eight religious treatises. He wrote these for those who

pression of devotion manifested throughout his Catholic writings.[40] Ieuan Ellis described this work as well as another sermon, Devotion to the Church, as giving "a psychic, mystical quality to Pius IX ... and expressed in his appallingly sentimental (but highly popular) poetry the emotional force of Ultramontanism."[41] *Devotion to the Pope* was translated into French, German, Spanish, and Italian, the latter at the Holy Father's request. Pope Pius read the Italian version's proof-sheets and made only one correction.[42] In this published sermon, Faber stated that since Jesus and Mary have now been withdrawn, the pope has been left to the church as:

> ... a third visible presence of Jesus amongst us ... The Pope is the Vicar of Jesus on earth, and enjoys among the monarchs of the world all the rights and sovereignties of the Sacred Humanity of Jesus. No crown can be above his crown. By divine right he can be subject to none.[43]

Catholic readership of this work was widespread and played a significant role in promoting neo-ultramontane ideals. The availability of the work in multiple languages, and papal approval prior to the council, illustrates the unique

---

desired to live spiritual lives while in the world. Chapman stated that his work displayed "almost every fault" but amidst the rubbish was gold. These works were mostly written when he was ill and for relaxation, not for literary style, and his anticipated audience was the laity. The disparity between Wordsworth's praise and Chapman's critique is intriguing. Chapman, *Father Faber*, 290, 96. Sheridan Gilley stated that these works "articulated the content of the neo-Ultramontane Devotional Revolution within English Catholicism." Gilley, *Newman and His Age*, 288. These works, as well as his sermons and hymns, would be fertile ground for a study of his neo-ultramontane ideals.

[40] Frederick William Faber, *Devotion to the Pope* (Baltimore: Murphy & Company Printers and Publishers, 1860). According to John Bowden, this "remarkable devotion to the Holy See" led, in the following year, to the founding of the Association of St. Peter, whose "sole object and duty ... was to offer prayers for the Sovereign Pontiff." John Edward Bowden, *The Life and Letters of Frederick William Faber, D.D.: Priest of the Oratory of St. Philip Neri*, 5th ed. (London: Burns & Oates, 1869), 369.

[41] Ieuan Ellis, "The Intellectual Challenge to 'Official Religion'," in *The British: Their Religious Beliefs and Practices 1800-1986*, ed. Terence Thomas (London: Routledge, 1998), 67. See also: Altholz, *The Liberal Catholic Movement*, 131.

[42] Bowden, ed., *The Life and Letters of Frederick William Faber*, 429-30. "Notices of Books: F. Faber on Devotion to the Pope," *Dublin Review* 9 (1867): 231. This text was published in Italian, French, and German in 1860. An 1880 Spanish edition was also produced. These texts are: *Devozione al papa* (1860, S.I.: s.n.), *De la dévotion au pape* (Paris: A. Bray, 1860, 1861), *Opferwillige Hingebung für den Papst* (Regensburg: Manz, 1860), and *Devocion al Papa* (Madrid: Hospicio, 1880).

[43] Faber, *Devotion to the Pope*, 21.

contribution of this convert in promoting an expansive theory of papal authority and devotion to the Holy Father. A summary of Faber's teaching concerning the papacy appeared in an article in the 4 October 1863 issue of *The Tablet*.[44]

Faber's sermon, which had a significant impact in the debates, was followed by another highly significant work by fellow convert and member of the London Oratory, Thomas Francis Knox (1822-1882). Knox was among those who were received into the Catholic Church with Frederick Faber on 16 November 1845, but he was not an Oxford Movement convert in the proper sense of the term since his degree was from Cambridge.[45] In 1848, Knox was the only novice among the founding members of the Birmingham Oratory.[46] Knox had vowed "special obedience" to Newman, his superior at the Birmingham Oratory, and was subsequently sent with Faber to found the London Oratory, saving Newman from Knox's "affection and devotion."[47]

Knox cultivated the neo-ultramontane position, and, while serving as the superior of the London Oratory, wrote his 1867 treatise *When Does the Church Speak Infallibly? or, The Nature and Scope of the Church's Teaching Office*.[48] This work reflected the same devotional priorities as Faber's books. As noted in the introduction to the Italian version, this "little" book was of general interest to the international community, and while not the only good book on the subject, "[e]verything is in this book and all is well done."[49] In William Ward's *Dublin Review*, the reviewer stated that "... on the whole it is the most complete and orthodox exposition of the Church's integral doctrine on Infallibility which has appeared in any part of Christendom."[50] The January-April 1870 issue of the

---

[44] Bowden quotes the summary as follows: "'He taught men to regard the Pope as their Father, and not as their King only; he could not bear to hear of rights, or privileges, or customs in any local Church, unless they had been allowed by the Holy See: for his obedience was a loyal love, that knew no questioning in the presence of a Father whose rights he would never measure.'" Bowden, *Life and Letters of Frederick William Faber*, 430.

[45] Windle, *Who's Who*, 156. Chapman, *Father Faber*, 113.

[46] Newman, *Newman the Oratorian*, 453.

[47] Gilley, *Newman and His Age*, 259. Chapman, *Father Faber*, 220.

[48] From the introduction of the 1870 Italian edition of *When does the Church speak Infallibly?*. quoted in "Notices of Books: *When does the Church speak Infallibly?* By Thomas Francis Knox, of the Oratory. 1867. Del Magistero Infallibile della Chiesa. Opuscolo di Tommaso Fransicso Knox, dell' Oratorio, tradotto dall' inglese. 1870," *The Dublin Review* 14 (1870): 523.

[49] Ibid.

[50] "Notices of Books: *When does the Church speak infallibly?* By Thomas Francis Knox of the Oratory. 2nd ed. London: Burns, Oates, & Co.," *Dublin Review* 15 (1870): 238.

Dublin Review republished the February *Civiltà* review of the pamphlet, which stated that while Dr. Murray of Ireland's College of Maynooth "had handled the subject scholastically in his great treatise *de Ecclesiâ*" and William Ward "had discussed it with greater fulness [sic] controversially in the *Dublin Review*," Knox, while using their works:

> followed a simpler method; and, avoiding all scholastic and controversial expressions, produced a work, at once learned and popular, brief and yet full; the very quintessence, so to speak, of doctrinal exposition.[51]

According to the reviewer, this text needed to be translated and distributed since the "learned ecclesiastics did not take long to run through the treatise, and soon came to an unanimous agreement that it was the very thing they wanted," since it covered every aspect that needed to be covered.[52] As stated in the July-October 1870 issue of the *Dublin Review*:

> Knox has sought to explain in a simple, positive, and uncontroversial manner the whole doctrine regarding infallibility, and he has succeeded admirably. In preference to reasonings and controversies, and the opinions of theologians, he has attached himself to the acts of the teaching of the Church and the Pope down to our own time; that is to say, he has gathered together what the teaching Church and the Pope, on the subject of infallibility, has declared concerning the object of infallibility and the questions connected with it.[53]

Further, the *Dublin Review* reported that the *Civiltà* of 18 June 1870 had declared:

> ... though the work embraces all the questions which relate to infallibility, it treats more especially of the object, which is evidently the same both for the Pope and for the teaching Church.[54]

This, according to the reviewer in the Dublin Review, is the "peculiar merit of F. Knox's work." Knox's approach was to explore "the Church's practice, and

---

[51] "Notices of Books: *When does the Church speak Infallibly?* By Thomas Francis Knox, of the Oratory. 1867. *Del Magistero Infallibile della Chiesa.* Opuscolo di Tommaso Francisco Know, dell' Oratorio, tradotto dall' inglese. 1870," *The Dublin Review* 14 (1870): 523.

[52] Ibid.

[53] "Roman Documents," *Dublin Review*, July-October (1870): 235.

[54] Ibid., 232. Emphasis in the original.

from the living exercise of her teaching office, rather than from the various opinions of theologians."[55] The reviewer explained:

> [a]fter establishing once for all the subject of the infallible teaching office, the author places, in a clear light, the principle that the object of the Church's infallibility can only be learnt authentically from the Church herself, that is, from the subject of infallibility itself.[56]

Indeed, in *When Does the Church Speak Infallibly?*, Knox stated "[she] declared the powers which she possessed by using them," and that through providence "the full extent of the Church's infallible authority as teacher," has been increasingly defined through the ages.[57]

In 1870, Knox received a special commendation from Pope Pius IX. Here again, an English convert influenced by the Oxford Movement went on to stand at the intellectual center of efforts to promote neo-ultramontane ideals. The fact that Knox's book was translated into Italian, published in Turin, and was reissued in English in an expanded version in 1870 demonstrates its importance in the debates.[58]

John Dobrée Dalgairns (1822-1876) followed Newman to Littlemore in 1842.[59] Dalgairns converted in 1844[60] and had been ordained to the priesthood by the time he participated in the founding of the Birmingham Oratory in 1849.[61] He was sent with Faber in 1850 to start the London Oratory.[62] Dalgairns displayed a tendency toward an unstable enthusiasm as early as 1842, and this enthusiasm led to difficulties within the London Oratory.[63] As early as 1848, Dalgairns and Newman disagreed sharply over issues of developing Catholic

---

[55] Ibid., 232, 35.

[56] Ibid., 231-2. Emphasis in the original.

[57] Thomas Francis Knox, *When Does the Church Speak Infallibly? or, The Nature and Scope of the Church's Teaching Office*, 2nd ed., enlarged (London: Burns and Oates, 1870), 50.

[58] Thomas Francis Knox, *Del Magistero Infallibile della Chiesa* (Turin: Pietro d. G. Marietti, 1870).

[59] Gilley, *Newman and His Age*, 211.

[60] Windle, *Who's Who*, 174.

[61] Newman, *Newman the Oratorian*, 455.

[62] Ibid., 457.

[63] Some of the difficulties in London centered around his eagerness to hear confessions. Chapman, *Father Faber*, 227.

education in England.[64] Differences over preferences in spirituality added to the increasing tension between Newman and Dalgairns.[65]

Dalgairns' contributions to the debate include his essay "The Bearing of Infallibility on Religious Truth," in Knowles's *The Contemporary Review* in 1871.[66] His concluding statement in this essay was:

> The issue and the meaning of the Vatican Council is the declaration on the part of the Church that by defining the infallibility given by Christ to the Holy See she assumes the attitude which will best enable her to fulfill her mission of preaching the Christian faith most clearly and most readily to the modern world.[67]

Dalgairns, along with Faber and Knox—all from the London Oratory, promoted a "maximalist" understanding of papal authority and provided devotional and intellectual support to the neo-ultramontane cause, which received papal support and patronage. This engagement by Oxford Movement converts provides further illustration of the impact of English converts and the support some of them provided to the neo-ultramontane side of the debates.

Yet not all minor Oxford Movement converts were drawn to the neo-ultramontanist cause. For some, liberal Catholicism provided the vital current of thought that animated their faith. St. George Jackson Mivart (1827-1900) provides an example of this type of Oxford Movement convert. Like Knox, Mivart was not an Oxford alumnus. He converted to Roman Catholicism before seeking admission to Oxford and thus was barred from attending. However, his conversion was due to the work of Tractarians.[68]

---

[64] Newman, *Newman the Oratorian*, 109.

[65] Ibid., 109, 144.

[66] John Dobrée Dalgairns, "The Bearing of Infallibility on Religious Truth," *The Contemporary Review* (1871). James Knowles, Fellow of the Royal Institute of British Architects and founder of the Metaphysical Society, was editor of the ecumenical intellectual monthly journal, *The Contemporary Review*. Thomas Humphry Ward, *Men of the Time: A Dictionary of Contemporaries, containing Biographical Notices of Eminent Characters of Both Sexes*, 12th ed. (London: Routledge and Sons, 1887), 615.

[67] Dalgairns, "The Bearing of Infallibility on Religious Truth," 22.

[68] The converts featured in Michael Clifton's *A Victorian Convert Quintet* include Robert Aston Coffin, Frederick Oakeley, Richard Waldo Sibthorp, and St. George Jackson Mivart. Sibthorp's contributions to the debates are not discussed in this essay. However, further study might bring to light additional publications or sermons that engaged the debates after his conversion. In particular, Sibthorp went on the record as being clearly against papal infallibility in 1828, thirteen years before his conversion. In his published sermon *The Character of the Papacy as Predicted by St. Paul in 2 Thess ... Chap II*

Mivart was trained as a biologist and zoologist, worked as a physician, and was well-respected both within the scientific community and as a lay apologist for the Catholic Church. He was praised by Newman for his 1871 work Genesis of Species in which he presented a modified Darwinism in which he "appended ... a long section on the reconcilability of the evolutionary idea with Catholic theology. Even conservative Catholics saw his work "as a valuable defense of religion against [the] materialistic theories of the age."[69]

Mivart anguished over the barrier that he saw being constructed between science and the Roman Catholic Church, as well as his concerns about interpretation of Scripture.[70] His protest against infallibility was expressed in his 1892 pamphlet, *Happiness in Hell*, which was condemned in 1893 and indexed as a forbidden book.

It was as a scientist and a lay apologist that he offered an interesting challenge to the infallibility debate by combining Newman's *Development of Doctrine* with the biological evolutionary process debate that was still raging in the scientific community in his 1899 essay, "What Church Has 'Continuity'?". In this essay he stated:

> But what should we say of biologists who insisted on adhering to the views of Ray, Linnaeus, or Buffon, rather than those of the most recent leaders of science? Newman has clearly shown Christians that they should look rather to the future than to the past, in order to obtain the clearest and fullest religious knowledge. However much we may venerate 'the Fathers,' it is their very remote descendants to whom we must have recourse for their fullest knowledge and best interpretation of the writings of their remote predecessors.[71]

In his 1900 article "Scripture and Roman Catholicism," Mivart continued the discussion he began in "What Church Has 'Continuity'?". In this essay, he ar-

---

verse 4 (London, 1828), he openly criticized the papacy for claiming virtual divine rights. Based upon Sibthorp's comment in a letter written in 1849, Clifton stated that 1849 was the start of Sibthorp's hostility to papal claims and that this attitude eventually led him to reject papal infallibility; however, this earlier sermon demonstrates that his thoughts were already developed twenty years earlier. Sibthorp continued to struggle with the concept of infallibility throughout his time as a Catholic. Michael Clifton, *A Victorian Convert Quintet* (London: The Saint Austin Press, 1998), 102, 107, 118-19, 171.

[69] John D. Root, "The Final Apostasy of St. George Jackson Mivart," *Catholic Historical Review* 71 (1985): 2. The quote originated from an anonymous review in *The Tablet*, 25 February, 1871: 232.

[70] Ibid., 442.

[71] St. George Mivart, "What Church Has 'Continuity'?," *Nineteenth Century*, 46 (1899): 210.

gued that not only has doctrine changed, but that the Catholic Church has not been consistent in its doctrine throughout the ages:

> If only Roman Catholic authorities could plainly and honestly declare that some of the dogmatic decrees of Florence, of Trent, and of the Vatican, though confirmed by the Pope, were entirely mistaken decrees and need not be obeyed, and if Leo the Thirteenth would withdraw his most unfortunate Encyclical, and own there are many errors in the Bible, the existing terrible state of tension would be relieved. This seems improbable, however, on account of the fatal character of Infallibility which the Roman Catholic Church claims, but which (most fortunately for herself) the Anglican Church does not.
> That character of Infallibility is, as I have elsewhere said, like the fatal garment of Nessus which, till Rome manages to shake it off, will cling to her and eat away her substance till she is reduced to a mouldering and repulsive skeleton. And yet that terrible claim, maintained for so many centuries, could hardly now be got rid of without causing otherwise fatal results.
> It is this pretension of Infallibility which carries with it the need of also pretending that Church dogma never has changed and never by any possibility can change, during all the ages of ages of the world's future existence.[72]

As a well-known lay apologist, Mivart's ideas were considered dangerous by the ecclesiastical hierarchy. While he did eventually accept the decree of papal infallibility in 1893 in his apologia regarding his indexed books,[73] he died unreconciled with the Catholic Church, unwilling to recant all of the beliefs that had caused his estrangement with the Church.[74]

These five Oxford Movement converts provide a sample of how obscure converts engaged in the infallibility debates through the spoken and written word. While the influence of some was minimal, others, most notably Faber and Knox, were able to influence the debates significantly. Of the five men discussed in this section, the three neo-ultramontanes were from the same religious order and the same house. Robert Wilberforce's early death suggests that his influence may have been more narrow, and limited to classifying Manning's theological ideas about the dangers of state intrusion on church affairs. Mivart, who did not pursue religious life but continued his work in the sciences and apologetics, stands as an example of converts who were drawn to liberal Catholic ideals. Mivart also represents those converts who struggled with the

---

[72] St. George Mivart, "Scripture and Roman Catholicism," *Nineteenth Century* 47 (1900): 439.
[73] Clifton, *A Victorian Convert Quintet*, 190.
[74] Root, "The Final Apostasy of St. George Jackson Mivart," 1.

definition of papal infallibility and continued to engage the debates, long after the definition had been declared.

Providing Access to the Council: Coffin and Talbot

No other English figure had more to do with defining papal infallibility than Henry Edward Manning. He was the only Oxford Movement convert at the First Vatican Council and a prominent leader of the Majority bishops. Yet this would not have happened without Robert Aston Coffin and George Talbot. Both played crucial roles in securing Manning's position as the de facto head of the Catholic Church in England, just fourteen years after his conversion.

Robert Aston Coffin (1819-1885) was one of the seven founding members of the Birmingham Oratory with Newman in 1848.[75] In October of 1849, he was one of the fathers sent to found the London house.[76] However, their relationship became strained when Coffin joined the neo-ultramontane Redemptorists in 1850.[77] In 1853, Manning arranged a meeting with Coffin to discuss Coffin's *The Mysteries—The Incarnation*. During this meeting Coffin confronted the older Manning concerning his lack of thorough instruction of converts. Because of this conversation and the "warm friendship" that subsequently developed between the two men, Coffin became Manning's confessor. Further, both men shared in the neo-ultramontanist cause.[78]

In 1865, Coffin was in Rome with the provincial of the English Redemptorists for an audience with the pope as part of the special meeting of the provincials and vice provincials in Rome.[79] During the audience, Coffin asked who would be the successor to Cardinal Wiseman. Coffin, thinking that the decision had already been made in William Clifford's favor, informed the pope of his concerns over what he considered a less than worthy choice for the position

---

[75] Coffin was received into the Catholic Church two months after Newman in 1845. Windle, *Who's Who*, 101-2.

[76] Newman, *Newman the Oratorian*, 455, 57.

[77] Clifton, *A Victorian Convert Quintet*, 19-20. The Redemptorists identified with the ultramontane cause with their lavish devotions and "fierce loyalty for, and obedience to, the Roman See." According to John Sharp, "Even before the definition, the Redemptorists strongly maintained belief in papal infallibility and would have extended the dogmatic definition to include the temporal power of the papacy." John Sharp, *Reapers of the Harvest: The Redemptorists in Great Britain and Ireland* (Dublin: Veritas, 1989), 96.

[78] Clifton, *A Victorian Convert Quintet*, 33, 45.

[79] At this meeting Coffin received his appointment as provincial of the Province of England and Ireland. Ibid., 35.

and "suggested that Manning would be an ideal candidate."[80] Thus, for Coffin, an opportunity to advance an old friend's ability to serve the church proved a factor in Manning being named archbishop of Westminster and *de facto* primate of England.

George Talbot (1816-1886)[81] was even more strategically placed to influence Manning's appointment.[82] Talbot was present at Oxford when the Tractarian Movement gained importance and he became acquainted with the leaders of the movement, either in person or through their writings.[83] He was among the earliest to be received into the Catholic Church,[84] was ordained to the priesthood 1846, and served as a priest in England until 1849 or 1850.[85] In 1850, Pius IX, desiring to lessen the influence of the Italians in the Curia, appointed Talbot, on Wiseman's commendation, as a papal chamberlain and a canon of the basilica.[86] Talbot exercised his diplomatic skills well in this position, mostly through indirect influence.[87] Despite his condition as a neophyte Catholic with a paucity of experience in pastoral care, Talbot gained the pope's trust and became his interpreter of English Catholicism. Furthermore, his relationship with Pius IX was such that when bad news was delivered to the Holy Father, it was typically Talbot who carried it to him.[88] As chamberlain, he served Pope Pius IX as his private secretary and confidant. According to Arnold Lund, "Talbot's motto was summed up in the words: 'Sentire cum Petro [to think with Peter] is

---

[80] Ibid., 34.

[81] Windle lists him as Monsignor Gilbert Chetwynd Talbot. Windle, *Who's Who*, 229. Research into Talbot's work within the Vatican could provide a wealth of information about this very neglected and misunderstood contributor to the debate.

[82] Odo van der Heydt begins his article by stressing that the absence of works on Talbot is not justified given his level of influence in ecclesiastical history between 1850 and 1869. Odo van der Heydt, "Monsignor Talbot de Malahide," *The Wiseman Review*, Winter (1964-5): 290.

[83] Ibid., 292.

[84] His date of reception is 1843. Ibid., 294. This places him among the earliest Oxford Movement converts, within the first five of the Oxford clergy. Gondon, *Conversion de cent cinquante ministres anglicans*, 86.

[85] Lund places this event in 1847. Van der Heydt provides the date of 1850 based upon a baptismal registry in his name. Arnold Lund, *Roman Converts* (Newcastle-upon-Tyne, UK: The Northumberland Press Ltd., 1925), 59-60. van der Heydt, "Monsignor Talbot de Malahide," 299.

[86] Ibid., 299.

[87] Ibid., 303.

[88] Ibid., 299.

always the safest side.' And to do him justice, he usually contrived to think to-day what Peter was going to think to-morrow."[89]

Talbot's role in the infallibility debates was achieved through his position in the Vatican; for he utilized his influence to both promote some and to impede others. Talbot served as Manning's confidant through the difficulties between Manning and other members of the Westminster Chapter.[90] In his unofficial capacity he supported the neo-ultramontane side of the debate, especially the work of Manning and Cardinal Wiseman.[91]

Two incidents demonstrate Talbot's support for and assistance to Manning. In 1857, Talbot used his influence with Pius IX to have Manning assigned to the position of Provost of the Westminster Chapter instead of the recommended candidate, Canon Maguire.[92] The second incident concerns Manning's lectures on the temporal power of the pope. Manning sent the lectures to Talbot in order for them to be translated and published, and he depended on Talbot for feedback when the lectures were censured with the threat of being indexed. Talbot provided insights on passages which created difficulty for the readership, traced the source of some of the antagonism against Manning, and acted as liaison by explaining to others what Manning had meant in his lectures.[93] According to van der Heydt, Talbot was not "the mere instrument of Manning," as others have suggested, for "it was quite often Talbot who told Manning how to act and what to do in many circumstances and not vice versa."[94] Thus, Talbot offered Manning invaluable assistance as a mentor and guide through curial politics.

Despite his great service to Manning, Talbot's penchant for intrigue and his frankness in correspondence with Manning led him to later describe Talbot as

---

[89] Lund, *Roman Converts*, 59-60, 104.

[90] Clifton, *A Victorian Convert Quintet*, 81.

[91] Talbot's ultramontanist agenda can be seen as early as December 1854, just prior to the announcement of the dogma of the Immaculate Conception of Mary. Talbot confided to Franz Knoodt that the manner in which the dogma was announced was more important than the dogma itself. He meant by this that a precedent had been established, in which a pope had made an *ex cathedra* definition apart from a council—on his separate authority. See: Johann Friedrich, *Ignaz von Döllinger*, 3 vols (Munich: C.H. Beck'sche, 1899-1901), 3:146-7. I am grateful to Kenneth Parker for this observation. Also see: Kenneth L. Parker, "Francis Kenrick and Papal Infallibility: How Pastoral Experience in the American Missions Transformed a Roman Ultramontanist," in *Tradition and Pluralism: Essays in Honor of William M. Shea*, eds. K.L. Parker, P. Huff, and M.J.G. Pahls (Lanham, MD: University Press of America, 2008).

[92] Shane Leslie, *Henry Edward Manning: His Life and Labours* (New York: P. J. Kenedy and Sons, 1921), 130.

[93] Purcell, *Manning*, 2:152-61.

[94] van der Heydt, "Monsignor Talbot de Malahide," 306.

"the most imprudent man who ever lived."[95] Lund suggested mischievously that one might argue that Talbot had been "providentially created in order to provide Protestants with the perfect specimen of the scheming Papist."[96] However, Lund argued that Talbot exemplified the espirit de corps of Catholicism. His loyalty was clearly to the Holy See, and his efforts were not for his own advancement:

> He was a whole-hearted Papalist, and, like Manning, fought, not for his own hand, but for the Ultramontane policy and for the Pope. Pius IX had the gift of evoking loyalty and affection. Monsignor Talbot's worst faults were committed not in his own interests but in the interests of the Holy See.[97]

Talbot assumed the role of "agent" and mediator for the English bishops, using his trusted position as confidant of Manning and Pius IX, as well as many of the cardinals at the Congregation of Propaganda.[98] However, the English bishops and clergy did not all receive equal consideration. Talbot's partiality to Wiseman[99] and Manning and his hindrance of others, most notably Newman—whom he once described as "the most dangerous man in England"—caused resentment among bishops and clergy who experienced his obstructions. Newman wrote to Ambrose St. John in 1867, concerning Catholic education at Oxford, that "Talbot, Vaughan, and Stonor besiege the Pope, and, if they can, will not let anyone come near him."[100] By August of 1867, St. John reported that he feared "a rising party" in Rome: "The more I think of my interview with Talbot the more I am struck with the constant expression of uneasiness and excitement in his countenance ... the refusal to dine was the signal for war."[101] Newman's reply on 24 August was that he agreed with St. John: "the Ultramontane party at Rome is in a great fix just now," and he feared personal consequences.[102]

Newman's concerns were not without cause. In May of 1868, Newman wrote to Edward Bouverie Pusey, "the Pope is just now approachable only through a few men, such as Mgr Talbot (who has done a great deal of harm)."[103]

---

[95] Leslie, *Henry Edward Manning*, xii.
[96] Lund, *Roman Converts*, 106.
[97] Ibid.
[98] Purcell, *Manning*, 2:86.
[99] Shane Leslie referred to Talbot as Wiseman's "Roman henchman." Leslie, *Henry Edward Manning*, 103.
[100] *LD*, 23:167.
[101] *LD*, 23:319, n. 1. From a letter dated 22 August 1867.
[102] *LD*, 23:319.
[103] *LD*, 24:79. Newman experienced Talbot's diffident use of Roman influence even in his first year as a Catholic. *LD*, 12:12-13.

Talbot's opposition to Newman can be seen in an incident in 1867 concerning debate among the English Catholics on the relative importance of the "preservation of the Papal States."[104] However, Newman, Acton, and Richard Simpson considered it to be a secondary matter. During this time, Monsignor Talbot accused Newman, through rumors, of supporting Garibaldi.[105] This was one of the "monstrous things" Talbot told Newman's close friend and confidant, Ambrose St. John.[106] These groundless rumors not only threatened Newman's reputation in Rome, but also exacerbated the rift among the former Tractarians.[107] However, the day after St. John wrote to Newman about Talbot's slander, St. John reported to Newman: "Talbot is entirely (so Neve says) Manning's tool and hears from him three times a week everything great and small. He is not all powerful with the Pope and the Pope snubs him."[108] Within a few days of St. John's letter concerning Talbot's slanderous statements, he wrote to Newman that Talbot was "excessively sorry for the estrangement[109]—he desires [Newman's] friendship very much [sic] could be of the greatest service to [Newman] in letting [him] know how things were felt at Rome." When Talbot declared that his actions toward Newman had been, in his eyes, with the best intentions, St. John reported that he confronted Talbot concerning the statements made earlier linking Newman to Garibaldi.[110] While Talbot was the primary reason Newman had "a cloud ... hanging over" him during Talbot's time as papal chamberlain, Talbot did reluctantly admit that his public distrust of Newman was "all due to a mistake" made in 1867.[111] Running afoul of Mgr Talbot, even through a mistake

---

[104] These lingering fears about Erastianism, or the intrusion of secular power in church affairs, clung to Ward and Manning from their Anglican days, and caused them to consider the issue to be "of almost doctrinal significance." Allitt, *Catholic Converts*, 98.

[105] Ibid.

[106] In St. John's letter to Newman, dated 1 May 1867. *LD*, 23:208.

[107] Allitt, *Catholic Converts*, 98.

[108] From a letter dated 2 May 1867. *LD*, 23:208.

[109] This estrangement dated back to the 1850s regarding Newman's "On Consulting the Faithful." I am grateful to Kenneth Parker for this observation.

[110] From a letter dated 6 May 1867. *LD*, 23:223. The context for this incident was whether Catholics should be educated at Oxford or not. But it is apparent that these types of incidents were due to multiple issues currently being debated at the time, so that motives and exact context for disagreements are sometimes difficult to discern. Lund, *Roman Converts*, 106.

[111] van der Heydt, "Monsignor Talbot de Malahide," 303. Van der Heydt noted that "Talbot regarded everyone in two ways; viz. in so far as each one had private and public obligations and capacities. Each one was a private person and a public one with corresponding occupations. As private persons, both Newman and Errington were Talbot's friends. This he wrote openly in his letters, he even told them of his admiration and ap-

on Talbot's part, had serious consequences which affected Newman's ability to engage in the debates.[112] Talbot might have not wished ill upon anyone, but as Newman wrote in 1867, "he is determined to bend or break all opposition. He has an iron will, and resolves to have his own way."[113]

Talbot's last curial appointment was given in April of 1868, when he became one of the council's central commission consultors.[114] This commission provided direction for sub-commissions preparing for the Vatican Council. Talbot wrote to Manning concerning potential English theologians for the council. Newman was listed as a probable appointee and Talbot "proffered advice about Manning's coming to Rome for preparatory work."[115] In a letter to Manning, dated 20 October 1868, Talbot despaired of the English theologians: "I must say that when one looks all over England it appears that there are few theologians up

---

preciation of them. As public persons, however, both Newman and Errington were Talbot's enemies." van der Heydt, "Monsignor Talbot de Malahide," 304. Newman's expression of this difference in private and public engagements can be seen in his letter to Talbot on 26 May 1867, in which he wrote the following: "When you first entered the Holy Father's immediate service, I used to say a Mass for you the first day of every month, that you might be prospered at your important post; and now I shall say Mass for you seven times, beginning with this week, when we are keeping the Feast of St Philip, begging him at the same time to gain for you a more equitable judgment of us and a kinder feeling towards us on the part of our friends, than we have of late years experienced." *LD*, 23:241-2. The majority of the content of the letter, with excerpts from Talbot's reply, can be found in Appendix B.

[112] van der Heydt noted that Newman's argument for consulting the faithful seemed ridiculous, possibly even heretical, to Talbot. "Newman ... was the most dangerous man in England because, if Newman's principles were right, Talbot's would be wrong. But how could the Roman policy be wrong? What then about the infallibility of the Roman Pontiff; what about the encyclicals?" Another area of disagreement was over mixed education. van der Heydt, "Monsignor Talbot de Malahide," 307.

[113] Letter from Newman to Emily Bowles dated 3 January 1867. *LD*, 23:8.

[114] van der Heydt listed some of his responsibilities as consultor for the Sacred Congregation of Rites, English College pro-protector (1867), and canon of St. Peter's. van der Heydt, "Monsignor Talbot de Malahide," 300. Talbot's appointments within Pius IX's *Hofprälaten* were: 1851-1857, *Camerieri segreti partecipanti ohne Spezial-Titel*; 1858-1866, *Segretario d'ambasciata*; 1867-1878, *Coppiere*. Christopher Weber, *Kardinäle und Prälaten in den letzten Jahrzehnten des Kirchenstaates: Elite- rekrutierung, Karriere-muster und soziale Zusammensetzung der kurialen Führungsschicht zur Zeit Pius IX (1846-1878)* (Stuttgart: Anton Hiersemann, 1978). I am grateful for Michael Shea's assistance in directing me to Weber's text.

[115] van der Heydt, "Monsignor Talbot de Malahide," 300. Purcell noted that either Pius IX "revoked his intention" or Talbot was misinformed. Purcell, *Manning*, 2:422, n. 1.

to the mark, and capable to stand by the Roman and German consultors. But you will do your best."[116]

George Talbot's influence and considerable activity at the Vatican was continuous until mental illness incapacitated him.[117] He was admitted to a private asylum at Passy[118] in 1869, on the eve of the council. The stress of preparations for Vatican I, combined with his ordinary duties as chamberlain to Pope Pius IX must have contributed to the timing of his decline. Whether this unfortunate turn of events was due to his taking on additional responsibilities at the English College, the weight of a vast "capacity for intrigue," or the stress of these two factors, the result was mental instability from which he never recovered. Purcell noted that Pius IX kept his apartments, which were close to his own, ready, hoping that his trusted chamberlain, friend, and constant companion would once again need them. However, while Mgr Talbot had periods of lucidity, he did not recover and died at Passy in 1886.[119]

Confidants and Correspondents: Oakeley, St. John, Giberne, and Bowles

While Coffin and Talbot exercised influence at the center of Roman Catholicism, other Oxford Movement converts exercised personal influence in correspondence and spiritual counsel. Despite differences over papal infallibility, many Oxford Movement converts maintained the bonds of friendship.

Frederick Oakeley (1802-1880) is one well-documented example. Oakeley managed to maintain friendships with all of the important Anglican converts he met prior to conversion, including Newman, Manning, and Ward. Oakeley's views on papal authority were evident prior to his conversion. In his letter dated 19 February 1845 and published 25 June, he wrote:

---

[116] Ibid., 423.

[117] van der Heydt, "Monsignor Talbot de Malahide," 302.

[118] Of the numerous private "lunatic asylums" in Paris which "catered for the rich and middle class," Doctor Blanche's at Passy was one of the two most celebrated. At this time, mental illness at this Parisian asylum was treated with restraints and a combination of potassium bromide and other narcotics, sedatives or anodynes as quieting agents. Charles A. Lee, "Foreign Correspondence. Letter XVII: Lunatic Asylums," *American Medical Times* 5, July to December (1862): 319. E. T. Wilkins, *Insanity and Insane Asylums: Report of E. T. Wilkins, M.D., Commissioner in Lunacy for the State of California, made to His Excellency H. H. Haight, Governor, December 9d, 1871* (Sacramento: T. A. Springer, 1872), 4, 183. Ian Robert Dowbiggin, *Inheriting Madness: Professionalization and Psychiatric Knowledge in Nineteenth Century France* (Berkeley: University of California Press, 1991), 15.

[119] Purcell, *Manning,* 2:485.

> It is Rome alone which seems to me to propose doctrines on the authority of the Church. As soon as I leave this firm basis I get adrift and am thrown in one way or another upon private judgement, private views of Scripture, or of Antiquity, or of both. If Our Lord has left a Church on earth, that Church must be toties quoties the authorized expositress of His Word and I see no Church but the Roman which even claims to fulfill this office for the Christian World.[120]

He was received into the Catholic Church with Newman in late 1845, ordained as a priest two years later, served as a parish priest, and after 1852, became a chapter canon of Westminster.[121]

Oakeley's influence in the infallibility debates flowed from his interactions with Manning and Ward. Since Oakeley was a gifted musician and deeply concerned with liturgical matters in his Oxford years, it is possible that he may have also exerted influence through his primary interest, the liturgy.[122] However, his actions on behalf of his fellow converts provides an example of how friendships formed among the converts continued after their conversions, as demonstrated by Oakeley's efforts as peacemaker between Newman and Manning in 1867.[123]

While Oakeley provides an example of those who struggled to maintain friendships across the lines of the infallibility debates, some converts became partisans, loyal to a specific person. Talbot's partisanship on behalf of Henry Manning has been discussed. Ambrose St. John, Maria Rosina Giberne, and Emily Bowles, all of whom stood outside the institutional structures of the Church, were loyal confidants of John Henry Newman.

Ambrose St. John (1815-1875) was Newman's most important confidant among his fellow converts. St. John was received into the Roman Catholic Church one month prior to Newman and was the Birmingham Oratory's school headmaster for decades.[124] According to Windle, he was Newman's closest friend (his *fidus Achates*); Newman wrote in a letter to a Mr. Dering that

---

[120] This letter followed Ward's *The Ideal of a Christian Church*. Clifton, *A Victorian Convert Quintet*, 74.

[121] Windle, *Who's Who*, 189. Clifton, *A Victorian Convert Quintet*, 78, 84.

[122] Windle, *Who's Who*, 188.

[123] Oakeley desired for the two men to be reconciled after their disagreement over mixed education, as demonstrated in letters between Oakeley and Newman, Oakeley and Manning, and Newman and Manning in the summer and fall of 1867. *LD,* 23:276-9, 305-312, 328-9. Whether these types of friendships, and Oakeley's attempt at reconciling Newman and Manning in particular, moderated or intensified the views of individuals would make for an interesting study.

[124] St. John also served first as curate to Henry Wilberforce then to Newman before his conversion to Catholicism. Windle, *Who's Who*, 211.

"[Ambrose St. John] had been my life, under God, for thirty-two years." In his *Apologia* Newman wrote that he considered St. John as a gift from God, the one upon whom he leaned and could always count.[125] In Newman's words:

> And to you, especially, dear Ambrose St. John, whom God gave me, when he took everyone else away; who are the link between my old life and my new; who have now for twenty-one years been so devoted to me, so patient, so zealous, so tender; who have let me lean hard upon you; who have watched me so narrowly; who have never thought of yourself, if I was in question.[126]

This is a fitting panegyric for a man who strove to defend his friend even with someone who had the ear of the pope. Correspondence between Newman and St. John was restricted to when the two were separated; for this reason we lack documentary evidence of the extent to which they discussed the issues around the infallibility debates and influenced each other's thoughts. Yet aspects of the intrigue of the inner workings of the Catholic Church's hierarchy are threaded throughout their correspondence.[127] Where we do have correspondence, Newman's open and frank remarks demonstrate the level of trust St. John enjoyed. An example of Newman working through his own struggles with assent to the dogma is found in a letter to St. John on 27 July 1870. This letter was marked as confidential. St. John was instructed at the end of the letter to either keep the letter or return it to Newman. Newman wrote:

> I have been thinking over the subject which just now gives you and me, with thousands of others, who care for religion, so much concern. First, till better advised, nothing shall make me say that a mere majority in a council, as opposed to a moral unanimity, in itself creates an obligation to receive its dogmatic decrees. This is a point of history and precedent; ... but I do not, cannot see, that a majority in the present council can of itself rule its own sufficiency, without such external authority.[128]

---

[125] *Apologia*, 252 [353].

[126] Ibid., 252 [353].

[127] For example, in a letter from St. John (in Rome) to Newman, dated 4 May 1867, when St. John was in Rome on behalf of Newman, St. John wrote to Newman that Talbot was not trustworthy since "he is under Manning's thumb." A postscript to the letter, in response to a letter from Newman that came prior to St. John mailing the 4 May letter contains the following: "Well I suppose you with your monkey up will be angry with us for talking to Talbot at all. But what can we do? We must go on when we are in a groove. ... Pray for us hard that we may make no mistakes." *LD*, 23:221.

[128] *LD*, 25:167. Emphasis in the original.

Newman then discussed the five means by which he could be "brought under obligation of receiving a doctrine as a dogma, that is, as part of the faith necessary for salvation," and which of these five held the most weight for him.[129] This letter illustrates the degree to which Newman trusted St. John with his interior theological struggles over papal infallibility.

While Newman's means of assenting to the dogma are intriguing in their own right, his personal wrestling with the issue cannot be abstracted from the anguished questions of spiritual disciples which served to shape and focus his attention. Newman's relationships with Maria Rosina Giberne and Emily Bowles exemplify this facet of his experience.

Through Newman's influence, Maria Rosina Giberne (1802-1885) rejected her family's evangelical position and became an enthusiastic Tractarian.[130] Newman accompanied her to the interview which led to her reception into the Catholic Church.[131]

In August 1868, Newman wrote to Giberne regarding what he called the "sad confusion" of the Anglicans, especially how English Catholics were instructing potential converts about the issue of papal infallibility. In this letter he wrote regarding Edward Bouverie Pusey's potential conversion: that if the evangelicals did challenge and convict him, in an ecclesiastical court, concerning three specific issues,[132] he will have gone "a good way towards leaving the Anglican Church." On papal infallibility Newman wrote:

> I should not despair of him, if English Catholics did not make it a point of faith for him to believe in the infallibility of the Pope. This bothers him. Of course if

---

[129] These are that the dogma is: 1) clearly demonstrated in Scripture, 2) is found "in primitive and uninterrupted tradition," 3) is high probability as reasoned from Scripture or tradition, 4) contains no definite contradiction in Scripture and is defined by "a legitimate Superior," or 5) "the consideration that the merciful Lord would, not care so little for His elect people, the multitude of the faithful as to allow their visible Head and such a large number of Bishops to lead them into error, and an error so great and so serious, if an error." Newman then stated that, based upon this consideration, he was led to "accept the dogma as a dogma, indirectly indeed from the council, but not as from a council, but as from the Pope and a large collection of bishops." Thus, Newman states that his assent to the dogma was not based on the council's pronouncement, but "the Pope's self-assertion." *LD*, 25:167-8.

[130] Sugg, *Ever Yours Affly*, 34.

[131] Giberne was received into the Roman Catholic Church in 1845. Ibid., 79. Giberne accepted the call to religious life as a nun and was in the Autun Order of the Visitation convent when she died. Windle, *Who's Who*, 128.

[132] "1. that Anglicans may not hold, the Eucharist Sacrifice—2. the *Objective* real presence—3 the duty of adoring the host." *LD*, 24:128.

the Ecumenical Council defined the Pope's Infallibility, that will be another thing, (not that I think it will) but, as things are, it is quite open to hold the Pope not infallible—but the Archbishop, Ward, etc etc. are clamorous on the point, and, while they are creating much uneasy feeling among lay converts, and unsettling their minds, they are hindering the chances of such as Pusey joining the church.[133]

In February 1870, Newman wrote to her that he was glad not to be at the council since he did not consider himself a theologian, and that she should accept this and not be annoyed about it.[134] Newman continued this pastoral tone in his 27 July 1870 letter to her which stated:

I feel how you will be disappointed, but our good God is trying all of us with disappointment and sorrow just now; —I allude to what has taken place at Rome—who of us would not have rejoiced if the Fathers of the Council had one and all felt it their duty to assent to the infallibility of the Holy Father? but a gloom falls upon one, when it is decreed with so very large a number of dissentient voices. It looks as if our Great Lord were in some way displeased with us. Indeed the look of public matters generally is very threatening, and we need the prayers of all holy souls, of all good nuns, to avert the evils which seem coming upon the earth. ... You will have to offer up this disappointment to our good Lord, and I shall give three Masses to your intention upon it.[135]

This letter was from the same day as the letter to St. John, quoted above, in which Newman had written of his own angst over the lack of unanimity. The context of the letter to his *fides Achates* seems clear; he had received indication of Giberne's distress and he had to first complete his own soul searching before offering spiritual guidance. Thus, while his personal wrestling was quite clear in the letter to St. John, his own concerns were not displayed for his disciple. To Giberne, his response was a recognition of her feelings, a call to obedience and prayer, and a promise of spiritual support to her in her struggles.

Newman was also a regular correspondent with Emily Bowles (1818-c 1904), sister of Oxford Movement convert Frederick Bowles.[136] While much of their correspondence dealt with her translation work as well as her poetry and prose, in September 1869 she "was anxious to hear Newman's opinion about the

---

[133] *LD*, 24:128. Emphasis in the original.
[134] *LD*, 24:212.
[135] *LD*, 25:116-7.
[136] Emily Bowles was received into the Catholic Church in 1843. Gondon, *Conversion de cent cinquante ministres anglicans*, 100. She served as the Oratory School's matron for a time. Windle, *Who's Who*, 90.

controversy over papal infallibility and its definition." In her *Memorials of John Henry Newman*, she reported that in September 1869, "... Newman insisted that even if the doctrine were defined 'in the face of the utmost protest of a large minority to be of faith then you will know that it is by the overruling of the Holy Ghost. God cannot leave His Church." To her concern that this doctrine could cause her faith to falter and to forsake the Church, Newman replied: "You will not. ... We all must go through that gate of obedience, simply as obedience. And mind, if the dogma is declared, you will find that it will not make the slightest difference to you."[137]

However, after the definition, Bowles pressed Newman to "take up the cause of the bishops of the Minority." In a letter dated 1 August 1870, she wrote:

> I enclose—after much consideration—a letter I had from Aubrey de Vere ... Mr Monsell has been most anxious you should put forth some letter on the definition of the Infallibility. There is an immense amount of unhappiness and discouragement about it. ... Still I suppose this definition might have been much worse?[138]

Newman's 12 August reply was, in a letter marked confidential, "I could not undertake the thing. It is above me. At present I wait to see what the minority will do. If they do nothing, I shall consider it a moral unanimity in favour of the definition."[139]

Newman encouraged and counseled those he mentored during days that were difficult and pastorally challenging. However, while he sought to comfort and guide those he discipled to remain in the life of the church, he had already complained to Ullathorne that the dogma was being forced upon the church by "an aggressive insolent faction." In his 28 January 1870 letter to Bishop Ullathorne, Newman wrote that this faction had been permitted to "'make the heart of the just to mourn.'" By listening to "the flattery of a clique of Jesuits, Redemptorists, and converts," the Holy See had stirred up considerable pastoral concerns for those tending to the faithful.[140]

---

[137] *LD*, 24:341, n. 1. This is connected in the text to a letter from Newman to Bowles, dated 29 September 1869.

[138] *LD*, 25:178, n. 3. Emphasis in the original.

[139] *LD*, 25:178.

[140] Letter from Newman to Ullathorne, dated 28 January 1870. The relevant excerpt from the letter is as follows: "When we are all at rest, and have no doubts, and at least practically, not to say doctrinally, hold the Holy Father to be infallible, suddenly there is thunder in the clear sky, and we are told to prepare for something we know not what to try our faith we know not how. No impending danger is to be averted, but a great diffi-

The Impact of Oxford Movement Converts on the Debates from the Periphery

Those who stand out in the historical narrative of the infallibility debates, as with any historical event, did not act alone. They were influenced, aided, agitated, and hindered by others who are typically forgotten in the narrative. Some Oxford Movement converts entered into the periphery of the debates directly through their writings, such as Wilberforce, Dalgairns, Faber, Knox, and Mivart. Their influence can be gauged by the reception of their work. Two of these men, both from the English Oratory, produced works that caught the attention of Rome. Faber's work, directed at personal piety, was published in three languages ten years before the council and approved by the Vatican. Knox's work provided a concise and timely summary of the neo-ultramontane position that, in an expanded second edition, continued to be of use to the neo-ultramontane cause after the council. Both of these works, as well as Dalgairns's writings, emerged from the neo-ultramontane ethos of the London Oratory. These publications, which range in genre, demonstrate that the spiritualities of the Birmingham and London Oratories were significantly different, especially on matters touching papal authority.

Faber's book, a demonstration of the London Oratory's spirituality, was reviewed in *The Tablet*, where another Oxford Movement convert, Robert Ornsby, was an assistant editor. Publishing summaries and reviews of works on both sides of the debate, as well as providing a venue for publishing essays, was an important function of these periodicals. Through the work of converts, even the

---

culty is to be created. Is this the proper work for an Ecumenical Council? As to myself, personally, please God, I do not expect any trial at all; but I cannot help suffering with the various souls which are suffering, and I look with anxiety at the prospect of having to defend decisions, which may be not difficult to my private judgment, but may be most difficult to maintain logically in the face of historical facts. What have we done to be treated, as the faithful never were treated before? When has definition of doctrine *de fide* been a luxury of devotion, and not a stern painful necessity? Why should an aggressive insolent faction be allowed to 'make the heart of the just to mourn, whom the Lord has not made sorrowful?' Why can't we be let alone, when we have pursued peace, and thought no evil? I assure you, my dear Lord, some of the truest minds are driven one way and another, and do not know where to rest their feet; one day determining to give up all theology as a bad job, and recklessly to believe henceforth almost that the Pope is impeccable; at another tempted to believe all the worst which a book like Janus [Döllinger's *The Pope and the Council*] says; others doubting about the capacity possessed by Bishops, drawn from all corners of the earth, to judge what is fitting for European society, and then again angry with the Holy See for listening to the flattery of a clique of Jesuits, Redemptorists, and converts." *LD*, 25:18.

liberal Catholic voice had an opportunity to engage the debates through the *Weekly Register* and *The Rambler*.

Some Oxford Movement converts, positioned as they were to influence major decisions behind closed doors, changed English Catholicism. Coffin, part of the London Oratory whose commitments and spirituality led him to an even more neo-ultramontane order, influenced the debates through his recommendation of Manning to replace Wiseman as archbishop of Westminster. Talbot, who was a young Oxford movement convert, moved from the periphery of the Oxford Movement to a highly privileged insider position in the Roman Curia and exercised his influence to promote a neo-ultramontane agenda. The fact that Talbot was incapacitated by mental illness does not detract from his influence and impact on the debates of the 1860s.

Moreover, it is important to consider how personal relationships among the Oxford Movement converts affected the key historical figures' doctrinal positions and ways of articulating those positions. While Oakeley's impact upon the stances taken by Newman and Manning is uncertain, the fact that he successfully navigated the politics of the debates to retain friendships across the divide between liberal and ultramontane views of authority is important to note. It indicates that additional research into the influence across the sides of the debate would aid in understanding the complexity of the events leading up to the council. The unalloyed affection between Newman and St. John appears to have been the exception, but yield crucial insights into the struggles over papal infallibility. These men did not operate in a world without laity or women. Through their questions and insights, Giberne and Bowles, as intelligent, insightful women engaged in the religious debates of the times, and provided opportunities for Newman to work out aspects of his position and means of articulating that position. Friendships and pastoral care provided means of influence from the periphery. Other connections, such as Faber's position within the Birmingham Oratory, may have been a source of agitation that helped clarify opposing positions.

Others influenced by the Oxford Movement, such as Mivart, were less connected to the inner circles of English Catholicism, yet strove to make their voices heard. Mivart also exemplifies those who continued to struggle against the definition of infallibility after Vatican I.

Along with their passion for Catholicism, the converts entered Rome with a desire to use their Oxford training to refine their new religious commitments. While unified in their background as Tractarians and their desire to assimilate into Catholicism, they also shared an anxiety about spiritual and secular authority, as seen in their concern about Erastianism and the secular control of the Papal States. However, this passion and anxiety was manifested in a diversity of views and multiplicity of influence. Mgr Talbot's illness and Mivart's agonizing defiance of infallibility serve as poignant examples of the ways that the Oxford Movement converts, both men and women, poured themselves into Catholicism, using whatever means at their disposal to fight for the true expression of Roman Catholicism, as they came to understand it. This quest for Christian Truth, which had originally drawn them together in the Oxford Movement, remained the bond that enabled them to hold fast to their Catholic faith, despite their differences.

Appendix A: A Summary of People and Contributions

Name	Year of Conversion	Key Relationships	Order or Organization	Contribution	Regarding Papal Infallibility[1]
Bowles, Emily (1818-c 1904)	1843	Disciple of Newman	Oratory School matron	Corresponded with Newman; encouraged Newman to engage the debate after the definition of infallibility	Liberal
Capes, Frederick (1816-1888)	1845	Brother of John Moore		Editor and founder (1848) of *The Rambler*	Liberal*
Capes, John Moore (1813-1889)	1845	Brother of Frederick		Part proprietor of *The Rambler*	Liberal*
Coffin, Robert Aston (1819-1885)	1845 (two months after Newman)	Manning's confessor from 1853	English Oratory (London) Redemptorist	Recommended Manning as archbishop of Westminster to Pius IX in 1865	Neo-ultramontane

[1] Those who worked as editors for publications with a specific orientation have been assumed to hold to that orientation. These have been marked with an asterisk.

189

Name	Year of Conversion	Key Relationships	Order or Organization	Contribution	Regarding Papal Infallibility
Faber, Frederick William (1814-1861)	1845 (received with Knox)	Strained relationship with Newman over management of the London Oratory	English Oratory (London)	*Devotion to the Pope* (1861)	Neo-ultramontane
Giberne, Maria Rosina (?-1885)	1845	Disciple of Newman	Autun Order of the Visitation	Received pastoral care from Newman regarding papal infallibility	Liberal
Knox, Thomas Francis (1822-1882)	1845 (received with Faber)	Devoted to Newman	English Oratory (London)	*When Does the Church Speak Infallibly? or, The Nature and Scope of the Church's Teaching Office* (1867)	Neo-ultramontane
Northcote, James Spencer (1821-1907)	1846 (the year after his wife)	Worked with the Capes brothers	Priest (1855)	Editor of *The Rambler* (1853-54)	Liberal*
Oakeley, Frederick (1802-1880)	1845	Friends with Newman, Manning, and very close friend of Ward	Parish priest and Chapter canon under Manning	Friendships maintained in spite of views on papal infallibility	Undetermined
Ornsby, Robert (1820-1889)	1847	Married J. D. Dalgairns's sister; Friend of Newman		Editor of *The Tablet* from 1847-1854	Neo-ultramontane

Name	Year of Conversion	Key Relationships	Order or Organization	Contribution	Regarding Papal Infallibility
St. John, Ambrose (1815-1876)	1843 (one month prior to Newman)	Newman's closest friend; curate to H. Wilberforce then Newman during Anglican years	English Oratory (Birmingham)	Newman's closest friend	Liberal
Talbot, George (1816-1886)	1843	Manning's curial collaborator Newman's bane	Curia (1850-1869)	Confidant of Pius IX, liaison for Manning, impediment for Newman	Neo-ultramontane
Wilberforce, Henry William (1807-1873)	1850	Brother to R. Wilberforce; close friend of Newman		Founded the *Weekly Register* and editor (1854 to 1863) contributor for *Dublin Review* after 1863	Liberal*
Wilberforce, Robert Isaac (1802-1857)	1853	Brother of H. Wilberforce; close friend of Newman; closer friend of brother-in-law Manning		*A Sketch of the History of Erastianism* (1851)	Undetermined

191

Appendix B: Correspondence between Newman and Talbot in May 1867

The following is the majority of the content of Newman's letter to Talbot on 26 May 1867:

> I know you have a good heart; I know you did me good service in the Achilli matter—and you got me a relic of St. Athanasius from Venice, which I account a great treasure; and for these reasons I have been the more bewildered at your having of late years taken so strong a part against me, without (I may say) any real ground whatever; or rather, I should have been bewildered were it not that, for now as many as thirty four years, it has been my lot to be misrepresented and opposed without any intermission by one set of persons or another. Certainly, I have desiderated in you, as in many others, that charity which thinketh no evil, and have looked in vain for that considerateness and sympathy which is due to a man who has passed his life in attempting to subserve the cause and interests of religion, and who, for the very reason that he has written so much, must, from the frailty of our common nature, have said things which had better not have been said, or left out complements and explanations of what he has said, which had better have been added.
>
> I am an old man, perhaps within a few years of my death, and you can now neither do me good nor harm. I have never been otherwise than well-disposed towards you. When you first entered the Holy Father's immediate service, I used to say a Mass for you the first day of every month, that you might be prospered at your important post; and now I shall say Mass for you seven times, beginning with this week, when we are keeping the Feast of St Philip, begging him at the same time to gain for you a more equitable judgment of us and a kinder feeling towards us on the part of our friends, than we have of late years experienced.[1]

On 31May 31 1867, Talbot's reply was that Newman had been misinformed, possibly by some "mischief makers ... whose chief occupation seems to be to make feuds amongst friends by reporting to one what the other may have said of him." Talbot could not approve of some of Newman's later writings and some of his actions, but goes on to say that,

---

[1] *LD*, 23:241-2.

a certain school in England have done you much harm by making many believe that you sympathized with their detestable views. You have also been more injured by your friends than your enemies. When I was in England three years ago, I heard some of them quoting your name in opposition to the Authority of the Holy See. I remarked that there was a party forming of what are called liberal Catholics, who wished to place you at their heard [sic], in preference of professing filial devotion for the Vicar of Christ, and a due veneration for the Chair of S. Peter. ... For twenty years I was your warm admirer and defender, and should be delighted to be so still, but when I found that there was a dangerous party rising in England, who quoted your name, I was obliged to modify my views, and stand up for Ecclesiastical authority in preference of worshipping great intellectual gifts.

As for yourself personally my love and affection has never varied. I may have lately criticized your public acts, as I have done those of many others of my friends, but this is no reason why any coldness should exist between friends who are all working for the same great end ... .[2]

---

[2] *LD*, 23:242. Emphasis in the original.

DEVELOPMENT IN THE SERVICE OF RECTIFICATION: JOHN HENRY NEWMAN'S UNDERSTANDING OF THE *SCHOLA THEOLOGORUM*

MICHAEL J. G. PAHLS

By the year 1874, reception of *Pastor Aeternus* was all but accomplished—even among those bishops who had maintained their opposition to the dogma of papal infallibility up to the casting of the final ballot. Two bishops who had voted *non placet* on July 18, 1870 affirmed their assent to the definition immediately following the vote. Others drafted similar expressions in the days and months immediately following.[1] Characteristic of these early reversals of opinion among the anti-infallibilist minority was that of the French bishop, Félix-François-Joseph Barthélémy de Las Cases (1805-84), who classically protested,

> As long as the Council had not spoken I remained firm in my conviction; on the morrow of the definition God gave me the grace to be able to say in all truth, in the depth and the calm of my faith: 'Today, I believe in infallibility as much as I disbelieved in it yesterday.'[2]

Only a few withheld formal reception and promulgation of the dogma beyond 1873.[3]

---

[1] The standard account of the First Vatican Council in English is Dom Cuthbert Butler's *The Vatican Council, 1869–1870: Based on Bishop Ullathorne's Letters*, ed. Christopher Butler (Westminster: Newman, 1962). See also the accounts of James Hennesy, *The First Council of the Vatican: The American Experience* (New York: Herder and Herder, 1963); Roger Aubert, *Vatican I* (Paris: Éditions de l'Orante, 1964); Klaus Schatz, *Vaticanum I, 1869-1870*, 3 vols (Paderborn: F. Schöningh, 1992).

[2] Johannes Dominicus Mansi, *Sacrorum conciliorum nova et amplissima collectio* Graz: Akademische Druck u. Verlagsanstalt, 1961) 53:1042C-1042D. Quoted in Margaret O'Gara, *Triumph in Defeat: Infallibility, Vatican I, and the French Minority Bishops* (Washington, D.C.: Catholic University of America Press, 1988), 190.

[3] Bishop MacQuaid of Rochester, New York, for example, announced his adherence to the dogma in 1875, but with the faint protest: "[T]o the last I opposed it; because somehow or other it was in my head that the Bishops ought to be consulted." Frederick J.

This task being largely accomplished, church leaders faced the rather more difficult task of defending the council against its Protestant and nationalist detractors. The stakes could not have been greater, as the subsequent history makes clear. Fearing the disloyalty of its Roman Catholic citizenry, whose consciences were thought to be captive to the policies of an ultramontane papacy, the German government made infallibility an occasion for its ideology of *Kulturkampf*. The Austrian government reacted in a similar manner, annulling its concordat with Rome. Catholics on the continent suffered grave social and political disenfranchisement as a result.[4] Similar fears were present in England where the deep cultural memory of Roman Catholic threats to the crown were rehearsed annually on Guy Fawke's Day.[5]

To stave off the boiling over of hostilities, occasioned by Prime Minister William Gladstone's (1809-1898) published suspicions of English Catholic loyalty in 1874, John Henry Newman (1801-1890) composed a rejoinder in the form of a letter addressed to Henry Fitzalan-Howard, the fifteenth Duke of Norfolk (1847-1917).[6] In the letter Newman took up Gladstone's charges one by one, allaying fears and correcting misunderstandings. By this he hoped to put the best possible face on the new Roman dogma and mitigate the more extreme agenda being spearheaded by Henry Edward Manning (1808-1892).

Zwierlein, *The Life and Letters of Bishop McQuaid*, 3 vols (Rochester: The Art Print Shop, 1925-1927) 2:63.

[4] Ibid.

[5] Celebrated every 5 November, Guy Fawkes Day marks the anniversary of the 1605 Gunpowder Plot—a conspiracy on the part of English Catholics to blow up the English Parliament and assassinate King James I.

[6] Gladstone's article, "Ritual and Ritualism," was published in an October 1874 edition of the *Contemporary Review* 24 (1874): 663-81. It dealt primarily with controversies over ritualism in Anglicanism, but the controversy gave Gladstone the opportunity to decry "the effort to Romanise the Church and people of England." Later in the article, he gestured to the conversion of long time political associate, Lord Ripon, to Roman Catholicism in September 1874 and wrote, "no one can become her [the Roman Church's] convert without renouncing his moral and mental freedom, and placing his civil loyalty and duty at the mercy seat of another; and when she has equally repudiated modern thought and ancient history." *LD*, 27:122, n. 3.

Gladstone later repeated and expanded on these charges in his 1874 pamphlet, "The Vatican Decrees in their Bearing on Civil Allegiance." The episode up to the publication of Newman's "Letter to the Duke of Norfolk" is ably chronicled by John R. Page, *What Will Dr. Newman Do? John Henry Newman and Papal Infallibility 1865-1875* (Collegeville, MN: Michael Glazier/Liturgical Press, 1994), 249-318. The Gladstone pamphlet and Newman's letter appear together in Alvan Ryan, ed., *Newman and Gladstone: The Vatican Decrees* (Notre Dame, IN: University of Notre Dame Press, 1962).

Most interesting in Newman's apologetic for the council, however, was an appeal to the subsequent interpretive work of theologians, arguing that they would establish the true sense of the council's definition. In his dedicatory remarks, Newman wrote the following:

> I deeply grieve that Mr. Gladstone has felt it his duty to speak with such extraordinary severity of our Religion and of ourselves. I consider he has committed himself to a representation of ecclesiastical documents which will not hold, and to a view of our position in the country which we have neither deserved nor can be patient under. None but the *Schola Theologorum* is competent to determine the force of Papal and Synodal utterances, and the exact interpretation of them is a work of time. But so much may be safely said of the decrees which have lately been promulgated, and of the faithful who have received them, that Mr. Gladstone's account, both of them and of us, is neither trustworthy nor charitable.[7]

While appearing quite infrequently and comparatively late in his writings, Newman's conception of the *schola theologorum* contributes significantly to his overall understanding of doctrinal development and, perhaps surprisingly, supplies us with a helpful interpretive perspective on Newman's prior work as a leader of the Oxford Movement.[8] This essay examines the scattered references to the *schola theologorum* and clarifies Newman's intended sense. I also consider Newman's prior contributions as a Tractarian, particularly displayed in the famous *Tract 90*, and highlight the manner in which members of the Oxford faculty functioned as a quasi-magisterial *schola*. Finally, I conclude with some reflections on how Newman's Anglican style of "development-by-rectification" emerge in the reception *Pastor Aeternus* by Vatican II.

---

[7] John Henry Newman, "Letter to the Duke of Norfolk," in *Certain Difficulties Felt By Anglicans in Catholic Teaching Considered*, 2 vols (London: Longmans, Green, and Co., 1900), 2:176.

[8] I acknowledge here my grateful indebtedness to the prior work of Paul Misner's prior work on Newman's conception of the *schola theologorum* in his *Papacy and Development: Newman and the Primacy of the Pope*, Studies in the History of Christian Traditions (Leiden: Brill, 1976). Professor Misner was also quite helpful in his suggestive formal responses to an earlier form of this essay presented at a meeting of the American Catholic Historical Association in 2007. His original essay treats Newman's thought on the subject only after his reception into the Roman Communion. While I accept many of his conclusions, I also wish to establish some important lines of continuity with his earlier Anglican period.

Newman's Conception of the Schola Theologorum

References to the importance of theologians and to the *schola theologorum* appear in the correspondence of Newman as early as 1863, but a proper context for those remarks was established in his preface to the third edition of the *Lectures on the Prophetical Office of the Church*, published in 1877.[9] The lectures themselves were very much the product of Newman's Anglican period, having been originally composed between 1834 and 1836, and substantially revised for publication in 1837. Significantly, the Catholic Newman later republished them without alteration, except for the added preface.[10] There Newman sketched out a fundamental ecclesiology patterned on the *triplex munus Christi*—the "threefold office"—of Christ as prophet, priest, and king. Within this scheme, the church as the mystical body of Christ manifests itself in three more or less distinct offices: the prophetical office of theology, the sacerdotal office of the ministerial priesthood, and the regal office of the ruling hierarchy. The text demonstrates his high regard for the place of theology, and for the way that he functionally subordinated the latter two to the former:

> I say, then, Theology is the fundamental and regulating principle of the whole Church system. It is commensurate with Revelation, and Revelation is the initia and essential idea of Christianity. It is the formal cause, the expression, of the Prophetical Office, and as being such, has created both the Regal Office and the Sacerdotal. And it has in a certain sense a power of jurisdiction over those offices, as being its own creations, theologians being ever in request and in employment in keeping within bounds both the political and popular elements in the Church's constitution,—elements which are far more congenial than itself to the human mind, are far more liable to excess and corruption, and are ever

---

[9] *The Via Media of the Anglican Church, Volume 1: Lectures on the Prophetical Office of the Church* (London: Longmans, Green, and Company, 1891), xv-xciv.

[10] Of the *Lectures*, Newman wrote, "This work employed me for three years, from the beginning of 1834 to the end of 1836, and was published in 1837. It was composed, after a careful consideration and comparison of the principal Anglican divines of the seventeenth century. It was first written in the shape of controversial correspondence with a learned French Priest; then it was re-cast, and delivered in Lectures at St. Mary's: lastly, with considerable retrenchments and additions, it was re-written for publication." *Apologia,* 67 [186]. Cf. Amelia Fleming, "The Role of the Theologian, *Donum Veritatis* and Newman," *Irish Theological Quarterly* 69 (2004): 276. For a close examination of Newman's revision of these lectures in the summer of 1837, see: Kenneth L. Parker, "Newman's Individualistic Use of the Caroline Divines in the *Via Media*," in *Discourse and Context: An Interdisciplinary Study of John Henry Newman,* ed. Gerard Magill (Edwardsville, IL: Southern Illinois University Press, 1993), 33-42.

struggling to liberate themselves from those restraints which are in truth necessary for their well-being.[11]

Against this backdrop, other witnesses to his understanding of the *schola theologorum* become intelligible.

In a letter dated 9 November 1865, Newman responded to a question addressed to him by Henry Nutcombe Oxenham regarding his precise understanding of the category. Oxenham was apparently perplexed by Newman's prior advocacy of the *schola* as "holding the Church together." Newman clarified by writing that the *schola theologorum* is in one sense a "generalization, for the decisions of theologians throughout the world."[12] On the other hand, however, the term has a more immediate, incarnational sense. He wrote that theologians exhibit a "natural tendency to collect into centers" and that these tend to manifest "a distinct character all their own, severally."[13] Newman then cited the competing patristic schools of Alexandria and Antioch as examples of his meaning and rather surprisingly admitted that various of these distinctive *scholae* were *not* represented in the *schola* of Rome.[14]

Four years later, Newman seemed to see the *schola theologorum* as exercising a ministry of subsequent clarification and even rectification of papal and conciliar decrees. In his 20 October 1869 letter to Mrs. Magdalene Helbert, he invoked the Augustinian maxim, "*Securus judicat orbis terrarum*"—glossed by Newman as "The Christian commonweath judges without misgiving"—and described the *schola* as serving the cause of the consent of the faithful.[15] It does this, not by simple promulgation of the given decree, but by clarifying its proper interpretation in dialogue with the faithful who assent to and accept it. As Newman wrote,

> The Christian commonwealth is one organized body—from time to time local disturbances rise in it—branches of it rise up separately from the rest, and claim to be heard in matters of discipline or doctrine—they appeal to the Fathers—so did the Donatists, so did the Arians, the Monophysites, the Protestants, the Anglicans—but the Christian State, Commonwealth, Kingdom judicat securus, has the right, the power, the certitude of deciding the rights and the wrongs of the matter.[16]

---

[11] Newman, *Lectures on the Prophetical Office of the Church*, xlvii-xlviii.
[12] Newman to Henry Nutcombe Oxenham, 9 November 1865, *LD*, 22:98.
[13] Ibid, 99.
[14] Ibid.
[15] Newman to Magdalene Helbert, 20 October 1869, *LD*, 24:354.
[16] Ibid., 354-5.

Newman then applied this principle to the impending First Vatican Council:

> How shall we know that the coming Council is a true Council—but by the after assent and acceptance of it on the part of that Catholic organization which is lineally descended, as one whole, from the first ages? —How can we interpret the decisions of that Council, how the Pope's decisions in any age, except by the *schola theologorum*, the great Catholic school of divines dispersed all over the earth?[17]

While Newman's understanding of the *schola theologorum* is uniquely expansive for its time, one may not construe his view as embracing a broader confessional scope than that of the Roman Communion. Indeed, Newman was quite parochial in his conception of who counted as part of his Christian "commonwealth" and *schola*. As his 1869 letter to Mrs. Helbert illustrated, "I put the validity of the Council upon its reception by the *orbis terrarum*, of which Greece [i.e. the Orthodox churches] and England [i.e. Protestant Anglicanism] are no part."[18]

Newman could not have known in 1869 how *Pastor Aeternus* would be explicitly worded to curtail full conciliar or gallican construals of the *sensus fidelium*—definitions of the Roman pontiff being "irreformable *of themselves*, and not by the consent of the church."[19] However, this does not mean that he was unaware of the debate. Indeed, Newman was pressured a decade earlier to nuance some of his more ambitious references to "consulting the faithful," published in a May 1859 issue of the *Rambler*.[20] In that article, he explained that the Catholic faithful represented the voice of the infallible Church and that this should be consulted when defining a dogma.[21] This article brought him into immediate conflict with John Gillow, Catholic professor of theology at Ushaw. Gillow objected that this construal of the relationship between the magisterium and the faithful would result in the faithful holding a kind of veto power over a

---

[17] Ibid., 355.

[18] Ibid.

[19] "First Dogmatic Constitution on the Church of Christ (*Pastor Aeternus*)" in *The Sources of Catholic Dogma,* ed. H. Denzinger, trans. R. Deferrari (Fitzwilliam, NH: Loretto, 2002), §1839, 457.

[20] The episode which was provoked by the May 1859 article has been chronicled in the introduction to *On Consulting the Faithful in Matters of Doctrine,* ed. J. Coulson (London: Geoffrey Chapman, 1961). Newman's July 1859 response to John Gillow as well as his "Appendix V: The Orthodoxy of the Faithful During the Supremacy of Arianism" from the 1871 edition of *The Arians of the Fourth Century* were reproduced in that volume.

[21] Ibid., 63.

given definition. Newman wrote again in July 1859 to clarify that his use of the word was intended as an inquiry into a matter of *fact*, rather than an appeal for *judgment*. Consultation of the faithful then, is an inquiry into the *sensus* rather than the *consensus* of the church.[22] This being said, the general thrust of his opinion of the *schola's* ministry, as an instrument of clarification and rectification in subsequent dialogue with *sensus fidelium,* was little modified by late 1871. On 10 December 1871, Newman described the *schola theologorum* as a quasi court of appeal: "All these are questions for the theological school—and the theologians will, as time goes on, settle the force and wording of the dogma, just as the courts of law solve the meaning and bearing of Acts of Parliament."[23] What Newman published in 1877, therefore, represented a *considered* opinion, developed in dialogue and dispute.

Newman's Concept in Historical Practice

Because Newman believed that the *schola theologorum* was extant throughout the entire history of the church, he claimed the above referenced patristic schools as ancient instantiations of the phenomena described. More immediate to his own mind, however, were the various medieval schools of Europe—especially the theological faculty of Paris. These theologians were not simply teachers associated with a university but a "self-perpetuating corporation of scholars" with formally granted power to "read, teach, interpret Holy Scripture in Paris and everywhere on earth by Pope Nicholas I."[24] As a corporation, they functioned in their own day with a canonical teaching authority and represented one of the primary incarnations of the Catholic magisterium prior to the "second Roman centralization" following the Council of Trent.[25] Gres-Gayer chronicled the manner in which these French doctors even made official doctrinal pronouncements and issued theological censures and condemnations as cases warranted.[26] Because faculties of this type constituted an "atemporal body, a repository of the authentic tradition of their Church," their "*avis doctrinal* was to be more than an opinion or a particular judgment of authorized specialists; it was to be an official utterance, consistent with previous pronouncements."[27]

---

[22] Newman wrote, "A physician consults the pulse of his patient; but not in the same sense in which his patient consults *him.*" Ibid., 54.

[23] Newman to William Henry Cope, 10 December 1871, *LD* 25:447.

[24] Jacques M. Gres-Gayer, "The Magisterium of the Faculty of Theology of Paris in the Seventeenth Century," *Theological Studies* 53 (1992): 425.

[25] Ibid., 424.

[26] Ibid., 449.

[27] Ibid.

It was this historical praxis that led Newman to conceive the *shola theologorum* as a teaching authority in the church. On 26 March 1863, Newman praised the liberty of theological debate among the medieval Parisian doctors, writing of the "free and fair play" of their theological discourse:

> ... disputants were not made to feel the bit in their mouths at every other word they spoke, but could move their limbs freely and expatiate at will. Then, when they went wrong, a stronger and truer intellect set them down—and, as time went on, if the dispute got perilous, and a controversialist obstinate, then at length Rome interfered—at length, not at first. Truth is wrought out by many minds working together freely.[28]

In the *Apologia* as well, Newman extolled this medieval precedent as an example of a way ecclesiastical authority and liberty of theological exploration may be harmonized:

> Perhaps a local teacher, or a doctor in some local school, hazards a proposition, and a controversy ensues. It smoulders or burns in one place, no one interposing; Rome simply lets it alone. Then it comes before a Bishop; or some priest, or some professor in some other seat of learning takes it up; and then there is a second stage of it. Then it comes before a University, and it may be condemned by the theological faculty. So the controversy proceeds year after year, and Rome is still silent. An appeal perhaps is next made to a seat of authority inferior to Rome; and then at last after a long while it comes before the supreme power. Meanwhile, the question has been ventilated and turned over and over again, and viewed on every side of it, and authority is called upon to pronounce a decision, which has already been arrived at by reason.[29]

In his letter to Robert Ornsby, Newman also mourned the abeyance of this procedure, especially after the French Revolution. He bemoaned the fact that by his own day, an "individual thinker in France, England, or Germany is brought into immediate collision with the most sacred authorities of the Divine Polity."[30]

This expression of regret suggests a more recent example of Newman's idea of the *schola theologorum*. Perhaps his work to establish the Oxford Movement as the authoritative voice of a rectified Anglicanism provided the best exemplar his vision for how a *schola* might function—an example his could not invoke. This is not to say that Oxford was an ideal situation for him. Indeed, the particular failures of the Tractarian Movement seemed to have led to a partial

---

[28] Newman to Robert Ornsby, 26 March 1863, *LD,* 20:425-6.

[29] *Apologia,* 238-9 [341].

[30] Newman to Robert Ornsby, 20:426.

moderation of his views. Nevertheless, the Catholic Newman's understanding of the *schola theologorum* bear striking similarity to the movement that Newman helped to lead at Oxford from 1833 to 1841.

The Oxford Movement as an Instantiation of Newman's Schola Theologorum

Newman dated the inception of the Tractarian Movement from John Keble's Assize sermon on national apostasy, delivered 14 July 1833.[31] From there began a series of meetings in the rectory of Hugh James Rose with John Keble, Newman, Hurrell Froude, William Palmer, and Arthur Perceval in attendance.[32] The immediate goal was a defense of Anglicanism against the precipitous loss of identity they perceived to be imminent in acts of the British Parliament from 1828 to 1833.[33] They sought to defend what they believed to be the two pillars of Anglicanism: the doctrine of apostolic succession and the integrity of the *Book of Common Prayer*. This resulted in the publication of *Tracts for The Times* between 1833 and 1841.[34]

Although the ninety tracts were the product of eighteen different authors, all but those by Edward Pusey were published anonymously under the corporate moniker, "Members of the University."[35] Their intended audience was alterna-

---

[31] *Apologia*, 43 [162].

[32] Ibid., 44 [163-4].

[33] The five years from 1828-1833 witnessed a perfect storm for Anglicanism. Evangelicals in the Church of England had produced Methodism and revitalized other nonconforming sects in the growing urban population centers. Coupled with the growing unrest among Irish Catholics, this produced an overwhelming wave of religious dissent, resulting in the 1828 repeal of the seventeenth-century Test and Corporation Acts. The Roman Catholic Relief Act followed in 1829. These laws had precluded non-Anglicans from holding public office and thereby from participating in parliamentary decisions concerning the Church of England—including decisions related to the liturgy of the *Book of Common Prayer*. The effect of these reforms was soon made clear by parliament's passage of the 1833 Irish Church Temporalities Bill, suppressing two archbishoprics and eight bishoprics in the Church of Ireland. For a fuller discussion see: Owen Chadwick, *The Victorian Church: An Ecclesiastical History of England*, 2 vols (New York: Oxford, 1966), 1:7-158.

[34] *Tracts for the Times by Members of the University of Oxford* (London: Rivington, 1834-1841).

[35] According to Frank M. Turner, Newman was author of thirty tracts. Keble had eight; Pusey, who insisted on initialing the his tracts, seven; John William Bowden, five. Thomas Keble and Benjamin Harrison penned four apiece. Froude, A.P. Perceval, and Isaac Williams each wrote three. Other contributors included Alfred Menzies, C.P. Eden, R.F. Wilson, Anthony Buller, Henry Manning, George Prevost, and Charles Marriott. Additional tracts were reprints of writings by past Anglican divines. *John Henry New-*

tively the common membership (*ad Populum*), clergy (*ad Clerum*), and theologians of the Church of England (*ad scholas*) who would be moved by the unanimous theological opinions of the sound, and thoroughly Anglican, Oxford University.

As fervor, focused on Parliament, began to abate, the topical scope of the tracts expanded beyond narrow concerns for the episcopate and liturgy. Eventualy embracing a comprehensive vision for the future of the Church of England, the Tracts differentiated the Oxford Movement vision from that of the traditional high and low parties. The Tractarians came to be identified with a high view of the ordained ministry, a concern for the centrality of the church and catholic ecclesiastical orders, the insistence on the divine liturgy and the sacraments as necessary for saving grace, and a pronounced opposition to evangelicalism.[36] As principal author and editor of the Tracts, Newman appeared to be answerable only to Keble. Despite their reverence for the episcopate, the Tractarians remained deliberately independent of the oversight of bishops. As Frank Turner observed, "The Tractarians actually distrusted the bishops, repeatedly challenged them, and whenever possible ignored them."[37]

As a kind of next phase in their development, the Oxford men moved to perpetuate themselves and their vision of Anglicanism among the next generation of clergy. While Edward Pusey did not attend the meetings at Rose's Hadleigh rectory or participate in the initial planning of the tracts, he joined the Oxford Movement in late 1833.[38] Together they reasoned that they could "raise up a new generation of clergy," who would "be brought into a clearer and more complete Christianity." Even if the English Church suffered disestablishment and schism, the result would be a "purer" Church of England.[39]

In late 1835, therefore, Pusey founded the "Theological Society" which met on Friday evenings at his residence. At these meetings, theologians gathered to read and discuss papers. Many of the papers, including one by Isaac Williams on the subject of the "Reserve in Communicating Religious Knowledge," later ap-

---

man: The Challenge to Evangelical Religion (New Haven: Yale University Press, 2002), 165. The balance of this early history of the Tractarian Movement is dependent on Turner's painstaking chronicle.

[36] Ibid., 165. See also Michael J. McClymond, "'Continual Self-Contemplation': John Henry Newman's Critique Of Evangelicalism" in *Tradition and Pluralism: Essays in Honor of William M. Shea*, eds. K.L. Parker, P. Huff, and M.J.G. Pahls (Lanham, MD: University Press of America, 2008), 303-28.

[37] Turner, *Newman*, 165.

[38] Ibid., 96.

[39] Newman to E.B. Pusey, 24 January 1836, *LD,* 5:215.

peared among the Tracts.[40] Over time, younger candidates for ordination took up residence with Pusey. By February 1837, Newman was hosting meetings in his Oriel rooms and raising money for the housing of students not elected to full fellowships. In the summer of 1839, Newman made this development permanent by arranging the founding of a separate house of study rented in St. Aldate's. According to Turner,

> These as well as other informal gatherings, pastoral conversations, and after 1838, private confessions provided the institutional settings for the rise of 'Newmania' in Oxford, whereby men generally younger than Newman came to look to him for personal counsel, theological guidance, and ecclesiastical leadership."[41]

Such meetings, by which Newman and the others perpetuated their "corporation of scholars," continued until Newman's publication of *Tract 90* in 1841, which led to a deepening breach between Newman and Pusey, and the resulting dissolution of the Theological Society.[42]

Viewed synoptically, many features of the Oxford Movement create an impression that the Tractarians aspired to become a new "Parisian faculty" for the Church of England. There was a self-conscious promotion of the Oxford Faculty, an organized approach to recruitment and self-perpetuation, a preservation of independence from the episcopate, and the *Tracts for the Times* project itself as the authoritative voice of their *avis doctrinal*. Perhaps the best witness to Newman's intention, however, is the content of *Tract 90* itself. Subtitled "Remarks on Certain Passages of the Thirty-nine Articles," the work represented a concerted effort to clarify the proper identity of Anglicanism. He did this through a revised interpretation of Anglicanism's confessional document.

Issued in 1571 by a convocation of the clergy of the Church of England, the *Thirty-nine Articles* appear on cursory reading to consolidate the essential reforms of Protestantism—particularly those of continental Calvinism. Until Newman's gloss in *Tract 90*, they were commonly understood to exclude doctrines and forms of devotion associated with Roman Catholicism. After a period studying the history of the Monophysite heresy in 1839, however, Newman grew more and more disillusioned with his evangelical and Protestant inheri-

---

[40] *Tract 80* and *Tract 87* in particular.

[41] Turner, *Newman*, 96.

[42] Ibid., 376. Newman's renewal of the Society's work in his Littlemore community testifies to the value he placed on this project.

tance.[43] This break with Calvinism corresponded to a deepening affection for what he described as the *"Catholic teaching* of the early centuries." This was contrasted with the *"formal dogmas of Rome"* and what he called the "dominant errors" of *"actual popular beliefs and usages* sanctioned by Rome and the countries in communion with it."[44] As he continued to study the history of the church, he came to the conclusion that "Roman doctrine" as such was not subject to the condemnation of the *Thirty-nine Articles*, but only the "dominant errors" and "some of the formal dogmas."[45]

As the Tractarians extended their influence throughout the Church of England, their Anglo-Catholic party became a real power. This growth in popularity led many to conclude that the Oxford Movement was a Trojan horse leading students and younger clergy to Roman Catholicism.[46] Newman recalled this increasing opposition in the *Apologia*,

> "I had been enjoined, I think by my Bishop, to keep these men straight, and I had wished so to do: but their tangible difficulty was subscription to the Articles: and thus the question of the Articles came before me. It was thrown in our teeth; 'How can you manage to sign the Articles? they are directly against Rome.' 'Against Rome?' I made answer, 'What do you mean by Rome?' and then I proceeded to make distinctions ... ."[47]

In the 1877 preface to *Tract 90*, in the uniform edition of his works, Newman outlined how the *Thirty-nine Articles* themselves made possible these distinctions:

> This Tract was written under the conviction that the Anglican Thirty-nine Articles of Religion, of which it treated, were, when taken in their letter, so loosely worded, so incomplete in statement, and so ambiguous in their meaning, as to need an authoritative interpretation; and that neither those who drew them up, nor those who imposed them were sufficiently agreed among themselves, or

---

[43] Newman had been converted to an evangelical and Reformed view of the Christian faith under the ministry of the Calvinist Oxford don, Walter Mayers of Pembroke College. Benjamin O'Connor ably chronicles this period in his essay in this volume. Also see Jay Hammond's essay in this volume, for a treatment of Newman's 1839 Monophysite crisis.

[44] *Apologia*, 79 [197]. Emphasis in the original.

[45] *Apologia*, 79 [197].

[46] Later remarks by Catholic convert, William Ward, seemed only to substantiate these fears among Protestant Anglicans. See the essay of Hudson Davis in this volume.

[47] *Apologia*, 78-9 [197].

clear and consistent in their theological views individually to be able to supply it.[48]

Newman then made a critical move in an appeal to the *sensus fidelium* as a key to the proper sense of the *Thirty-nine Articles*:

> There was but one authority to whom recourse could be had for such interpretation—the Church Catholic. She had been taught the revealed truth by Christ and His Apostles in the beginning, and had in turn taught it in every age to her faithful children, and would teach it on to the end. And what she taught, all her branches taught; and this the Anglican Church *did* teach, *must* teach, if it was a branch of the Church Catholic....[49]

Newman concluded that this *sense* was embodied in the First and Second *Books of Homilies*, commended in Article 35 as, "containing a godly and wholesome Doctrine." Because the use of the homilies in public worship had been advocated by the *Thirty-nine Articles* themselves, Newman reasoned that their advocacy of many putatively "Roman" ideas were part of the *lex orandi* that informed and gave rise to the *lex credendi* of the Church of England. He thus used the homilies as an interpretive commentary to open up possibilities for a good faith profession of what he called "moderate Catholicism" or "Roman doctrine, as far as it was Catholic" within Anglicanism.[50] The homilies thus allowed him to embrace the Roman numbering of the sacraments, its version of the canon of the scriptures, the efficacy of penance, prayers for the dead, devotion to Mary, and many other points.[51]

It is crucial to emphasize here the connections with the Catholic Newman's vision of the *schola theologorum*. Here is a theologian, as part of a recognized community of theologians, serving the cause of the faithful by determining the force of a synodal utterance and advocating a rectified interpretation of it by reflection on its historical and ecclesial situation. The continuity of Newman's later reflections on the *schola theologorum* with his Tractarian agenda are compelling.

The reception of the Oxford "magisterium" was ultimately unsuccessful. Perhaps, this had less to do with the particular merits of the Tractarian claims on Anglican history than with the highly politicized and partisan rhetoric of both sides. Whatever the reasons, the publication of *Tract 90* succeeded in alienating

---

[48] John Henry Newman, *Via Media*, 2:261.
[49] Ibid.
[50] Ibid., 263.
[51] Ibid., 264.

evangelicals, traditional high churchmen, and other members of the Oxford Movement. After its publication, Thomas Arnold wrote Archibald Tait—who later became archbishop of Canterbury—that Newman had knowingly suborned the confusion of the Tractarians, and that his positions were "far more objectionable morally than theologically," because of their "utter Perversion of Language ... according to which a Man may subscribe to an Article when he holds the very opposite opinions—believing what it denies and denying what it affirms."[52] This judgment was shared by the heads of houses and by others in authority at the Oxford University. At the personal request of Richard Bagot, bishop of Oxford, the publication of the Tracts came to an end.

Even this defeat seemed to factor into Newman's later conceptions of the *schola theologorum*. By the time of his 1877 "Preface," the mature Newman looked back on these controversies and judged that "theology cannot always have its own way."[53] He stated, "sometimes it has a conflict or overthrow, or has to consent to a truce or a compromise, in consequence of the rival force of religious sentiment or ecclesiastical interests; and that, sometimes in great matters, sometimes in unimportant."[54] Moreover, while he maintained a strong sense of the independence of theology—what he called mental "elbowroom" in faith and thought—he gained a pronounced, pastoral appreciation for human limitation. This sentiment was expressed in his 1852 *Idea of a University*:

> Once more, ... there must be great care taken to avoid scandal, or shocking the popular mind, or unsettling the weak; the association between truth and error being so strong in particular minds that it is impossible to weed them of the error without rooting up the wheat with it.[55]

Though these comments were made regarding the sciences, Newman's appreciation of the intellectual rigors and exactitude associated with theology make them readily applicable to the his ideal *schola* as well.

---

[52] Thomas Arnold to Archibald Tait, 11 March 1841, in *The Life of Archibald Campbell Tait, Archbishop of Canterbury*, eds. R.T. Davidson and W. Benham, 2 vols (London: Macmillan, 1891), 1:86-87.
[53] Newman, *Via Media*, 1:xlviii.
[54] Ibid., li.
[55] John Henry Newman, *The Idea of a University, Defined and Illustrated* (London: Longmans, Green, and Co., 1921), 74.

Newman's Schola Theologorum *and the Fate of* Pastor Aeternus

Newman's 1875 *Letter to the Duke of Norfolk*, in its dealings with the *schola theologorum*, conveys the ambiguity of his beliefs concerning the dogma of papal infallibility. Usually he is portrayed as one who possessed private belief in the dogma, but who considered it inopportune.[56] Newman had expressed great disappointment over the tactics used by many who were in favor of the definition and judged that the "violence and cruelty of journals and other publications" resulted in "unsettling the weak in faith, throwing back inquirers, and shocking the Protestant mind."[57] These words and others have led biographer, Ian Ker, to conclude that for Newman, "while not to be dismissed as an unmitigated disaster, the definition was at best a necessary evil."[58] Others, however, detect much more substantial objection than the label "inopportunist" suggests. John Page, the most exhaustive chronicler of this period in Newman's life, has noted how he often expressed grave doubts concerning the truth of the doctrine.[59]

Whatever private reservations one might ascribe to Newman, it remains important to note how his public expressions of submission to the definition of papal infallibility make considerable space for the role of history and for the process of interpretation following all dogmatic definitions. In May of 1871, Newman wrote,

> As to the definition, I grieve you should have been tried with it. The dogma has been *acted on* by the Holy See for centuries—the only difference is that now it is actually *recognised*. I know this is a difference—for at first sight it would seem to invite the Pope to use his now recognised power. But we must have a little faith. Abstract propositions avail little—theology surrounds them with a variety of limitations, explanations, etc. No truth stands by itself—each is kept in order and harmonized by other truths. The dogmas relative to the Holy Trinity and the Incarnation were not struck off all at once—but piecemeal—one Council did one thing, another a second—and so the whole dogma was built up. And the first portion of it looked extreme—and controversies rose upon it—and these controversies led to the second, and third Councils, and they did not *reverse* the first, but *explained* and *completed* what was first done. So will it be now. Future Popes will explain and in one sense limit their own power. This

---

[56] This is the so-called "received picture" described by Page, *Dr. Newman*, 2.

[57] Newman, *Letter to the Duke of Norfolk*, 300.

[58] Ian Ker, *John Henry Newman: A Biography* (Oxford: Oxford University Press, 1988), 683.

[59] Page notes, for example, Newman's journal entry of 12 December 1869: "Save the church, O my fathers, from a danger as great as any that happened to it." Page, *Dr. Newman*, 78.

would be unlikely, if they merely acted as men, but God will overrule them. Pius has been overruled—I believe he wished a much more stringent dogma than he has got. Let us have faith and patience.[60]

Given that theological interpretation is for Newman's an integral, not intrusive part of the church's infallibility, it does no violence to his view to imagine a third possibility between the above-stated categories of "explanation" and outright "reversal." Between the two lies the possibility of "rectification"—a series of theological modifications that ultimately lead to fundamental course *corrections* regarding a defined doctrine. If rectification is the historical standard—as Newman argued—it is possible to imagine interpretations of papal infallibility that appropriate non-contradictory criticisms of Catholic, Orthodox and Protestant theologians, and perhaps even open the door to an expanded ecumenical role for the Bishop of Rome.

Epilogue

When the Second Vatican Council took up the definitions of *Pastor Aeternus*, the ecclesiological landscape had changed. Almost a century of theological reflection called for a clarified—and rectified—reception of papal infallibility. *Pastor Aeternus* had dealt exclusively with papal primacy and with infallibility as a necessary corollary. *Lumen Gentium*, on the other hand, subordinated its treatment of the hierarchy (chapter 3) to its treatment of the church as divine mystery (chapter 1) and the church as the people of God (chapter 2). This shift served to reconfigure the papacy as an office bound to the faithful rather than functioning apart from it. When it finally came to treating the doctrine of papal infallibility itself, this connection was made explicit by a creative appeal to the work of Bishop Vincenz Gasser (d. 1879), principal author of *Pastor Aeternus*. Working with Gasser's writings, the theologians of Vatican II corrected the ultramontane imbalance of the prior definition by making clear how papal infallibility related to the faith of the whole church and the close, collegial cooperation between pope and bishops in the process of defining dogma. Most importantly, *Lumen Gentium* made explicit that the assent of the church (*sensus fidelium*) can never be wanting in an authentic definition.[61]

In his classic study, *The Bishop of Rome*, J.-M. R. Tillard observed of *Lumen Gentium* how,

---

[60] Newman to Mary Holmes, 15 May 1871, *LD*, 25:330.

[61] *Dogmatic Constitution on the Church: Lumen Gentium* (Boston: Pauline Books and Media, 1967), 47.

... the *receptio* of Vatican I by Vatican II amounts to a re-reading of the former which exemplifies 'dogmatic development' along a different line from that which, since Newman, has been regarded as normal, and which many of the Vatican I fathers accepted. The difference lies in the idea of development not by the addition of new truths but by clarification.[62]

In light of this study, one must conclude that the assumed "normal" reading of Newman here is erroneous. Whatever subsequent Catholic interpreters would wish to attribute to Newman's doctrine of development, a fuller assimilation of his teaching on the *schola theologorum* reveals the perfect coherence of a council developing doctrine through progressive clarification. One might also note that this perspective on development is not solely attributable to the *Catholic* Newman. Rather, at the far side of this consideration of the Oxford Movement as a *schola theologorum*, it becomes entirely possible to argue that the theological work of Vatican II, was perfectly coherent within the *Anglican* Newman's theological frame of reference.

---

[62] J.-M. R. Tillard, *The Bishop of Rome*, trans. John de Satgé (Wilmington, DE: Michael Glazier, 1983), 39.

AUTHORITY HISTORY AND DOGMA:
A BIBLIOGRAPHY OF SELECT AND CITED SOURCES

The editors and contributors have assembled this bibliography as a help to introductory research, but it is necessarily limited to select and cited works. Literature on the Oxford Movement is voluminous and new works continue to appear at a brisk pace. Readers who desire a more comprehensive guide to the literature are encouraged to consult the published bibliography of Lawrence Crumb, *The Oxford Movement and its Leaders: A Bibliography of Secondary and Lesser Primary Sources* (Metuchen, N.J./ London: ATLA/Scarecrow, 1988) and its supplementary volume, *The Oxford Movement and its Leaders: A Bibliography of Secondary and Lesser Primary Sources: Supplement* (Metuchen, N.J./ London: ATLA/Scarecrow, 1993).

Manuscripts

Birmingham Oratory, Birmingham, MS A.91.
                        MS B.2.8.c "Defection of Apollinarius;"
                                        "Apolinarius History;"
                                        "Apollinarianism;"
                                        Untitled Apollinarianism MS.

Bodleian Library, Oxford, MS Eng. Misc.d.1278.
                        MS Eng. Lett.c. 655, 656, 662.

British Library, London, Add. MS 44249.

Cambridge Univerity Library, Cambridge, Add. MS 5542.

Pitts Library Archives, Emory University, Atlanta, GA, Manning Collection.

Select and Cited Sources

A Member of the House of Commons. "Thoughts on Foreign Relations." *The Church of England Quarterly Review* 33 (1853): 380-410.

Addington, Raleigh, ed. *Faber Poet and Priest: Selected Letters by Frederick William Faber, 1833-1863*. Cowbridge and Bridgend, Glamorgan: D. Brown and Sons, 1974.

Allitt, Patrick. *Catholic Converts: British and American Intellectuals Turn to Rome*. Ithaca, NY: Cornell University Press, 1997.

Altholz, Josef Lewis. *The Liberal Catholic Movement in England: The "Rambler" and Its Contributors, 1848-1864*. London: Burns and Oates, 1962.

Artz, Johannes. "Entstehung und Auswerkung von Newmans Theorie der Dogmenentwicklung." *Theologische Quartalschrift* 148 (1968): 63-104, 167-98.

Aubert, Roger. *Le pontificat de Pie IX (1846-1878), Histoire de l'église depuis les origins jusqu'à nos jours*. Volume 21. Paris: Bloud & Gay, 1952.

_____. *Vatican I*. Paris: Éditions de l'Orante, 1964.

von Arx, Jeffrey P. "Archbishop Manning and the *Kulturkampf*," *Recusant History* 21 (1992): 254-266.

Barr, Colin. *Paul Cullen, John Henry Newman, and the Catholic University of Ireland, 1845-1865*. Notre Dame, IN: University of Notre Dame, 2003.

Battiscombe, Georgina. *John Keble: A Study in Limitations*. London: Constable, 1963.

Bebbington, David W. *William Ewart Gladstone: Faith and Politics in Victorian Britain*. Grand Rapids, MI: Eerdmans, 1993.

Beek, Wilhelm. *John Keble's Literary and Religious Contribution to the Oxford Movement*. Nijmegen: Academic Centrale, 1959.

Biemer, Günter. *John Henry Newman, 1801-1890: Leben und Werk*. Mainz: Matthias-Grünewald-Verlag, 1989.

Blehl, Vincent F. "Newman's Conversion of 1845: A Fresh Approach," in *By Whose Authority?: Newman, Manning, and the* Magisterium, edited by V. Alan McClelland, 123-135. Bath, UK: Downside Abbey, 1996.

_____. *Pilgrim Journey: John Henry Newman 1801-1845*. New York: Paulist Press, 2001.

Bodley, John. *Cardinal Manning. The Decay of Idealism in France. The Institute of France: Three Essays*. London: Longmans, Green, and Co., 1912.

Bowden, John Edward. *The Life and Letters of Frederick William Faber, D.D.: Priest of the Oratory of St. Philip Neri*. 5th ed. London: Burns & Oates, 1869.

Brendon, Piers. *Hurrell Froude and the Oxford Movement*. London: Paul Elek, 1974.

Brent, Allen. "Newman and Perrone: Unreconcilable Theses on Development." *Downside Review* 102 (1984): 276-289.

_____. "The Hermesian Dimension to the Newman-Perrone Dialogue." *Ephemerides Theologicae Lovanienses* 61 (1985): 73-99.

Breviarium romanum ex decreto sacrosancti Concilii Tridentini restitutum. Edited by H. Dessain and P.J. Hanicq. Mechelen, Belgium: Summi Pontificis, S. Congregationis de Propaganda Fide et Archiep. Typographi, 1861.

Brilioth, Yngve. *The Anglican Revival: Studies in the Oxford Movement*. New York: Longmans, Green and Co., 1933.

Brock, M.G. "The Oxford of Peel and Gladstone, 1800-1833." In *The History of the University of Oxford*, edited by M.G. Brock and M.C. Curthoys, 6:7-71. Oxford: Clarendon Press, 1997.

Brose, O.J. *Church and Parliament: The Reshaping of the Church of England: 1828-60*. London: Oxford University Press, 1959.

Brownson, Orestes, ed. "Article I.: The Immaculate Conception." *Brownson's Quarterly Review* 16 (1859): 417-436.

Burgon, John William. *Lives of Twelve Good Men*. 2 Volumes. London: Scribner & Welford, 1888.

Butler, Cuthbert. *The Vatican Council, 1869–1870: Based on Bishop Ullathorne's Letters*. Edited by Christopher Butler. Westminster, MD: The Newman Press, 1962.

Butler, Perry. *Gladstone: Church, State, and Tractarianism*. Oxford: Clarendon Press, 1982.

_____, ed. *Pusey Rediscovered*. Oxford: Oxford University Press, 1983.

Callam, Daniel. "Christopher Dawson on the Oxford Movement: The Relationship of Development to Authority." *Communio* 22 (1995): 488-501.

Cappellari, Mauro. *Il Trionfo della Santa Sede e della Chiesa contro gli assalti dei novatori combattuti e respinti colle stesse loro armi*. Rome, 1799.

Chadwick, Owen. *From Bossuet to Newman*. 2nd ed. London: Cambridge University Press, 1987.

_____, ed. *The Mind of the Oxford Movement*. Palo Alto, CA: Stanford University Press, 1960.

_____. *The Secularization of the European Mind in the Nineteenth Century*. Cambridge: University of Cambridge Press, 1990.

_____. *The Spirit of the Oxford Movement: Tractarian Essays*. Cambridge: Cambridge University Press, 1990.

_____. *The Victorian Church: An Ecclesiastical History of England*. 2 Volumes. New York: Oxford, 1966.

Chandler, Michael. *An Introduction to the Oxford Movement*. London: Society for Promoting Christian Knowledge, 2003.

Chapman, Mark D. "Bischofsamt und Politik: zur Begründung des Bishofsamtes in der Anglikanischen Kirche." *Zeitschrift für Theologie und Kirche* 97 (2000): 434-462.

Chapman, Raymond. *Faith and Revolt: Studies in the Literary Influence of the Oxford Movement*. London: Weidenfeld and Nicolson, 1970.

Chapman, Ronald. *Father Faber*. Westminster, MD: The Newman Press, 1961.

Chapeau, Alphonse. "Manning the Anglican." In *Manning: Anglican and Catholic*, edited by John Fitzsimons, 1-39. London: The Catholic Book Club, 1952.

Church, Richard William. *The Oxford Movement: Twelve Years, 1833-1845*. London: Macmillan and Co., 1891.

――――. *Life and Letters of Dean Church*. London: Macmillan and Co., 1895.

Clancy, Raymond. "American Prelates in the Vatican Council." *Historical Record and Studies* 28 (1937): 459-474.

Clark, J.C.D. *English Society, 1688-1832: Ideology, Social Structure, and Political Practice During the Ancien Regime*. Cambridge: Cambridge University Press, 1985.

Clifton, Michael. *A Victorian Convert Quintet: Studies in the Faith of Five Leading Victorian Converts to Catholicism from the Oxford Movement*. London: Saint Austin Press, 1998.

Clough, Arthur. *The Oxford Diaries of Arthur Hugh Clough*. Edited by Anthony Kenny. Oxford; New York: Oxford University Press, 1990.

Connolly, John. *John Henry Newman: A View of Catholic Faith for the New Millennium*. Lanham, MD: Rowman & Littlefield, 2005.

Cooper, Austin R. "Ireland and the Oxford Movement." *Journal of Religious History* 19 (1995): 62-74.

Cox, R. David. "Newman, Littlemore, and a Tractarian Attempt at Community." *Anglican and Episcopal History* 62 (1993): 343-376.

Crosthwaite, John Clarke. *Modern Hagiology: An Examination Of The Nature and Tendency of Some Legendary and Devotional Works Lately Published Under The Sanction of the Rev. J. H. Newman, the Rev. Dr. Pusey, and the Rev. F. Oakeley.* London: J.W. Parker, 1846.

Cwiekowski, Fredrick. *The English Bishops and the First Vatican Council.* Louvain: Publications Universitaires de Louvain, 1971.

Dalberg-Acton, John Emerich Edward. *Letters of Lord Acton to Mary, Daughter of the Right Hon. W. E. Gladstone.* London: George Allen, 1904.

_____. *History of Freedom and Other Essays.* London: Macmillan and Co., Ltd., 1907.

Davidson, R.T. and Benham, W., eds. *The Life of Archibald Campbell Tait, Archbishop of Canterbury.* London: Macmillan and Co., 1891.

Dawson, Christopher. *The Spirit of the Oxford Movement.* New York: Sheed and Ward, 1933.

Dessain, Stephen. "The Reception Among Catholics of Newman's Doctrine of Development, Newman's own Impressions." *Newman Studien* 4 (1964): 179-191.

Disraeli, Benjamin. *The Works of Benjamin Disraeli, Earl of Beaconsfield.* Edited by Edmund Gosse and Robe Arnot. London: M.W. Dunne, 1904.

Dowbiggin, Ian Robert. *Inheriting Madness: Professionalization and Psychiatric Knowledge in Nineteenth-Century France.* Berkeley: University of California Press, 1991.

Drexler, Charles. *The Authority to Teach: A Study in the Ecclesiology of Henry Edward Manning.* Washington, DC: University Press of America, 1978.

Dulles, Avery. "Newman, Conversion, and Ecumenism." *Theological Studies* 51 (1990): 717-31.

Dupuy, Bernard. "Newman's Influence in France." In *The Rediscovery of Newman: An Oxford Symposium,* edited by J. Coulson, and A. Allchin, 147-73. London: Sheen and Ward, 1967.

Edgecombe, Rodney. *Two Poets of the Oxford Movement: John Keble and John Henry Newman.* Madison, NJ: Fairleigh Dickinson University Press, 1996.

Ellis, Ieuan. "The Intellectual Challenge to 'Official Religion.'" In *The British: Their Religious Beliefs and Practices 1800-1986*, edited by Terence Thomas, 48-71. London: Routledge, 1998.

Erb, Peter, ed. *The Correspondence of Henry Edward Manning and William Ewart Gladstone, 1833-1891.* 3 Volumes. Forthcoming.

———. "Henry Edward Manning, Priscilla Maurice, and the Pastoral Care of the Sick." In *Victorian Churches and Churchmen: Essays Presented to Vincent Alan McClelland*, edited by Sheridan Gilley, 12-27. Suffolk: Boydell Press, 2005.

Faber, Geoffrey. *Oxford Apostles: A Character Study of the Oxford Movement*, 2nd ed. London: Faber and Faber, 1974.

Faber, Frederick William. *Devotion to the Pope.* Baltimore: Murphy & Company Printers and Publishers, 1860.

Fairweather, Eugene R., ed. *The Oxford Movement: A Library of Protestant Thought.* New York: Oxford University Press, 1964.

Faught, C. Brad. "The Oxford Movement and Politics: Church and State and Social Action." PhD diss., University of Toronto, 1996.

———. *The Oxford Movement: A Thematic History of the Tractarians and Their Times.* University Park, PA: Pennsylvania State University Press, 2003.

_____. "Tractarianism on the Zambezi: Bishop Mackenzie and the Beginnings of the Universities Mission to Central Africa." *Anglican and Episcopal History* 66 (1997): 303-328.

Félix, Joseph, S.J. "Opuscule théologique du R. P. Perrone, sur l'Immaculée Conception." *L'Ami de la religion: Journal ecclésiastique, politique, et littéraire* 35 (1847): 261-266.

Ferguson, Thomas. "The Enthralling Power: History and Heresy in John Henry Newman." *Anglican Theological Review* 85 (2003): 641-662.

Fessler, Joseph. *The True and False Infallibility of the Popes: A Controversial Reply to Dr. Schulte*. New York: The Catholic Publication Society, 1875.

Finley, A. Gregg. "'Habits of Reverence and Awe:' Bishop John Medley and the Promise of Ecclesiology." *Journal of the Canadian Church Historical Society* 35 (1993): 3-22.

Fleming, Amelia. "The Role of the Theologian, *Donum Veritatis* and Newman." *Irish Theological Quarterly* 69 (2004): 263-279.

Forrester, David. *Young Doctor Pusey*. London: Mowbray, 1989.

Franklin, Ralph William. "Puseyism in the Parishes: Leeds and Wantage Contrasted." *Anglican and Episcopal History* 62 (1993): 377-395.

Friedrich, Johann. *Ignaz von Döllinger*. 3 Volumes. Munich: C.H. Beck, 1899-1901.

Froude, Richard Hurrell. *The Remains of the late Reverend Richard Hurrell Froude*. 4 Volumes. London: Rivington, 1838.

Galloway, Peter. *A Passionate Humility: Frederick Oakeley and the Oxford Movement*. Leominster: Gracewing, 1999.

Gasquet, R.J. *Cardinal Manning*. London: Catholic Truth Society, 1895.

Gilley, Sheridan. *Newman and His Age*. Westminster, MD: Christian Classics, 1991.

_____. "The Ecclesiology of the Oxford Movement: A Reconsideration." In *From Oxford to the People: Reconsidering Newman and the Oxford Movement*, edited by Paul Vaiss, 60-75. Leominster: Gracewing, 1996.

Gladstone, William. *Gleanings of Past Years 1843-1879.* 7 Volumes. London: John Murray, 1879.

_____. "The Vatican Decrees in their Bearing on Civil Allegiance." In *Rome and the Newest Fashions in Religion*, vii-lxxxi. Leipzig: Bernhard Tauchnitz, 1875.

Goldstein, Jan and John W. Boyer. *Nineteenth-Century Europe: Part Eight: Liberalism and Its Critics.* Chicago: University of Chicago Press, 1988.

Gondon, Jules. *Conversion de soixante ministres Anglicans ou membres des universities anglaises, et de cinquante personnes de distinction, avec une notice sur mm. Newman, Ward, Oakeley.* Tournai, Belgium: Casterman, 1846.

_____. *Du movement religieux en Angleterre: ou les progress du catholicisme et le retour de l'église anglicaine à l'unité.* Paris: Signier et Bray, 1844.

Goslee, David. *Romanticism and the Anglican Newman.* Athens: Ohio University Press, 1996.

Grave, S. A. *Conscience in Newman's Thought.* Oxford: Clarendon Press, 1989.

Gray, Donald. *The Influence of Tractarian Principles On Parish Worship 1839-1849.* London: Alcuin Club, 1984.

Gray, Robert. *Cardinal Manning: A Biography.* London: Weidenfeld and Nicolson, 1985.

Greenfield, R.H. *The Attitude of the Tractarians to the Roman Catholic Church: 1833-1850*, D.Phil. thesis, Oxford University, 1956.

Gres-Gayer, Jacques M. "The Magisterium of the Faculty of Theology of Paris in the Seventeenth Century." *Theological Studies* 53 (1992): 424-50.

Griffin, John. *John Keble: Saint of Anglicanism.* Macon, GA: Mercer University Press, 1987.

_____. "The Anglican Response to Newman's Conversion." *Faith and Reason* 3 (1977): 17-34.

_____. *The Oxford Movement: A Revision*, 1833-1983. Edinburgh, Scotland: Pentland Press, 1984.

Härdelin, Alf. *The Tractarian Understanding of the Eucharist.* Uppsala, 1965.

Hastings, Adrian. *A History of Anglo-Catholicism, 1920-1985.* London: Collins, 1986.

Haugaard, William P. "A Myopic Curiosity: Martin Luther and English Tractarians." *Anglican Theological Review* 66 (1984): 391-401.

Harrold, Charles Frederick. "John Henry Newman and the Alexandrian Platonists." *Modern Philology* 37 (1940): 279-91.

Heimann, Mary. *Catholic Devotion in Victorian England.* Oxford: Clarendon Press, 1995.

Hennessy, Paul. "A Prelude to Vatican I: American Bishops and the Definition of the Immaculate Conception." *Theological Studies* 25 (1964): 409-419.

_____. "Infallibility in the Ecclesiology of Peter Richard Kenrick." *Theological Studies* 45 (1984): 702-714.

Hennesy, James. *The First Council of the Vatican: The American Experience.* New York: Herder and Herder, 1963.

Hergenröther, Joseph. *Anti-Janus: An Historico-Theological Criticism of the Work Entitled: "The Pope and the Council" By Janus.* Translated by J. B. Robertson. Dublin: W. B. Kelly, 1870.

Herring, George. *What Was the Oxford Movement?* New York: Continuum, 2002.

Hill, Roland. *Lord Acton*. New Haven: Yale University Press, 2000.

Hogben, Brian and Jonathan Harrison. *The Oxford Movement: Nineteenth-Century Books and Pamphlets in Canterbury Cathedral Library*. Canterbury: Dean and Chapter, Canterbury Cathedral, 1999.

Holmes, J. Derek. "Cardinal Newman and the First Vatican Council." *Annuarum Historiae Conciliorum* 1 (1969): 374-398.

_____. "How Newman Blunted the Edge of Ultramontanism." *Clergy Review* 53 (1968): 353-62.

Hoppen, K. Theodore. "Church, State, and Ultramontanism in Mid-Victorian England: The Case of William George Ward." *Journal of Church and State* 18 (1976): 289-309.

_____. "W. G. Ward and Liberal Catholicism." *Journal of Ecclesiastical History* 23 (1972): 323-44.

_____. "William George Ward and Nineteenth-Century Catholicism." PhD diss., University of Cambridge, 1966.

Hutton, Arthur W. *Cardinal Manning*. London: Methuen and Co., 1892.

Hylson-Smith, Kenneth. *High Churchmanship in the Church of England: From the Sixteenth Century to the Late Twentieth Century*. Edinburgh: T & T Clark, 1993.

Imberg, Rune. *In Quest of Authority: The "Tracts For The Times" and the Development of the Tractarian Leaders 1833-1841*. Lund, Sweden: Lund University Press, 1987.

_____. *Tracts For the Times: A Complete Survey of All the Editions*. Lund, Sweden: Lund University Press, 1987.

Jaki, Stanley. *Newman's Challenge*. Grand Rapids, MI: Eerdmans, 1999.

Jay, Elisabeth. *The Evangelical and Oxford Movements*. New York: Cambridge University Press, 1983.

Johnson, Margaret. *Gerard Manley Hopkins and Tractarian Poetry.* Brookfield, VT: Ashgate, 1997.

Johnson, Maria Poggi. "Probability the Guide of Life: The Influence of Butler's Analogy on Keble and Newman." *Anglican and Episcopal History* 70 (2001): 302-323.

Kaiser, James. "The Concept of Conscience According to John Henry Newman." PhD diss., The Catholic University of America, 1958.

Kasper, Walter. *Die Lehre von Tradition in der Römische Schule.* Freiburg im Breisgau: Herder, 1962.

Keble, John. "A Letter from England: John Keble to Benjamin Holmes, 10 July 1833." *Anglican and Episcopal History* 70 (2001): 438-450.

Kelly, Edward. "Newman, Ward, And Modernism: Problems With Infallible Dogmatic Truth." In *John Henry Newman and Modernism*, edited by Arthur Hilary Jenkins, 168-179. Sigmaringendorf, Germany: Glock & Lutz, 1990.

Kent, John. "Anglican Evangelicalism in the West of England, 1858-1900." In *Protestant Evangelicalism: Britain, Ireland, Germany and America, c.1750-c.1950*, edited by Keith Robbins, 179-200. Oxford: Blackwell, 1990.

Ker, Ian. *John Henry Newman: A Biography.* Oxford: Oxford University Press, 1988.

_____. *The Achievement of John Henry Newman.* Notre Dame, IN: University of Notre Dame Press, 1990.

_____, ed. *Newman and Conversion.* Notre Dame, IN: University of Notre Dame Press, 1997.

Ker, Ian and Alan G. Hill, eds. *Newman After a Hundred Years.* Oxford: Clarendon, 1990.

Ker, Ian and Terrence Merrigan, eds. *Newman and Faith.* Grand Rapids, MI: Eerdmans, 2004.

Knox, Thomas Francis. *When Does the Church Speak Infallibly? or, The Nature and Scope of the Church's Teaching Office.* London: Burns and Oates, 1870.

Lash, Nicholas. *Newman on Development: The Search for an Explanation in History.* Shepherdstown, WV: Patmos Press, 1975.

Lathbury, D.C. ed. *The Ecclesiastical and Religious Correspondence of William Ewart Gladstone.* 2 Volumes. New York: Macmillan and Co., 1910.

Laurentin, Rene. "The Role of the Papal Magisterium in the Development of the Dogma of the Immaculate Conception." In *The Dogma of the Immaculate Conception, History and Significance,* edited by E. O'Connor, 271-324. Notre Dame, IN: University of Notre Dame Press, 1958.

Leslie, Shane. *Cardinal Manning: His Life and Labours.* New York: P.J. Kenedy and Sons, 1921.

Leslie Ollard, Sydney. *The Anglo-Catholic Revival.* London: A. R. Mowbray & Co. Ltd., 1963.

Liddon, Henry. *The Life of Edward Bouverie Pusey.* 4 Volumes. London: Longmans, Green, & Co., 1893-97.

Locke, Kenneth A. "Antiquity As a Guide to Orthodoxy: A Critical Appraisal of Newman's *Via Media*." In *The Future of Anglicanism*, edited by Robert Hannaford, 118-30. Leominster: Gracewing, 1996.

Lund, Arnold. *Roman Converts.* Newcastle-upon-Tyne, UK: The Northumberland Press Ltd., 1925.

Lynch, M. J. "Was Gladstone a Tractarian? W.E. Gladstone and the Oxford Movement, 1833-45." *Journal of Religious History* 13 (1975): 364-89.

Lynch, T., ed. "The Newman-Perrone Paper on Development." *Gregorianum* 16 (1935): 402-447.

McClelland, V. Alan. *By Whose Authority?: Newman, Manning and the Magisterium.* Bath: Downside Abbey, 1996.

McClymond, Michael J. "'Continual Self-Contemplation': John Henry Newman's Critique Of Evangelicalism." In *Tradition and Pluralism: Essays in Honor of William M. Shea*, edited by K.L. Parker, P. Huff, and M.J.G. Pahls. Lanham, MD: University Press of America, 2008.

McGrath, Mark. "The Vatican Council's Teaching on the Evolution of Dogma: A Study in Nineteenth Century Theology." PhD diss., Pontificium Athenaeum Angelicum, 1960.

Mandle, William Frederick. "Newman and His Audiences: 1825-1845." *Journal of Religious History* 24 (2000): 143-158.

Manning, Henry. *A Charge Delivered at the Ordinary Visitation of the Archdeaconry of Chichester, July 1848*. London: John Murray, 1848.

_____. *Miscellanies*. 3 Volumes. London: Burns and Oates, 1877.

_____. *Religio Viatoris*. London: Burns and Oates, nd.

_____. *Sermons*. 4 Volumes. London: William Pickering, 1850.

_____. *Sermons on Ecclesiastical Subjects*. 2 Volumes. London: Burns, Oates, and Co., 1872.

_____. *The English Church: Its Succession, and Witness for Christ*. London: Rivington, 1835.

_____. *The Grounds of Faith*. London: Burns and Lambert, 1852.

_____. *The Oecumenical Council and the Infallibility of the Roman Pontiff*. London: Longmans, Green, and Co., 1869.

_____. *The Rule of Faith: Appendix to a Sermon*. London: Rivington, 1839.

_____. *The Temporal Mission of the Holy Ghost*. New York: D. and J. Sadlier, 1887.

_____. *The Workings of the Holy Spirit in the Church of England, A Letter to the Reverend E.B. Pusey, D.D*. London: Burns & Oates, 1864.

Mansi, Joannes Dominicus, ed. *Sacrorum conciliorum nova et amplissima collection*. 54 Volumes. Paris: H. Welter, 1901-1927.

Maret, Charles-Henri. *Du concile général et de la paix religiouse: memoir soumis au prochain concile oecumenique du Vatican*. 2 Volumes. Paris: Henri Plon, 1869-1870.

Marlett, Jeffrey. "Conversion Methodology and the Case of Cardinal Newman." *Theological Studies* 58 (1997): 669-85.

Martin, Brian W. *John Keble: Priest, Professor, and Poet*. London: Croom Helm, 1976.

Matthew, H.C.G. "Edward Bouverie Pusey: From Scholar to Tractarian." *Journal of Theological Studies* 32 (1981): 101-24.

_____. *The Gladstone Diaries: With Cabinet Minutes and Prime-Ministerial Correspondence*, edited by M.R.D. Foot and H.C.G. Matthew. 14 Volumes. Oxford: Oxford University Press, 1968-94.

Maurice, Frederick, ed. *The Life of Frederick Denison Maurice, Chiefly Told in His Own Letters*. 2 Volumes. London: Macmillan and Co., 1884.

May, J. Lewis. *The Oxford Movement: Its History and its Future, A Layman's Estimate*. London: John Lane The Bodley Head, 1933.

Merrigan, Terrence. "*Numquam Minus Solus, Quam Cum Solus*—Newman's First Conversion: Its Significance for His Life and Thought." *The Downside Review* 103 (1985): 99-116.

Misner, Paul. "The 'Liberal' Legacy of John Henry Newman." In *Newman and the Modernists*, edited by Mary Jo Weaver, 3-24. Lanham, MD: University Press of America, 1985.

_____. *Papacy and Development: Newman and the Primacy of the Pope*. Leiden: Brill, 1976.

Mivart, St. George. "Scripture and Roman Catholicism." *Nineteenth Century* 47 (1900): 425-42.

_____. "What Church Has 'Continuity'?" *Nineteenth Century* 46 (1899): 203-12.

Morris, Jeremy. "The Regional Growth of Tractarianism: Some Reflections." In *From Oxford to the People: Reconsidering Newman & the Oxford Movement.* Edited by Paul Vaiss. Leominster: Gracewing, 1996.

Mozley, Thomas. *Reminiscences: Chiefly of Oriel College and the Oxford Movement.* Boston: Houghton, Mifflin and Co., 1882.

Newman. John Henry. *An Essay in Aid of a Grammar of Assent.* Edited by Ian Ker. Oxford: Clarendon, 1985.

_____. *An Essay on the Development of Christian Doctrine.* London: James Toovey, 1845.

_____. *Apologia Pro Vita Sua and Six Sermons.* Edited by Frank Turner. New Haven: Yale University Press, 2008.

_____. *Discussions and Arguments on Various Subjects.* London: Rivington, 1873.

_____. *John Henry Newman: Selected Writings To 1845.* Edited by Albert Radcliffe. New York: Routledge, 2002.

_____. *Lectures on the Doctrine of Justification.* London: Longmans, Green, and Co., 1897.

_____. *The Letters and Diaries of John Henry Newman.* Volumes 1-10 edited by T.Gornall, I. Ker, G. Tracey, and F. J. McGrath. Oxford: 1978-2006; Volumes 11-31 edited by C.D. Dessain, E. E. Kelly, and T. Gornall. London, 1961-71; 1973-7.

_____. *Newman the Oratorian: His Unpublished Oratory Papers.* Edited by Placid Murray. Leominster: Gracewing, 2006.

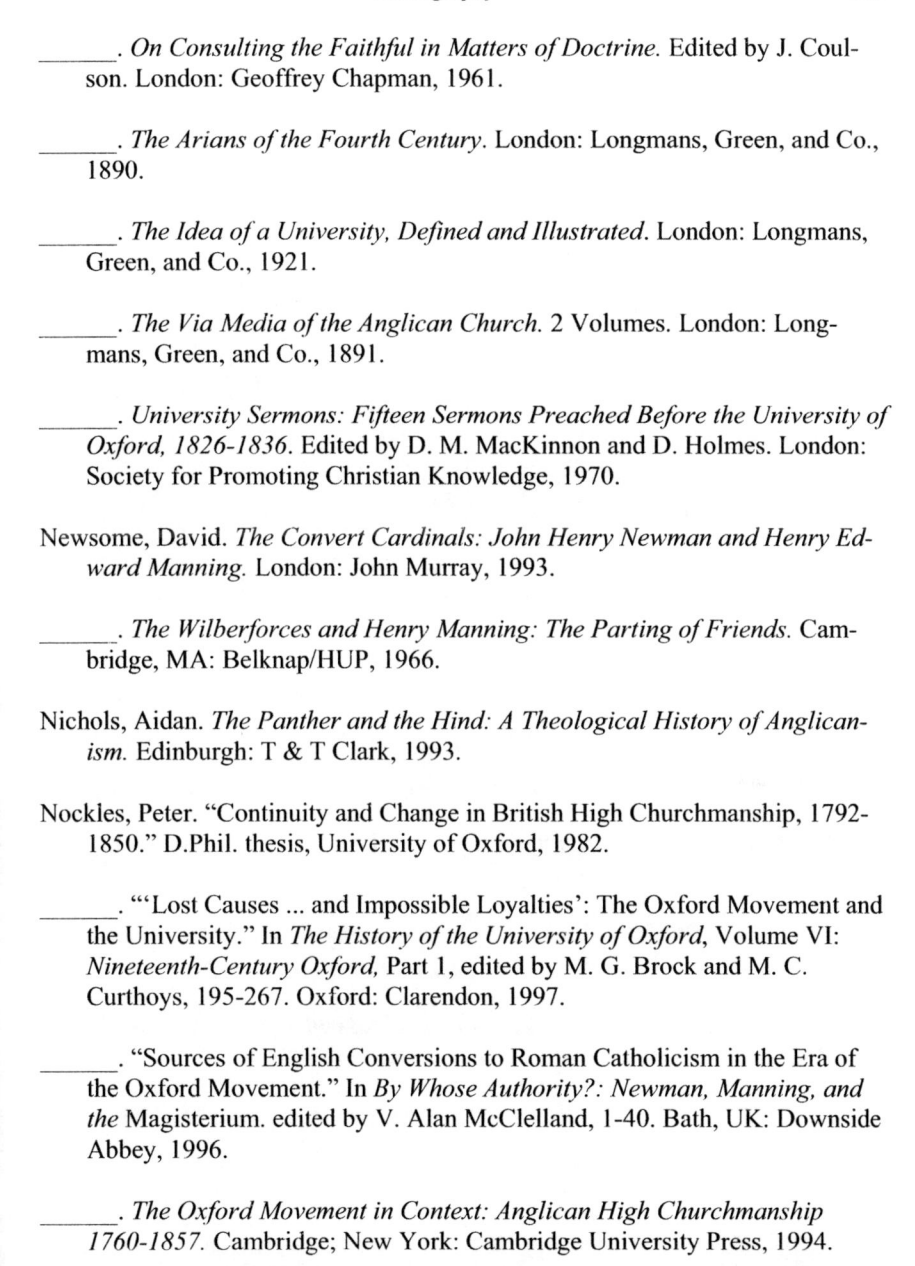

_____. *On Consulting the Faithful in Matters of Doctrine.* Edited by J. Coulson. London: Geoffrey Chapman, 1961.

_____. *The Arians of the Fourth Century.* London: Longmans, Green, and Co., 1890.

_____. *The Idea of a University, Defined and Illustrated.* London: Longmans, Green, and Co., 1921.

_____. *The Via Media of the Anglican Church.* 2 Volumes. London: Longmans, Green, and Co., 1891.

_____. *University Sermons: Fifteen Sermons Preached Before the University of Oxford, 1826-1836.* Edited by D. M. MacKinnon and D. Holmes. London: Society for Promoting Christian Knowledge, 1970.

Newsome, David. *The Convert Cardinals: John Henry Newman and Henry Edward Manning.* London: John Murray, 1993.

_____. *The Wilberforces and Henry Manning: The Parting of Friends.* Cambridge, MA: Belknap/HUP, 1966.

Nichols, Aidan. *The Panther and the Hind: A Theological History of Anglicanism.* Edinburgh: T & T Clark, 1993.

Nockles, Peter. "Continuity and Change in British High Churchmanship, 1792-1850." D.Phil. thesis, University of Oxford, 1982.

_____. "'Lost Causes ... and Impossible Loyalties': The Oxford Movement and the University." In *The History of the University of Oxford,* Volume VI: *Nineteenth-Century Oxford,* Part 1, edited by M. G. Brock and M. C. Curthoys, 195-267. Oxford: Clarendon, 1997.

_____. "Sources of English Conversions to Roman Catholicism in the Era of the Oxford Movement." In *By Whose Authority?: Newman, Manning, and the* Magisterium. edited by V. Alan McClelland, 1-40. Bath, UK: Downside Abbey, 1996.

_____. *The Oxford Movement in Context: Anglican High Churchmanship 1760-1857.* Cambridge; New York: Cambridge University Press, 1994.

Nye, George Henry Frederick. *The Story of the Oxford Movement: A Book for the Times*. London: Bemrose and Son, Ltd., 1899.

O'Connell, Marvin R. *The Oxford Conspirators*. New York: Macmillan and Co., 1969.

_____. "Ultramontanism and Dupanloup." *Church History* 53 (1984): 200-217.

O'Gara, Margaret. *Triumph in Defeat: Infallibility, Vatican I, and the French Minority Bishops*. Washington, D.C.: Catholic University of America Press, 1988.

Oakes, Edward. "Newman's Liberal Problem." *First Things* 132 (2003): 43-50.

Official Documents Connected with the Definition of the Dogma of the Immaculate Conception of the Virgin Mary. Baltimore, MD: John Murphy & Co., 1855.

Ollard, S.L. *A Short History of the Oxford Movement*. Reprint. London: Faith Press Reprints, 1963.

Ong, Walter. "Newman's Essay on Development in Its Intellectual Milieu." *Theological Studies* 7 (1946): 2-45.

Ornsby, Robert. *Memoirs of James Hope-Scott*. 2 Volumes. London: John Murray, 1884.

Page, John. *What Will Dr. Newman Do?: John Henry Newman and Papal Infallibility, 1865-1875*. Collegeville, MN: Liturgical Press, 1994.

Palmer, William. *A Narrative of Events Connected with the Publication of the Tracts for the Times*, 2nd ed. London: Mowbray, 1883.

_____. *A Treatise on the Church of Christ*. 2 Volumes. Oxford: Rivington, 1838.

"Pareri dell": Episcopato Cattolico sulla definizione dogmatica dell' immacolato concepimento della B.V. Maria. 10 Volumes. Rome, 1851-1854.

Parker, Kenneth. "Francis Kenrick and Papal Infallibility: How Pastoral Experience in the American Missions Transformed a Roman Ultramontanist." In *Tradition and Pluralism: Essays in Honor of William M. Shea*, edited by K.L. Parker, P. Huff, and M.J.G. Pahls. Lanham, MD: University Press of America, 2008.

_____. "Newman's Individualistic Use of the Caroline Divines in the *Via Media*." In *Discourse and Context: An Interdisciplinary Study of John Henry Newman*, edited by Gerard Magill, 33-42. Edwardsville, IL: Southern Illinois University Press, 1993.

_____. "The Role of Estrangement in Conversion: The Case of John Henry Newman." In *Christianity and the Stranger: Historical Essays*, edited by Francis Nichols, 169-201. Atlanta: Scholars Press, 1995.

Parry, Jonathan Philip. *Democracy and Religion: Gladstone and the Liberal Party, 1867-1875*. Cambridge: Cambridge University Press, 1986.

Pattison, Robert. *The Great Dissent: John Henry Newman and the Liberal Heresy*. New York: Oxford University Press, 1991.

Pereiro, James. *"Ethos" and the Oxford Movement: At the Heart of Tractarianism*. Oxford: Oxford University Press, 2008.

Perrone, Giovanni. *De Immaculato B. V. Mariae*. Rome: Ioannes Baptista Marini and Bernardus Morini, 1847.

Pottmeyer, Hermann Joseph. *Unfehlbarkeit und Souveränität: die Päpstliche Unfehlbarkeit im System der Ultramontanen Ekklesiologie des 19. Jahrhunderts*. Mainz: Mattias Grünewald Verlag, 1975.

Purcell, Edmund. *Life of Cardinal Manning*. 2 Volumes. London: Macmillan and Co., 1895-96.

Pusey, Edward Bouverie. *Case as to the Legal force of the Judgment of the Privy Council, in re Fendall v. Wilson; with the Opinion of the Attorney-General and Sir Hugh Cairns, and a Preface to those who love God and his Truth.* Oxford: Parker; London: Rivington, 1864.

_____. *The Spiritual Letters of Edward Bouverie Pusey.* Edited by J.O. Johnston and W.E. Newbolt. London: Longmans, Green & Co., 1898.

Rainbow, Bernarr. *The Choral Revival in the Anglican Church (1839-1872).* New York: Oxford University Press, 1970.

Ramm, Agatha. "Gladstone's Religion." *The Historical Journal* 28 (1985): 327-40.

Reardon, Bernard. *Religious Thought in the Victorian Age: A Survey From Coleridge to Gore.* London; New York: Longman Group, 1995.

Reed, John Shelton. *Glorious Battle: The Cultural Politics of Victorian Anglo-Catholicism.* Nashville: Vanderbilt University Press, 1996.

Root, John D. "The Final Apostasy of St. George Jackson Mivart." *Catholic Historical Review* 71 (1985): 1-25.

Rowell, Geoffrey. *Tradition Renewed: The Oxford Movement Conference Papers.* Allison Park, PA: Pickwick Publications, 1986.

_____. *The Vision Glorious: Themes and Personalities of the Catholic Revival in Anglicanism.* Oxford: Oxford University Press, 1983.

Rule, Philip C. *Coleridge and Newman: The Centrality of Conscience.* New York: Fordham University Press, 2004.

Ryan, Alvan, ed. *Newman and Gladstone: The Vatican Decrees.* Notre Dame, IN: University of Notre Dame Press, 1962.

Sardi, Vincenzo, ed. *La solenne definizione del Dogma dell'Immacolato Concepimento di Maria Santissima: Atti e documenti.* 2 Volumes. Rome: Tipografia Vaticana, 1905.

Schatz, Klaus. "Päpstliche Unfehlbarkeit und Geschichte in den Diskussionen des Ersten Vatikanums." In *Dogmengeschichte und katholische Theologie*, edited by W. Löser et al., 187-250. Würzburg: Echter Verlag, 1985.

_____. *Vaticanum I (1869-1870)*. 3 Volumes. Paderborn: Ferdinand Schöningh, 1992-1994.

Scheeben, Matthias, "Die theologische und praktische Bedeutung des Dogmas von der Unfehlbarkeit des Papsts, besonders in seiner Beziehung auf die heutige Zeit." In *Immaculata und Päpstliche Unfehlbarkeit*, 13-87. Paderborn: Ferdinand Schöningh, 1954.

Schmidt, Paul. "Newman's Conversion: Loss and Elegiac Longing." *Renascence* 36 (1984): 203-18.

Scotland, Nigel Source. "Evangelicals, Anglicans and Ritualism in Victorian England." *Churchman* 111 (1997): 249-265.

Selén, Mats. *The Oxford Movement and Wesleyan Methodism in England 1833-1882: A Study In Religious Conflict*. Lund, Sweden: Lund University Press, 1992.

Sharp, John. *Reapers of the Harvest: The Redemptorists in Great Britain and Ireland*. Dublin: Veritas, 1989.

Sidenvall, Erik. *After Anti-Catholicism: John Henry Newman and Protestant Britain, 1845-c. 1890*. London/New York: T & T Clark, 2005.

Skinner, S A. "Newman, the Tractarians and the British Critic." *Journal of Ecclesiastical History* 50 (1999): 716-759.

_____. *Tractarians and the "Condition of England": The Social and Political Thought of the Oxford Movement*. Oxford: Clarendon Press, 2004.

Smith, David. "Church and Society in Britain: A Mid-Nineteenth-Century Analysis." *Evangelical Quarterly* 61 (1989): 141-158.

Stanley, Arthur P. *Essays Chiefly on Questions of Church and State: From 1850 to 1870*. London: John Murray, 1884.

Strong, Rowan. *Alexander Forbes of Brechin: The First Tractarian Bishop.* Oxford: Clarendon Press; Oxford; New York: Oxford University Press, 1995.

Sugg, Joyce. *Ever Yours Affly: John Henry Newman and His Female Circle.* Leominster: Gracewing Publishing, 1996.

Tennyson, George B. *Victorian Devotional Poetry: The Tractarian Mode.* Cambridge, MA: Harvard University Press, 1981.

The Bull 'Ineffabilis' or, Immaculate Conception of the Most Blessed Virgin Mary. Edited by U. Bourke. Dublin: John Mullany, 1868.

Thirlwall, John. "John Henry Newman: His Poetry and Conversion." *Dublin Review* 242 (1968): 75-88.

Thomas, Stephen. *Newman and Heresy: The Anglican Years.* Cambridge; New York: Cambridge University Press, 1991.

Tillard, J.-M. R. *The Bishop of Rome.* Translated by John de Satgé. Wilmington, DE: Michael Glazier, 1983.

Toon, Peter. *Evangelical Theology 1833-1856: A Response to Tractarianism.* Atlanta: John Knox Press, 1979.

Tracts for the Times by Members of the University of Oxford. 5 Volumes. London: Rivington, 1834-1841.

Turner, Frank. *John Henry Newman: The Challenge to Evangelical Religion.* New Haven, CN: Yale University Press, 2002.

Ullathorne, William. *The Immaculate Conception of the Mother of God: An Exposition.* London: Richardson and Son, 1855.

Vaiss, Paul, ed. *From Oxford to the People: Reconsidering Newman & the Oxford Movement.* Leominster: Gracewing, 1996.

_____. *Newman—Sa vie, sa pensée et sa spiritualité: Première période, 1801-1832.* Paris: Harmattan, 1991.

van der Heydt, Odo. "Monsignor Talbot de Malahide." *The Wiseman Review* Winter (1964-5): 290-308.

Varley, Elizabeth. *The Last of the Prince Bishops: William Van Mildert and the High Church Movement of the Early Nineteenth Century.* Cambridge; New York: Cambridge University Press, 1992.

Vitello, John "The Conversion of John Henry Newman." *Review for the Religious* 36 (1977): 715-28.

Voll, Dieter. *Catholic Evangelicalism: The Acceptance of Evangelical Traditions by the Oxford Movement During the Second Half of the Nineteenth Century.* Translated by Veronica Ruffer. London: The Faith Press 1963.

Walgrave, Jan H. *Newman the Theologian.* New York: Sheed & Ward, 1960.

_____. *Unfolding Revelation: The Nature of Doctrinal Development.* London: Hutchinson; Philadelphia: Westminister, 1972.

Wallace, Charles, Jr. "The Oxford Movement and Wesleyan Methodism in England, 1833-1882: A Study in Religious Conflict." *Church History* 64 (1995): 506-507.

Walsh, Leo Joseph. "William G. Ward and the 'Dublin Review.'" PhD diss., Columbia University, 1966.

Ward, Wilfrid Philip. *The Life of John Henry Newman Based on His Private Journals and Correspondence.* 2 Volumes. London: Longmans, Green, & Co., 1912.

_____. *William George Ward and the Oxford Movement.* New York: Macmillan and Co., 1889.

_____. *William George Ward and the Catholic Revival.* New York: Longmans, Green, and Co., 1912.

Ward, William. "Mr. Brownson on Developments." *The Dublin Review* 23 (1847): 373-405.

_____. *Essays on the Church's Doctrinal Authority*. London: Burns & Oates, 1880.

_____. *The Ideal of a Christian Church Considered in Comparison with Existing Practice*. London: James Toovey, 1844.

_____. *On Nature and Grace: A Theological Treatise*. London: Burns and Lambert, 1860.

Ward, Thomas Humphry. *Men of the Time: A Dictionary of Contemporaries, containing Biographical Notices of Eminent Characters of Both Sexes*, 12th ed. London: Routledge and Sons, 1887.

Webb, C.C.J. *Religious Thought in the Oxford Movement*. London: Society for Promoting Christian Knowledge, 1928.

Weber, Christopher. *Kardinäle und Prälaten in den letzten Jahrzehnten des Kirchenstaates: Elite-rekrutierung, Karriere-muster und soziale Zusammensetzung der kurialen Führungsschicht zur Zeit Pius' IX (1846-1878)*. 2 Volumes. Stuttgart: Anton Hiersemann, 1978.

Whisenant, James. *A Fragile Unity: Anti-Ritualism and the Division of Anglican Evangelicalism in the Nineteenth Century*. Waynesboro, GA: Paternoster Press, 2003.

Wilberforce, Robert Isaac. *A Sketch of the History of Erastianism; Together with Two Sermons on the Reality of Church Ordinances, and on the Principle of Church Authority*. London: John and Charles Mosley, 1851.

Willam, Franz Michel. "John Henry Newman und P. Perrone." *Newman Studien* 2 (1954): 120-145.

Williams, N. P. and C. Harris, eds. *Northern Catholicism: Centenary Studies in the Oxford and Parallel Movement*. London: Society for Promoting Christian Knowledge, 1933.

Windle, Bertram C.A. *Who's Who of the Oxford Movement*. New York: The Century Co., 1926.

Wiseman, Nicholas. *The Last Four Popes*. Boston: Patrick Donahoe, 1858.

Yates, Nigel. *The Oxford Movement and Anglican Ritualism*. London: Historical Association, 1983.

_____. *The Oxford Movement and Parish Life: St. Saviour's, Leeds, 1839-1929*. University of York: Borthwick Institute, 1975.

_____. *The Religious Condition of Ireland: 1770-1850*. New York: Oxford University Press, 2006.

Zaniello, Tom. "The Divided Victorian Church: Butterfield and the Anglo-Catholic Compromise." *Religion and the Arts* 5 (2001): 172-184.

INDEX

A

Acton, John Dalberg (Lord Acton), 6, 102, 107, 124, 177
Altholz, Joseph, 175
Apologia Pro Vita Sua, 18, 23, 29-39, 45, 48-53, 55-60, 65-67, 73-81, 99, 129, 151, 154, 166-167, 199, 218, 223-224, 227-228, 250
The Arians of the Fourth Century (1833), 51, 59-61, 68, 83, 221
Arnold, Thomas, 146, 229

B

Bentham, Jeremy, 145
Bowden, J.W., 21
Bowles, Emily, 167-168, 175, 196, 199, 201-202
Brownson, Orestes, 87, 97

C

Capes, Frederick, 173-174, 178
Capes, John Moore, 74, 177
Chadwick, Owen, 10, 12, 17, 86-87, 93, 98, 101, 148, 224
Church of England, 4-5, 9, 13-16, 19-20, 24, 26, 28-30, 32-39, 41-46, 59, 66, 78, 98, 112, 115-118, 120-121, 126-134, 137-138, 152, 156, 179-180, 224-229, 235, 249

Church Temporalities Act (1833), 5, 14, 16, 44-45, 59, 224
Church, Richard William, 15, 19, 143, 166
Coffin, Robert Aston, 174, 188, 190
Council of Trent, 115, 132-134, 222

D

Dalgairns, John Dobrée, 174, 176, 187
disciplina arcani, 62-65
Disraeli, Benjamin, 39, 240
von Döllinger, Ignaz, 1, 99-100, 107, 138-139, 159, 165, 193, 242
The Dublin Review, 31, 48, 74, 91, 133, 143-144, 148, 150, 157-159, 163, 165-166, 170, 175, 177, 183, 185-186, 210, 256-257
Dupanloup, Felix-Antoine-Philibert, 17, 97, 100, 102, 168, 252

E

Eastern Orthodoxy, 134
Erastianism, 5, 14-15, 19-20, 26, 29, 37, 43, 45-46, 79, 115, 180-181, 195, 206, 210
An Essay in Aid of a Grammar of Assent, 54, 83, 250
Essay on the Development of Christian Doctrine, 4, 37, 39, 51, 57, 80-82, 86, 250
Essays and Reviews, 128

239

F

Faber, Frederick William, 174, 181, 182-183, 235, 237
First Vatican Council, 1, 46, 85-88, 98, 100, 106-107, 123-124, 143, 173, 190, 215, 220, 240, 245
Froude, Richard Hurrell, 13-14, 26-27, 224, 242

G

Giberne, Maria Rosina, 173, 175, 199, 201
Gillow, John, 221
Gladstone, William Ewart, 18, 46, 106-107, 111-112, 116-120, 124, 126, 136-140, 145, 165-166, 181, 216-217, 237-241, 247, 249, 253-254
Gorham Controvery (Gorham v. Bishop of Exeter, 1850), 13, 42-45, 118, 120, 127-129, 137

H

Hampden, Renn Dickson, 23, 66, 114
Harrison, Benjamin, 21, 225

I

Immaculate Conception, 6, 86, 90-100, 103, 133, 193, 237, 244, 247, 252, 256
Ineffabilus Deus (1854), 133

J

Jerusalem Bishopric Controversy, 44, 56, 78-79

K

Keble, John , 5, 13, 15-16, 74, 116, 132, 224, 236

Keble, Thomas, 21, 225
Kenrick, Peter, 1, 102, 107
Ker, Ian, 48, 54, 231, 250
Knox, Thomas Francis, 174, 184-186, 247

L

liberalism, 11, 15, 17-19
Liddon, Henry, 122, 133

M

Manning, Henry Edward, 1-5, 32, 44, 74, 105-111, 116, 119, 122-123, 126-127, 136, 143, 174-176, 179, 190, 193-194, 199, 217, 225, 241, 248, 251
Maurice, Frederick Denison, 117
Menzies, Alfred, 21, 225
Mill, John Stuart, 145
Mivart, G.J., 4
Möhler, Johann Adam , 103
Moore, John, 174, 177, 207

N

"National Apostasy" (1833), 5, 16, 18
Newman, John Henry, 2-6, 11-13, 17-42, 43-74, 75 92, 93-97, 99-112, 114, 117, 121-122, 124, 127, 129, 131-132, 135, 138, 144-146, 148-154, 155 -191, 194-258
Nockles, Peter, 11, 24
Northcote, James Spencer, 174, 178

O

Ornsby, Robert, 113, 174, 176, 205, 223, 252
Oxford Movement, 2-8, 9-42, 43-45, 47, 57, 65-66, 85, 87, 105, 107, 115, 122, 124, 128, 132, 144-146, 148-153, 155-156, 159, 168, 170-171,

Index 241

173-177, 181-182, 184, 186, 188, 190, 192, 198, 202, 204-206, 217, 223-229, 233, 237, 240-242, 249-252, 257-258

P

Palmer, William, 23, 29, 109, 137, 224
papal infallibility, 1, 3, 5, 8, 12, 17, 45-46, 85, 98, 100, 103-104, 106, 110, 113, 123-124, 126, 132-135, 137, 140, 143-144, 157-158, 160, 162, 164, 166-169, 174, 176, 179, 188, 190-191, 198, 201-202, 205, 208-209, 215, 230-232
Papal States, 1, 5-6, 98, 138, 195
Pastor Aeternus (1870), 47, 135, 137, 168, 215, 218, 221, 230, 232
Peel, Robert, 14
Pereiro, James, 10, 117, 130, 253
Perrone, Giovanni, 87, 121, 122
Phillpotts, Henry, 34, 43-44, 127
Pius IX (Giovanni Maria Mastai-Ferretti), 6, 88, 91, 94, 97, 99-100, 114-116, 122-123, 126-127, 133, 139, 150, 161-165, 183, 186, 192-194, 196-197, 207, 210
Pusey, Edward Bouverie, 4, 13, 21-27, 30, 39-46, 74, 116, 126, 128-136, 140, 152, 165, 194, 201-202, 225-226, 249, 253

R

The Rambler, 6, 17, 94, 175, 177-178, 205, 207, 209, 221, 235
Reform Act (1832), 14, 59
Roman Catholicism, 4, 9, 12, 30, 37, 45-46, 51, 52, 66, 73, 78-81, 83, 106, 108, 112, 126-127, 134, 136-140, 173, 188-190, 198, 206, 216, 227-228, 250-251

S

schola theologorum, 47, 217-223, 229, 230, 233
sensus fidelium, 221, 228, 232
Simpson, Richard, 4, 178
Syllabus of Errors (1864), 17, 162

T

The Tablet, 175-177, 184, 188, 205, 209
Talbot, George, 2, 4-6, 122, 174, 190, 191, 197
Thirty-nine Articles (*The Articles of Religion*), 23, 32, 33, 34, 41, 77, 116, 153, 227-228
Tract 90, 23, 32-36, 41, 43, 51, 77-78, 81, 132, 153, 155, 218, 226-229
Tractarianism. *See* Oxford Movement
Tracts for the Times, 9, 19-21, 23, 32-34, 70, 77, 224, 227, 256
Turner, Frank, 48

U

ubi Petrus, ibi ecclesia, 4, 107
Ubi Primum (1849), 133
Ullathorne, William Bernard, 2, 5, 97, 170, 203-204, 215, 237, 256
University of Oxford, 9, 13, 18, 21, 24, 71, 180, 224, 237, 251, 256
Utilitarianism, 145, 182

V

Via Media, 23, 28-32, 36, 51, 65-68, 71, 73, 75-79, 151-152, 218, 230, 251

W

Ward, William George, 2, 4, 13, 91, 130-131, 144, 146, 157, 185, 228

The Weekly Register, 129, 175-177, 205, 210
Who's Who of the Oxford Movement, 10
Wilberforce, Henry William, 174, 176
Wilberforce, Robert Isaac, 44, 74, 79, 111, 113, 114, 115, 116, 118, 120, 121, 174, 176, 179-180, 258
Wilberforce, Samuel, 25, 118, 127

Williams, Isaac, 15, 19, 32, 40, 72, 225-226
Windle, Bertram, 10, 173
The Workings of the Holy Spirit in England (1864), 129